STAR·WARS

DARTH VADER

DARK LORD OF THE SITH

LEGACY'S END

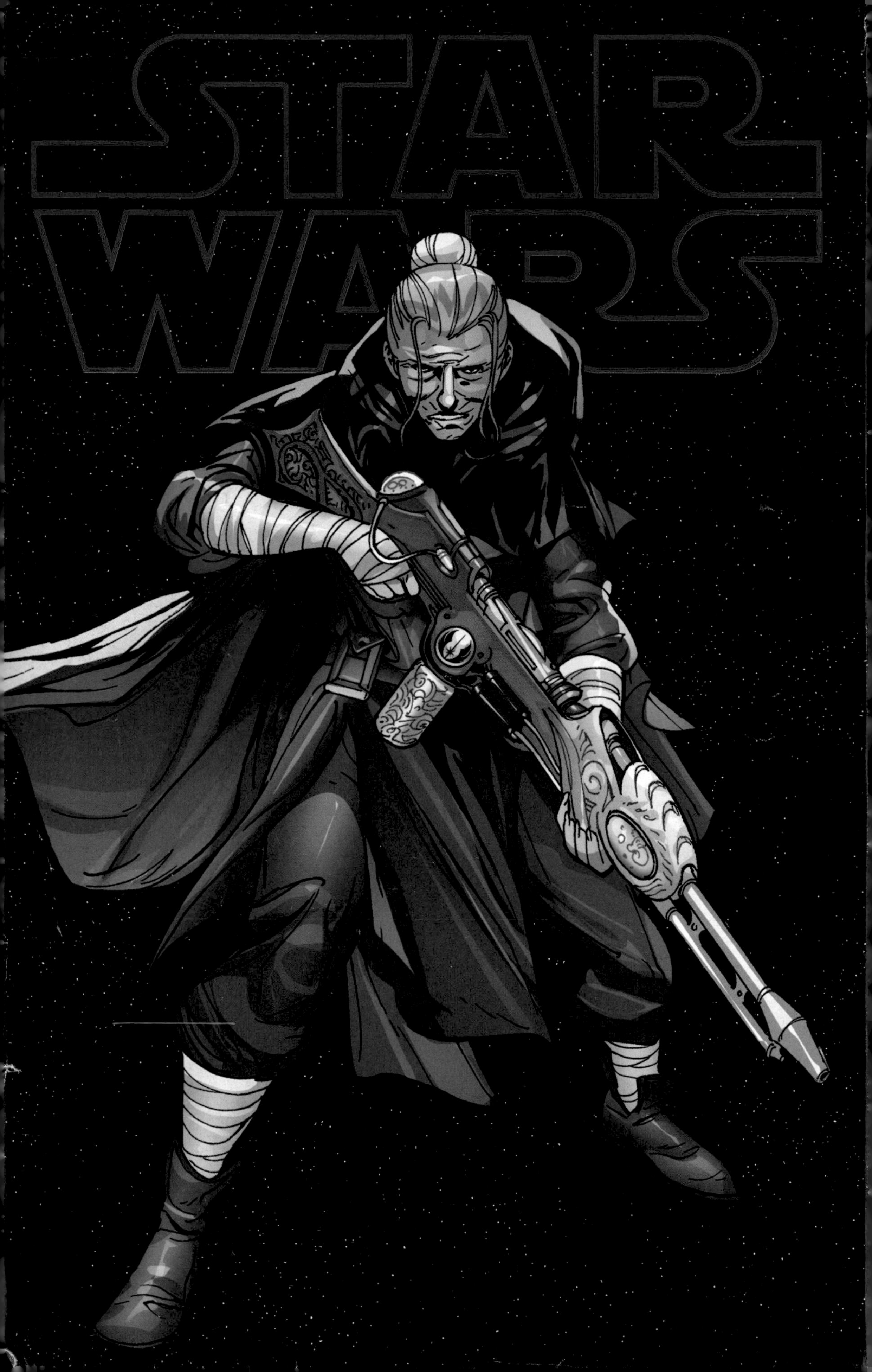
STAR
WARS

DARTH VADER

DARK LORD OF THE SITH

LEGACY'S END

Writer CHARLES SOULE
Penciler GIUSEPPE CAMUNCOLI
Inker DANIELE ORLANDINI
Colorist DAVID CURIEL
Letterer VC's JOE CARAMAGNA
Cover Art GIUSEPPE CAMUNCOLI & FRANCESCO MATTINA

Assistant Editor HEATHER ANTOS
Editor JORDAN D. WHITE

Editor in Chief C.B. CEBULSKI
Chief Creative Officer JOE QUESADA
President DAN BUCKLEY

For Lucasfilm:

Assistant Editor NICK MARTINO
Senior Editor JENNIFER HEDDLE
Creative Director MICHAEL SIGLAIN
Lucasfilm Story Group JAMES WAUGH, LELAND CHEE, MATT MARTIN

Collection Editor JENNIFER GRUNWALD
Assistant Editor CAITLIN O'CONNELL
Associate Managing Editor KATERI WOODY
Editor, Special Projects MARK D. BEAZLEY
VP Production & Special Projects JEFF YOUNGQUIST
SVP Print, Sales & Marketing DAVID GABRIEL
Book Designer ADAM DEL RE

STAR WARS: DARTH VADER: DARK LORD OF THE SITH VOL. 2 — LEGACY'S END. Contains material originally published in magazine form as DARTH VADER #7-12. First printing 2018. ISBN 978-1-302-90745-7. Published by [illegible] Printed in Canada. [illegible]

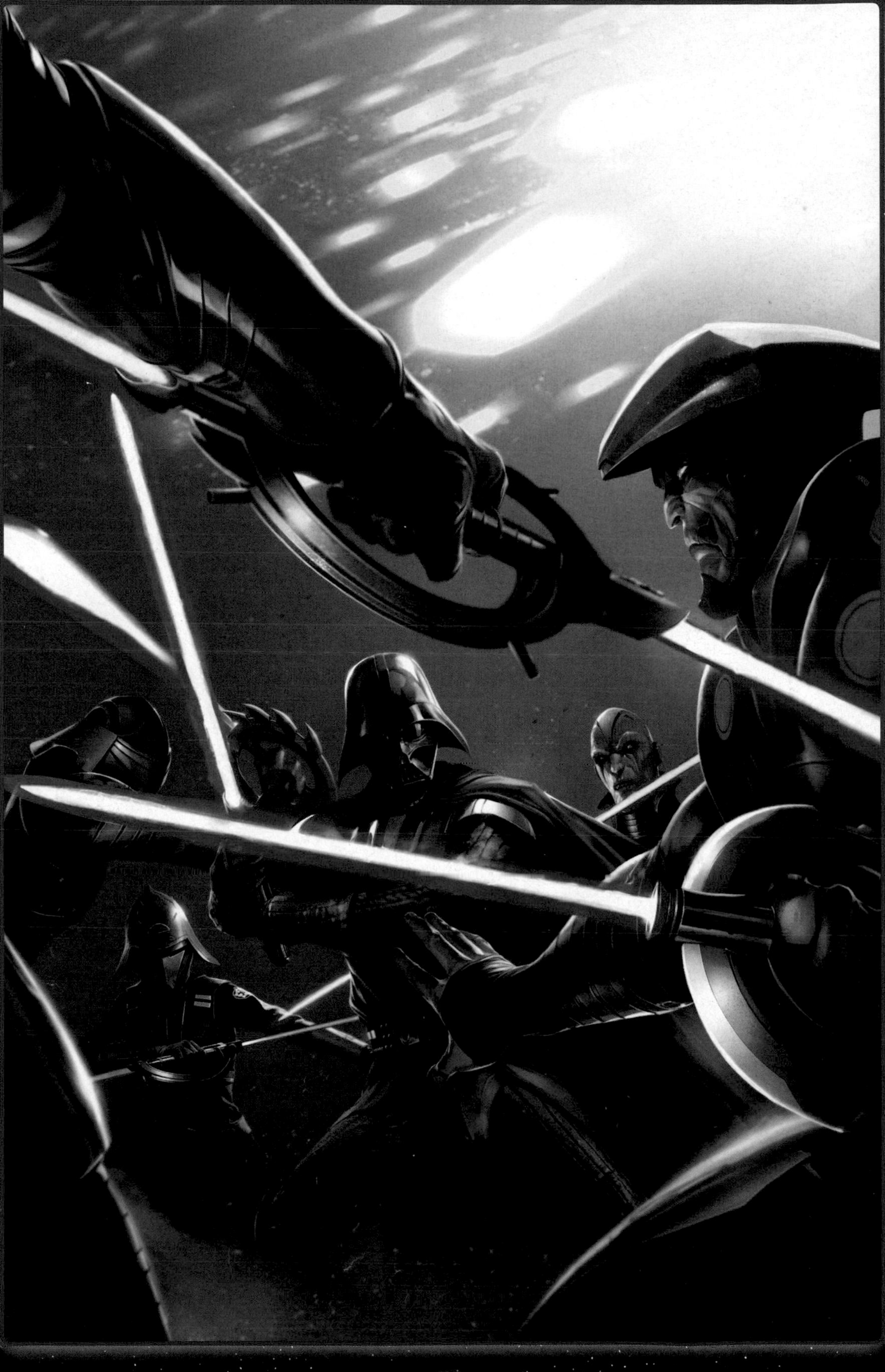

THE DYING LIGHT

The fledgling Empire has only just begun across the galaxy. As Emperor Palpatine firms up his grip on the reins of rulership, it falls to those under him to make sure the transition goes smoothly.

Lord Darth Vader, Palpatine's Sith apprentice, struggles to come into his own in this new Empire. Formerly a Jedi Knight known as Anakin Skywalker, Vader betrayed the Jedi Order and took the lead in their slaughter.

Now, Vader has been put in charge of the Inquisitorius, a group of former Jedi fallen to the dark side. Their mission: continue what Vader began and wipe out the remaining Jedi who have thus far evaded capture....

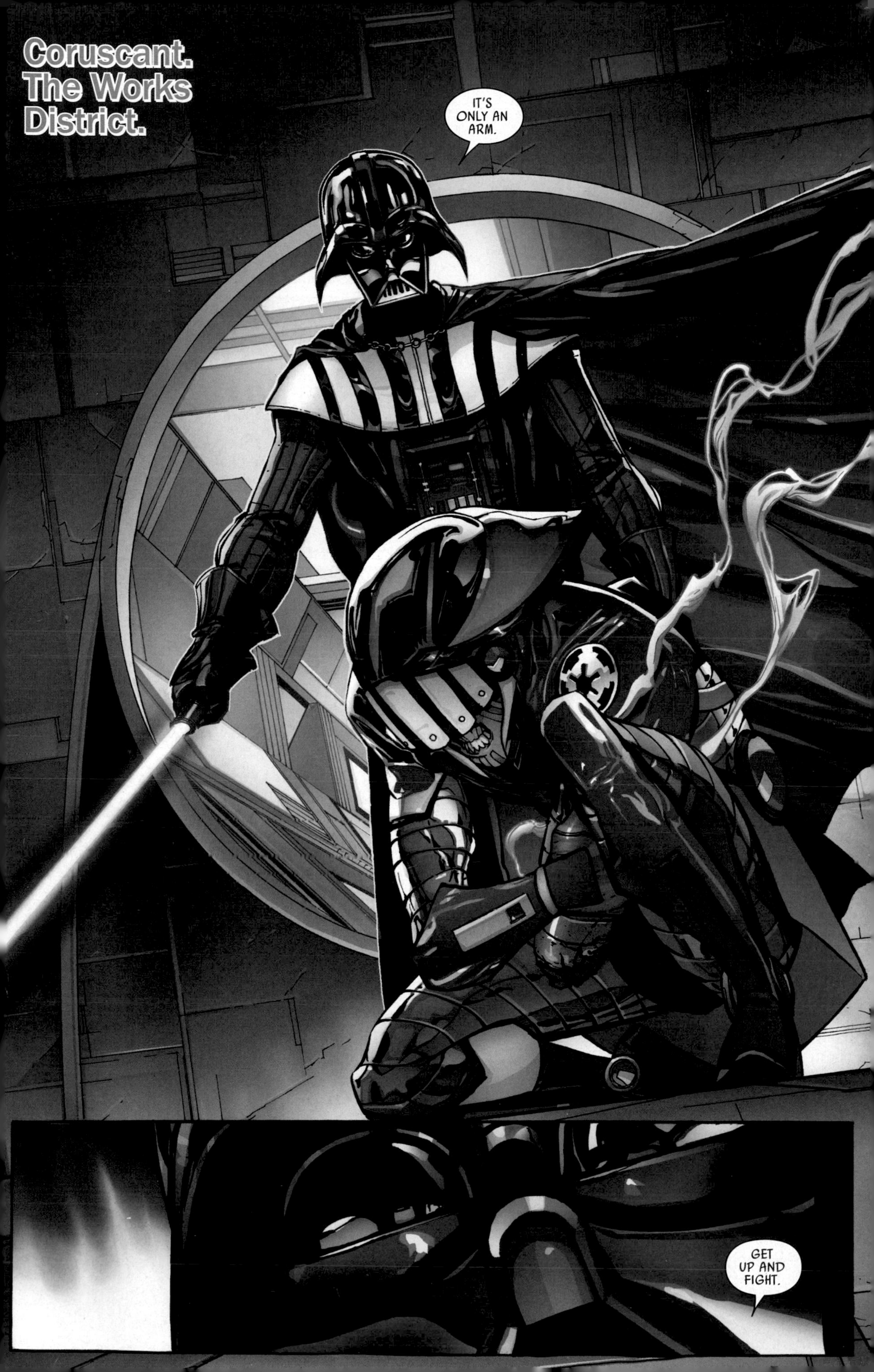
Coruscant. The Works District.
IT'S ONLY AN ARM.
GET UP AND FIGHT.

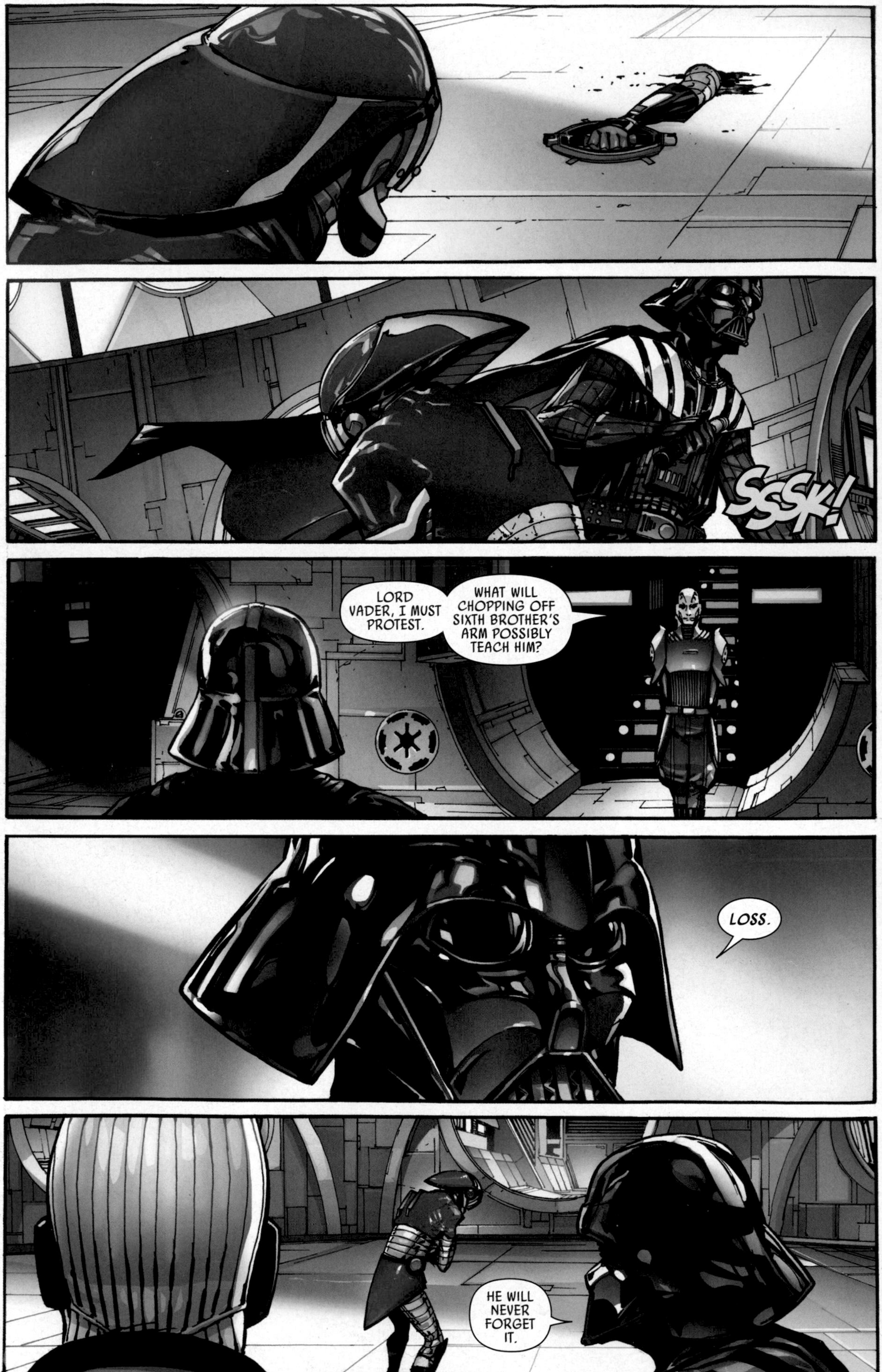
SSSK!
LORD VADER, I MUST PROTEST.
WHAT WILL CHOPPING OFF SIXTH BROTHER'S ARM POSSIBLY TEACH HIM?
LOSS.
HE WILL NEVER FORGET IT.

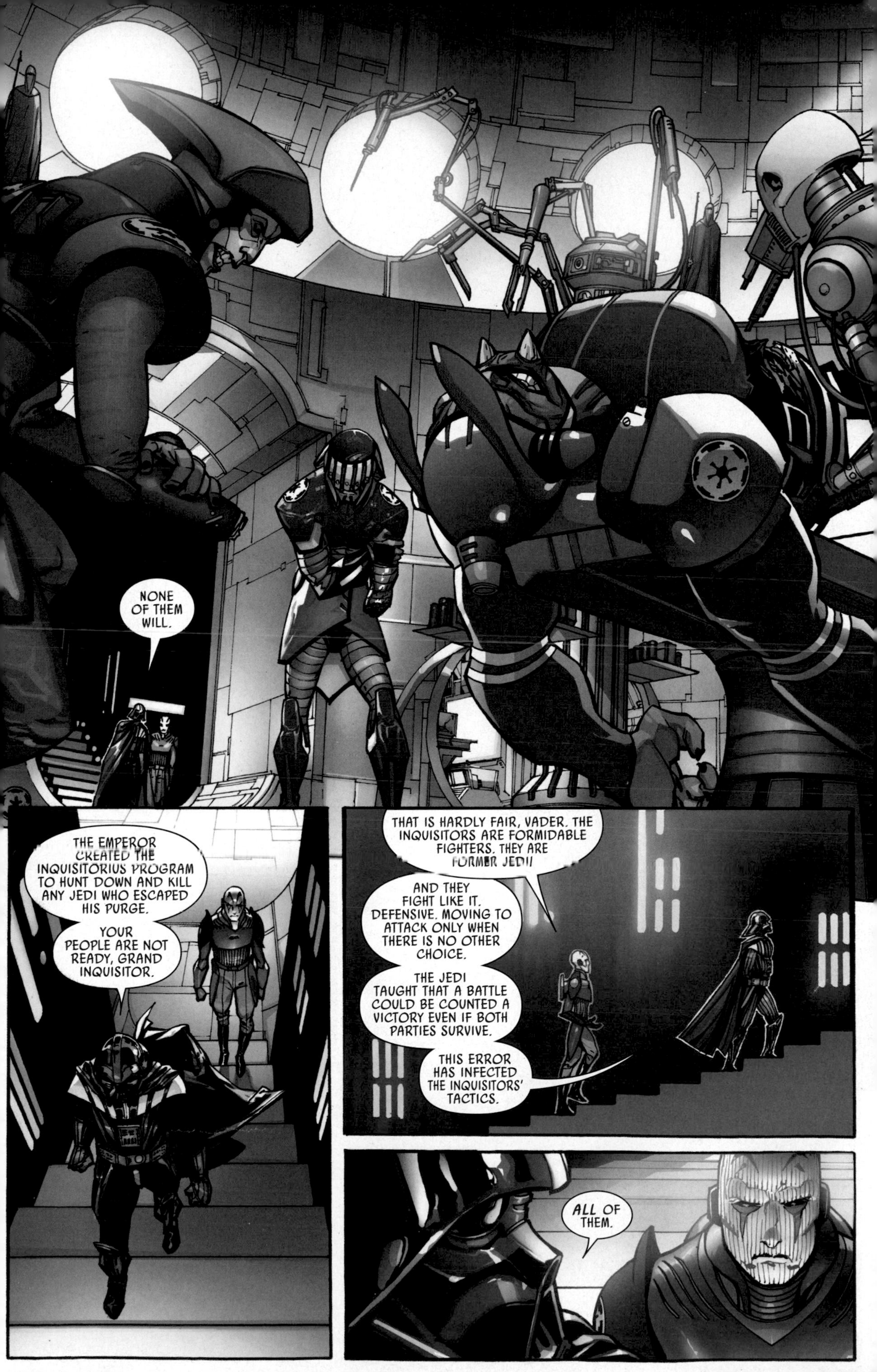
NONE OF THEM WILL.
THE EMPEROR CREATED THE INQUISITORIUS PROGRAM TO HUNT DOWN AND KILL ANY JEDI WHO ESCAPED HIS PURGE.
YOUR PEOPLE ARE NOT READY, GRAND INQUISITOR.
THAT IS HARDLY FAIR, VADER. THE INQUISITORS ARE FORMIDABLE FIGHTERS. THEY ARE FORMER JEDI!
AND THEY FIGHT LIKE IT. DEFENSIVE. MOVING TO ATTACK ONLY WHEN THERE IS NO OTHER CHOICE.
THE JEDI TAUGHT THAT A BATTLE COULD BE COUNTED A VICTORY EVEN IF BOTH PARTIES SURVIVE.
THIS ERROR HAS INFECTED THE INQUISITORS' TACTICS.
ALL OF THEM.

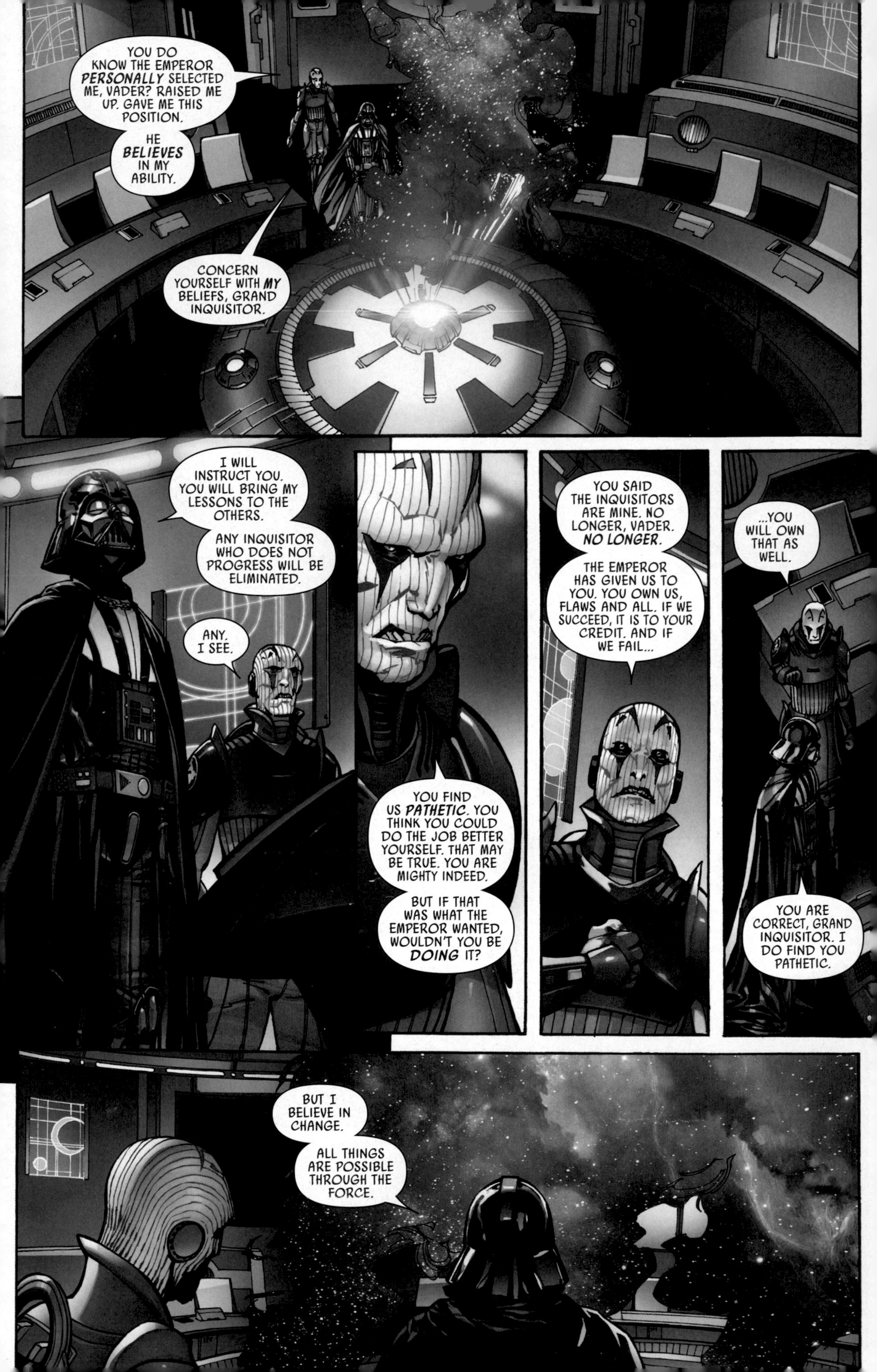
YOU DO KNOW THE EMPEROR PERSONALLY SELECTED ME, VADER? RAISED ME UP. GAVE ME THIS POSITION.
HE BELIEVES IN MY ABILITY.
CONCERN YOURSELF WITH MY BELIEFS, GRAND INQUISITOR.
I WILL INSTRUCT YOU. YOU WILL BRING MY LESSONS TO THE OTHERS.
ANY INQUISITOR WHO DOES NOT PROGRESS WILL BE ELIMINATED.
ANY. I SEE.
YOU FIND US PATHETIC. YOU THINK YOU COULD DO THE JOB BETTER YOURSELF. THAT MAY BE TRUE. YOU ARE MIGHTY INDEED.
BUT IF THAT WAS WHAT THE EMPEROR WANTED, WOULDN'T YOU BE DOING IT?
YOU SAID THE INQUISITORS ARE MINE. NO LONGER, VADER. NO LONGER.
THE EMPEROR HAS GIVEN US TO YOU. YOU OWN US, FLAWS AND ALL. IF WE SUCCEED, IT IS TO YOUR CREDIT. AND IF WE FAIL...
...YOU WILL OWN THAT AS WELL.
YOU ARE CORRECT, GRAND INQUISITOR. I DO FIND YOU PATHETIC.
BUT I BELIEVE IN CHANGE.
ALL THINGS ARE POSSIBLE THROUGH THE FORCE.

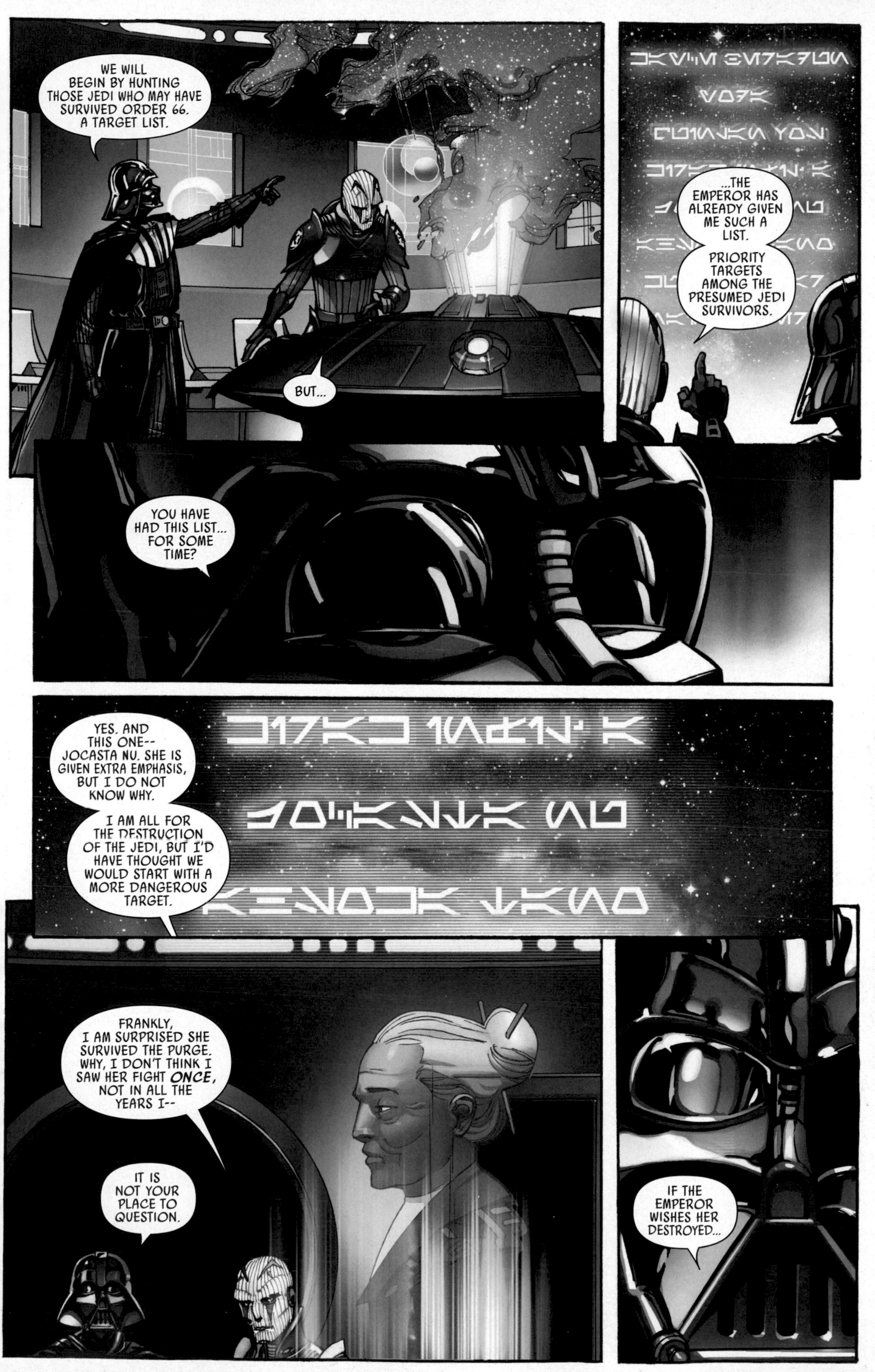
WE WILL BEGIN BY HUNTING THOSE JEDI WHO MAY HAVE SURVIVED ORDER 66. A TARGET LIST.
BUT...
...THE EMPEROR HAS ALREADY GIVEN ME SUCH A LIST.
PRIORITY TARGETS AMONG THE PRESUMED JEDI SURVIVORS.
YOU HAVE HAD THIS LIST... FOR SOME TIME?
YES. AND THIS ONE-- JOCASTA NU. SHE IS GIVEN EXTRA EMPHASIS, BUT I DO NOT KNOW WHY.
I AM ALL FOR THE DESTRUCTION OF THE JEDI, BUT I'D HAVE THOUGHT WE WOULD START WITH A MORE DANGEROUS TARGET.
FRANKLY, I AM SURPRISED SHE SURVIVED THE PURGE. WHY, I DON'T THINK I SAW HER FIGHT *ONCE*, NOT IN ALL THE YEARS I--
IT IS NOT YOUR PLACE TO QUESTION.
IF THE EMPEROR WISHES HER DESTROYED...

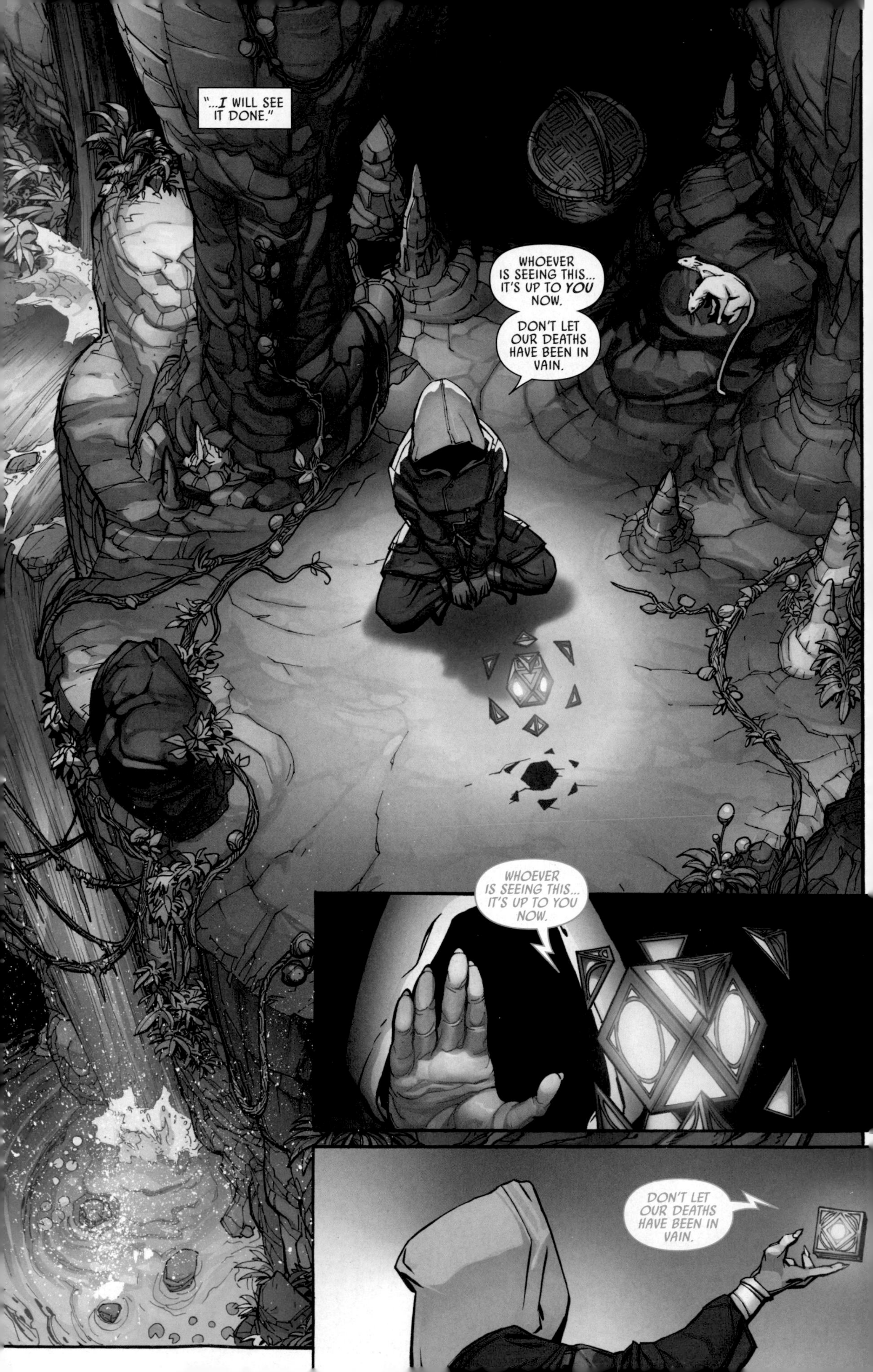
"...*I* WILL SEE IT DONE."
WHOEVER IS SEEING THIS... IT'S UP TO *YOU* NOW.
DON'T LET OUR DEATHS HAVE BEEN IN VAIN.
WHOEVER IS SEEING THIS... IT'S UP TO YOU NOW.
DON'T LET OUR DEATHS HAVE BEEN IN VAIN.

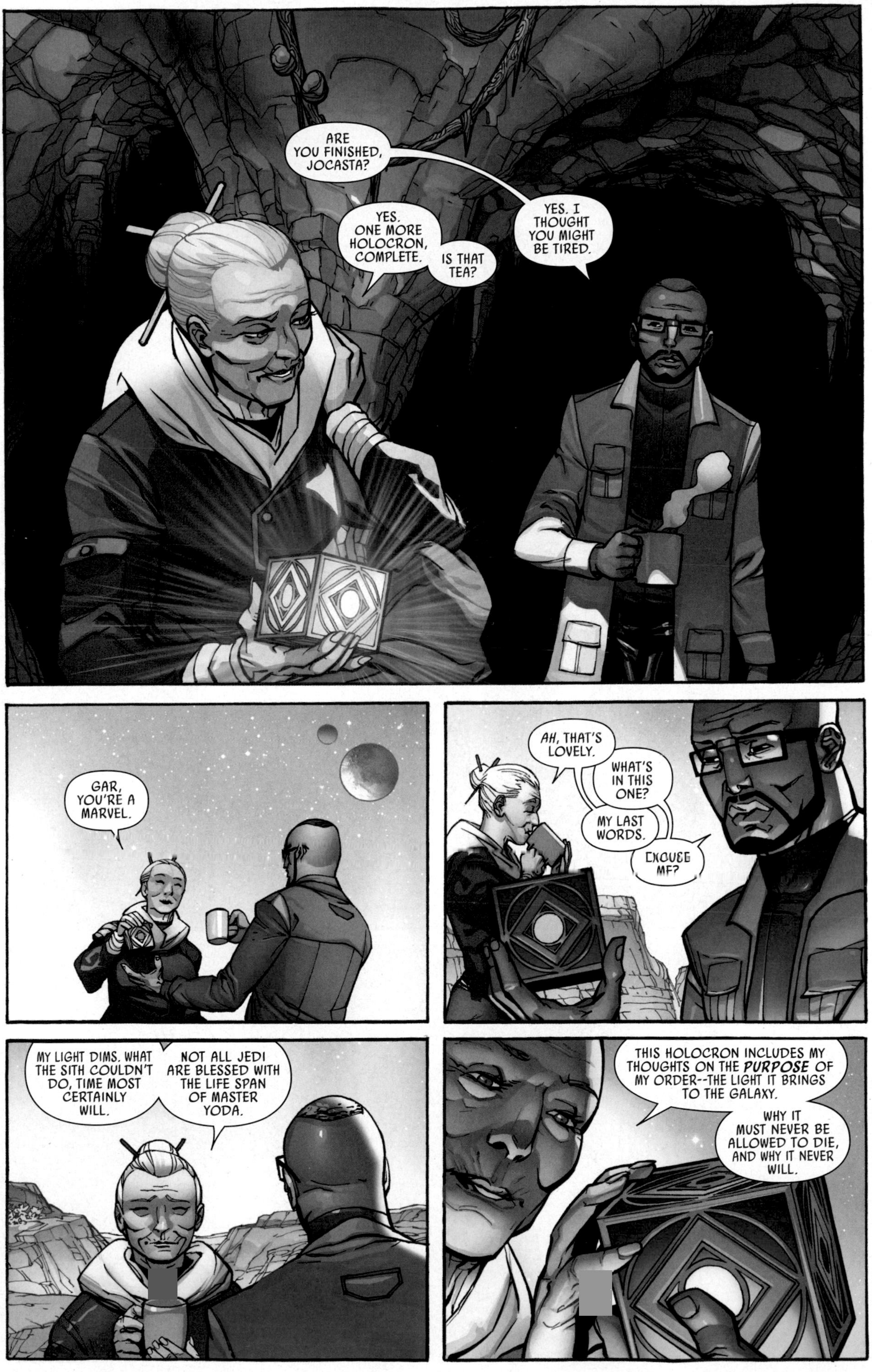
ARE YOU FINISHED, JOCASTA?
YES. ONE MORE HOLOCRON, COMPLETE.
IS THAT TEA?
YES. I THOUGHT YOU MIGHT BE TIRED.
GAR, YOU'RE A MARVEL.
AH, THAT'S LOVELY.
WHAT'S IN THIS ONE?
MY LAST WORDS.
EXCUSE ME?
MY LIGHT DIMS. WHAT THE SITH COULDN'T DO, TIME MOST CERTAINLY WILL.
NOT ALL JEDI ARE BLESSED WITH THE LIFE SPAN OF MASTER YODA.
THIS HOLOCRON INCLUDES MY THOUGHTS ON THE PURPOSE OF MY ORDER--THE LIGHT IT BRINGS TO THE GALAXY.
WHY IT MUST NEVER BE ALLOWED TO DIE, AND WHY IT NEVER WILL.

PLEASE PUT IT WITH THE OTHERS.

YOU AREN'T COMING? I THOUGHT PERHAPS...

OH NO, MY FRIEND.

I HAVE MORE WORK TO DO.

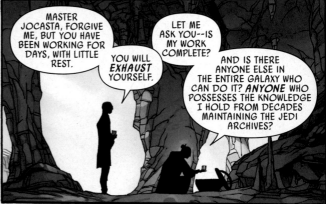

MASTER JOCASTA, FORGIVE ME, BUT YOU HAVE BEEN WORKING FOR DAYS, WITH LITTLE REST.

YOU WILL EXHAUST YOURSELF.

LET ME ASK YOU--IS MY WORK COMPLETE?

AND IS THERE ANYONE ELSE IN THE ENTIRE GALAXY WHO CAN DO IT? ANYONE WHO POSSESSES THE KNOWLEDGE I HOLD FROM DECADES MAINTAINING THE JEDI ARCHIVES?

WELL, NO, I SUPPOSE NOT, BUT...

IF MY WORK IS NOT COMPLETE, THEN I MUST WORK.

BUT I WOULDN'T SAY NO TO A BIT MORE TEA.

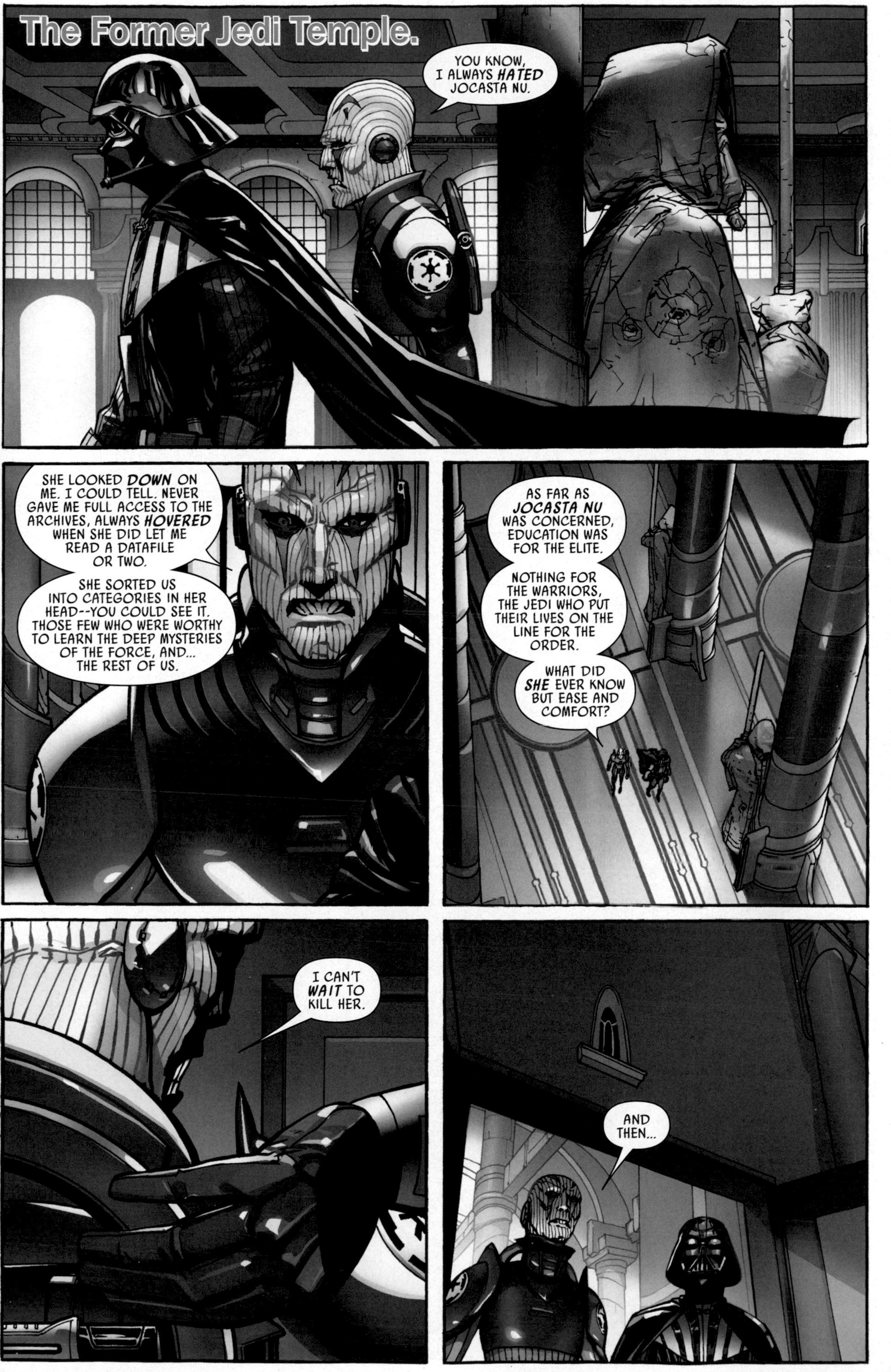
The Former Jedi Temple.
YOU KNOW, I ALWAYS HATED JOCASTA NU.
SHE LOOKED DOWN ON ME. I COULD TELL. NEVER GAVE ME FULL ACCESS TO THE ARCHIVES, ALWAYS HOVERED WHEN SHE DID LET ME READ A DATAFILE OR TWO.
SHE SORTED US INTO CATEGORIES IN HER HEAD--YOU COULD SEE IT. THOSE FEW WHO WERE WORTHY TO LEARN THE DEEP MYSTERIES OF THE FORCE, AND... THE REST OF US.
AS FAR AS JOCASTA NU WAS CONCERNED, EDUCATION WAS FOR THE ELITE.
NOTHING FOR THE WARRIORS, THE JEDI WHO PUT THEIR LIVES ON THE LINE FOR THE ORDER.
WHAT DID SHE EVER KNOW BUT EASE AND COMFORT?
I CAN'T WAIT TO KILL HER.
AND THEN...

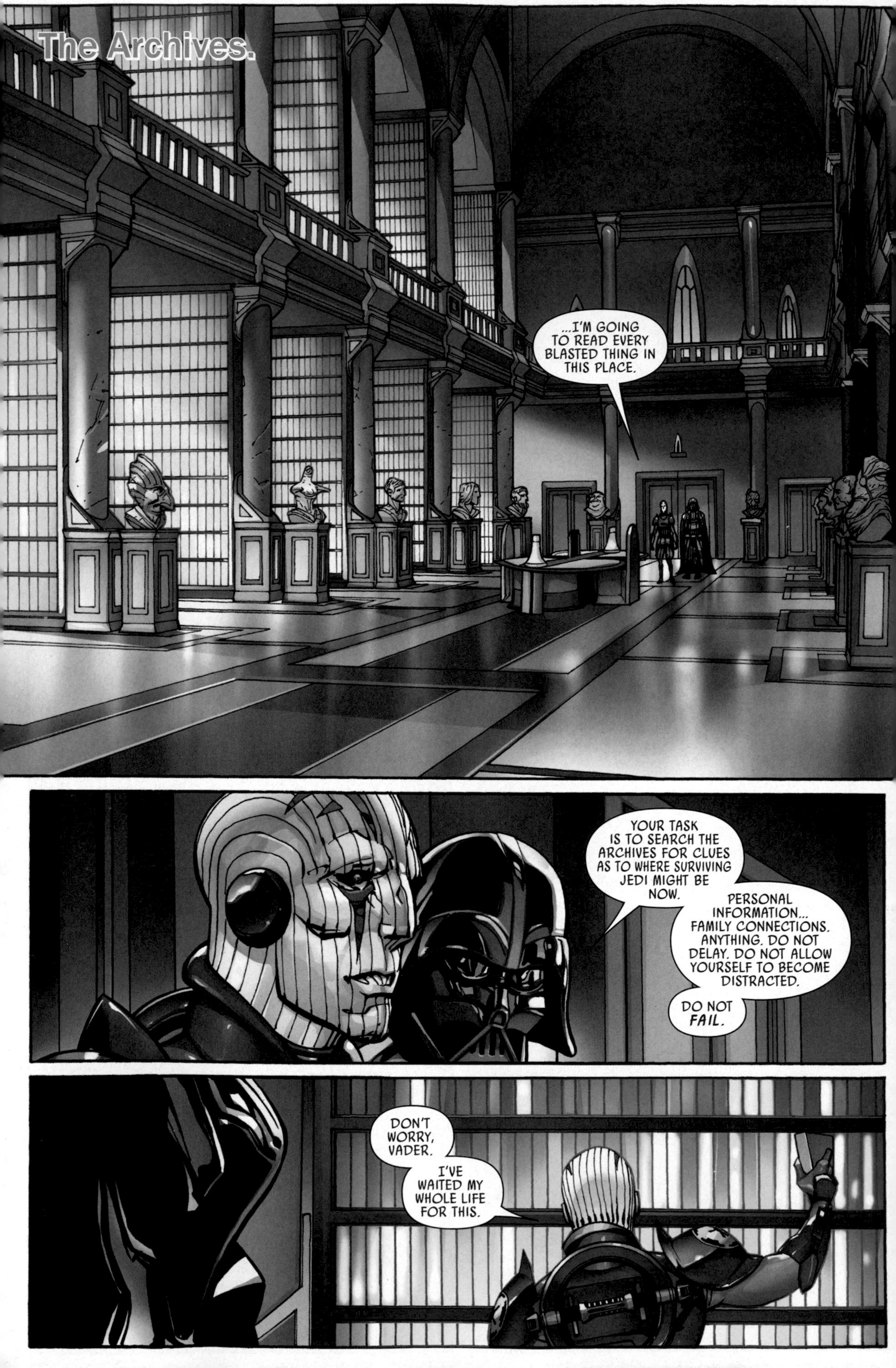
The Archives.
...I'M GOING TO READ EVERY BLASTED THING IN THIS PLACE.
YOUR TASK IS TO SEARCH THE ARCHIVES FOR CLUES AS TO WHERE SURVIVING JEDI MIGHT BE NOW.
PERSONAL INFORMATION... FAMILY CONNECTIONS. ANYTHING. DO NOT DELAY. DO NOT ALLOW YOURSELF TO BECOME DISTRACTED.
DO NOT FAIL.
DON'T WORRY, VADER.
I'VE WAITED MY WHOLE LIFE FOR THIS.

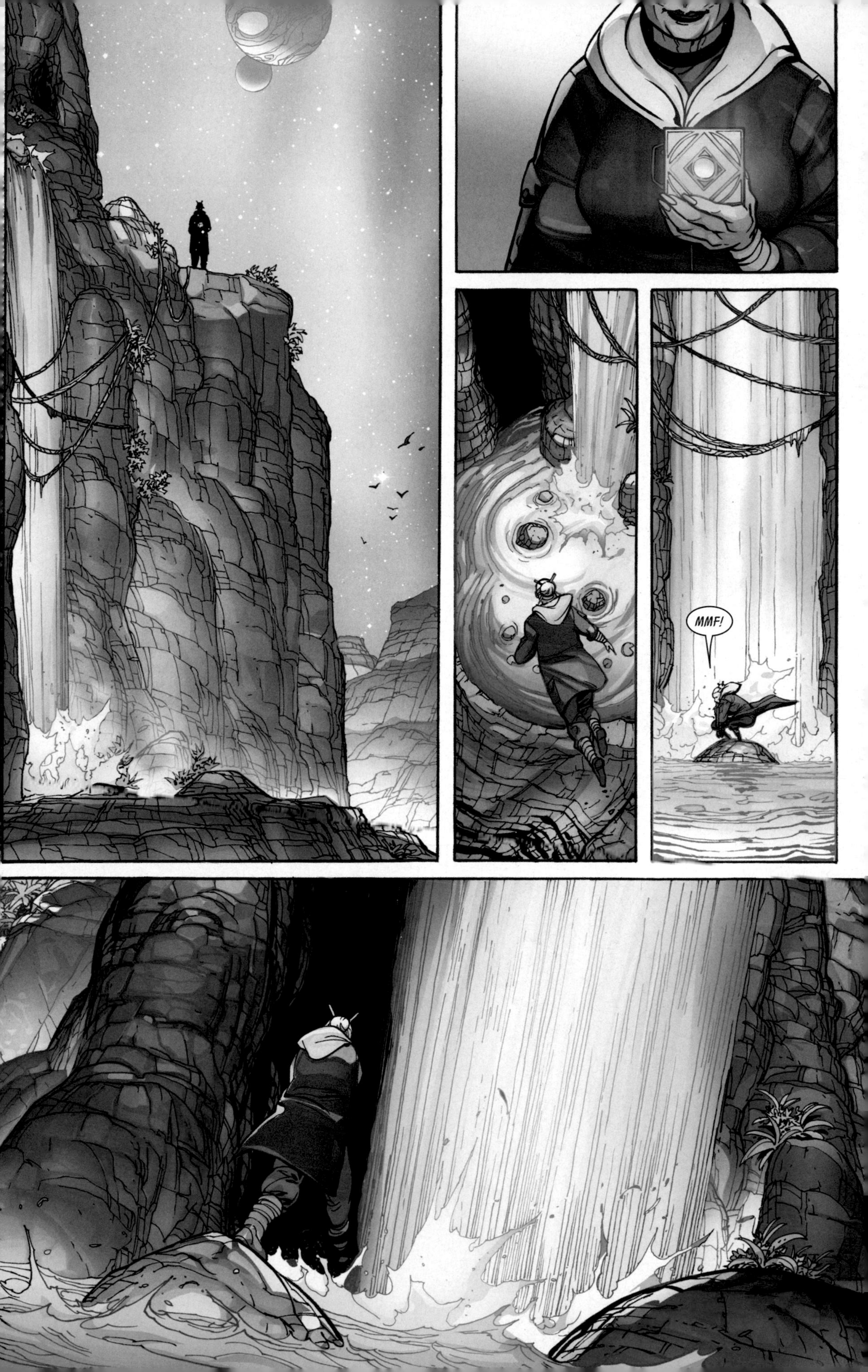
MMF!

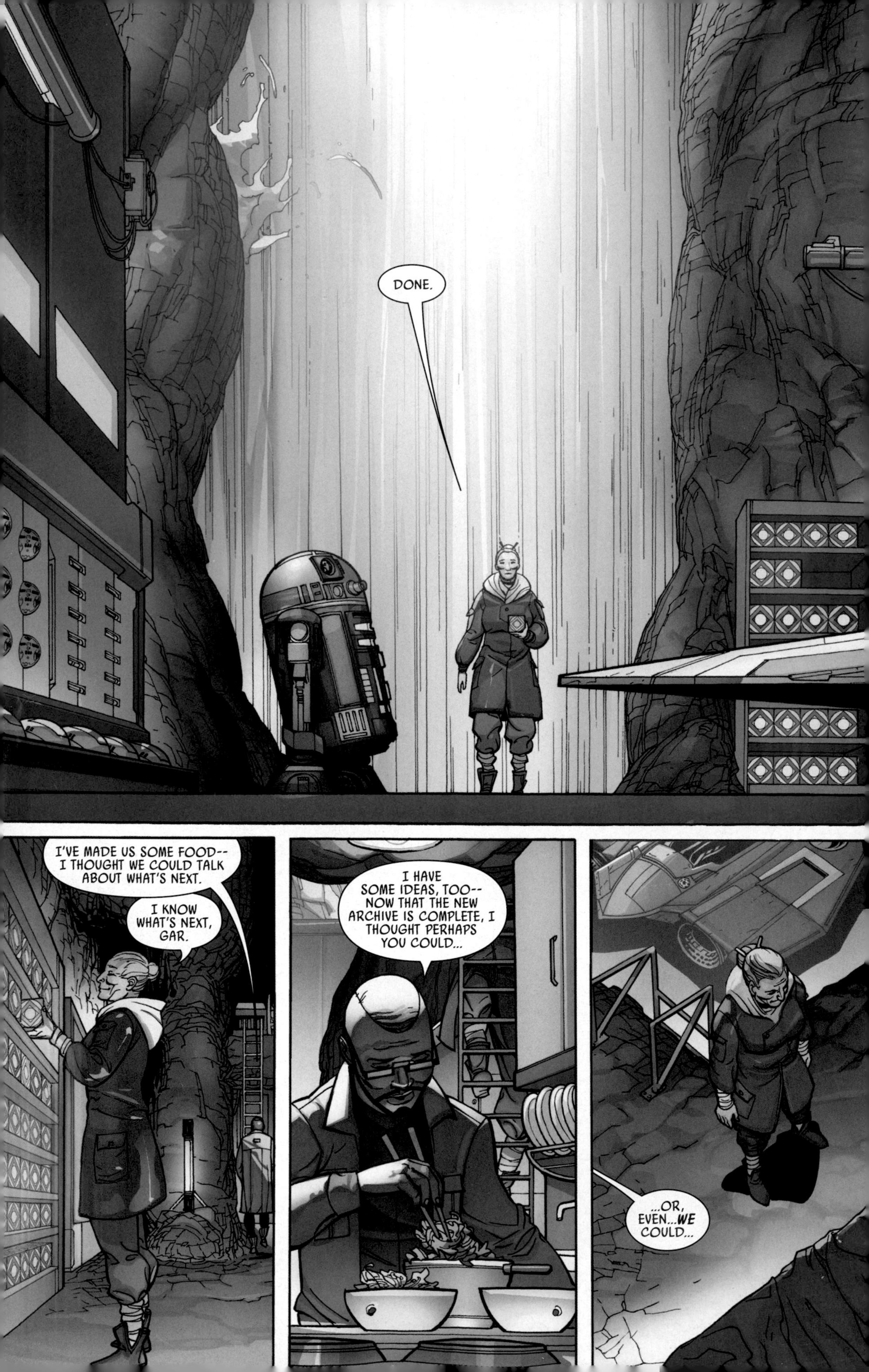
DONE.
I'VE MADE US SOME FOOD-- I THOUGHT WE COULD TALK ABOUT WHAT'S NEXT.
I KNOW WHAT'S NEXT, GAR.
I HAVE SOME IDEAS, TOO-- NOW THAT THE NEW ARCHIVE IS COMPLETE, I THOUGHT PERHAPS YOU COULD...
...OR, EVEN...*WE* COULD...

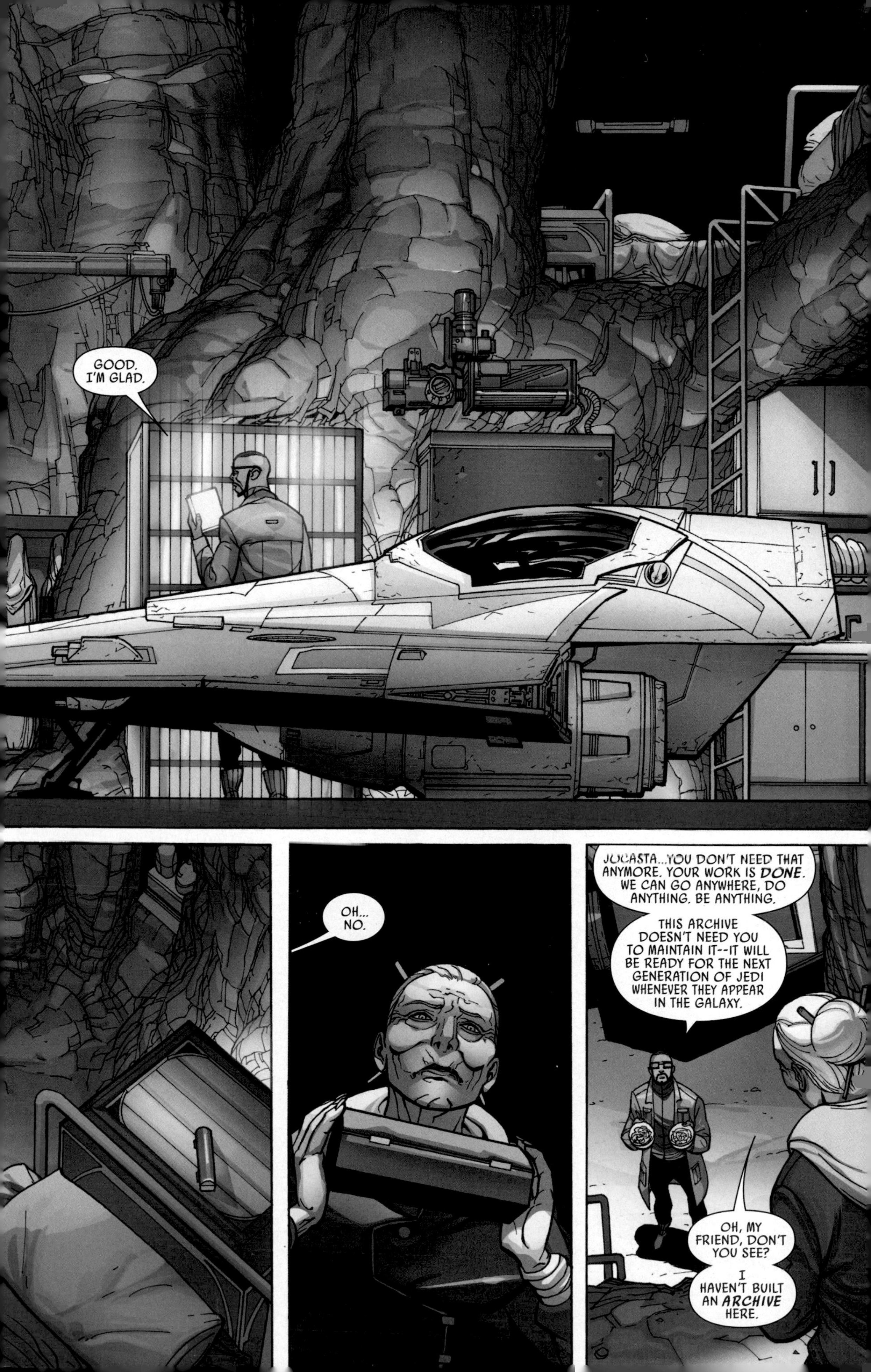
GOOD. I'M GLAD.
OH... NO.
JOCASTA...YOU DON'T NEED THAT ANYMORE. YOUR WORK IS DONE. WE CAN GO ANYWHERE, DO ANYTHING. BE ANYTHING.
THIS ARCHIVE DOESN'T NEED YOU TO MAINTAIN IT--IT WILL BE READY FOR THE NEXT GENERATION OF JEDI WHENEVER THEY APPEAR IN THE GALAXY.
OH, MY FRIEND, DON'T YOU SEE?
I HAVEN'T BUILT AN ARCHIVE HERE.

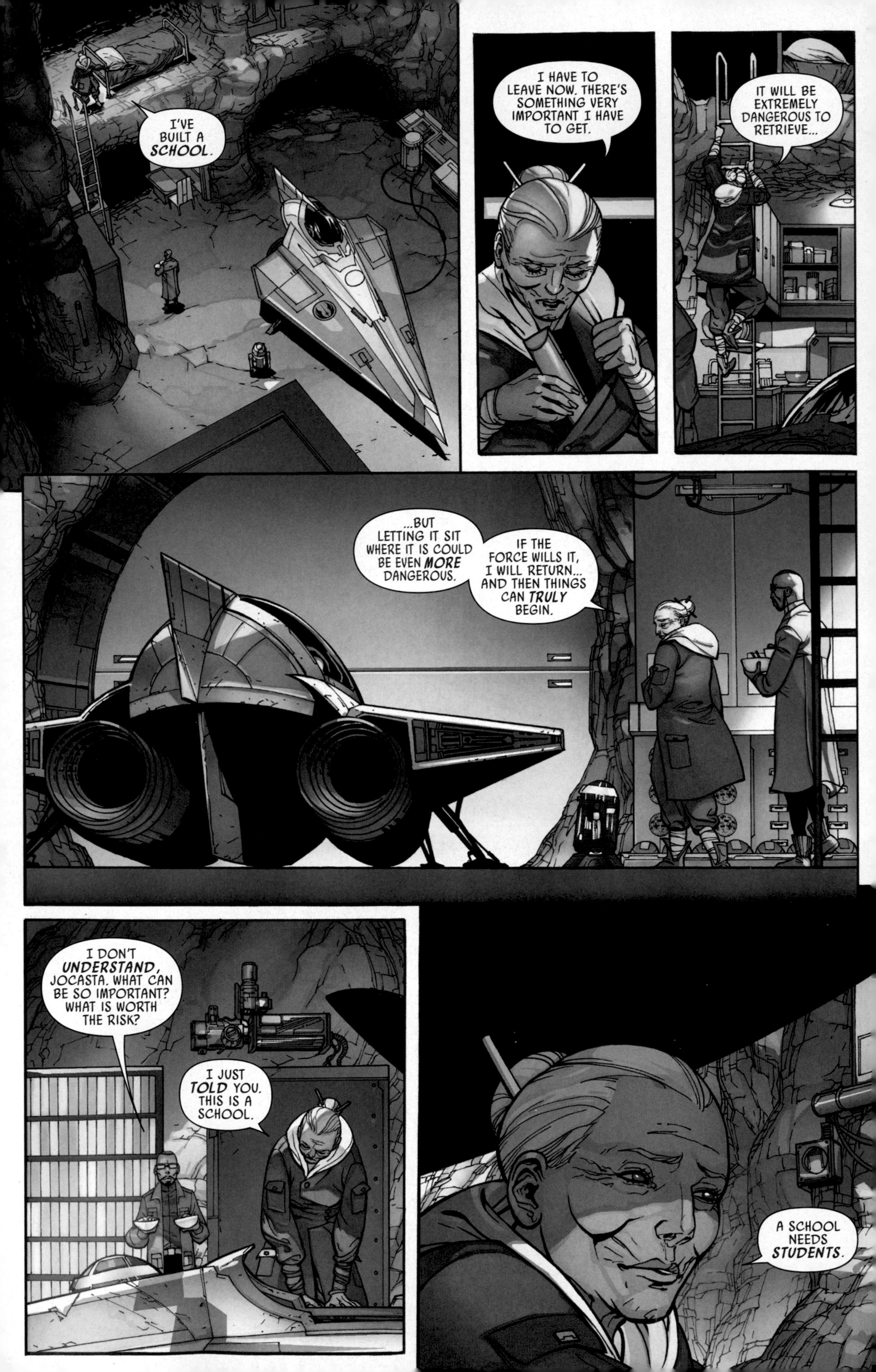
I'VE BUILT A SCHOOL.
I HAVE TO LEAVE NOW. THERE'S SOMETHING VERY IMPORTANT I HAVE TO GET.
IT WILL BE EXTREMELY DANGEROUS TO RETRIEVE...
...BUT LETTING IT SIT WHERE IT IS COULD BE EVEN MORE DANGEROUS.
IF THE FORCE WILLS IT, I WILL RETURN... AND THEN THINGS CAN TRULY BEGIN.
I DON'T UNDERSTAND, JOCASTA. WHAT CAN BE SO IMPORTANT? WHAT IS WORTH THE RISK?
I JUST TOLD YOU. THIS IS A SCHOOL.
A SCHOOL NEEDS STUDENTS.

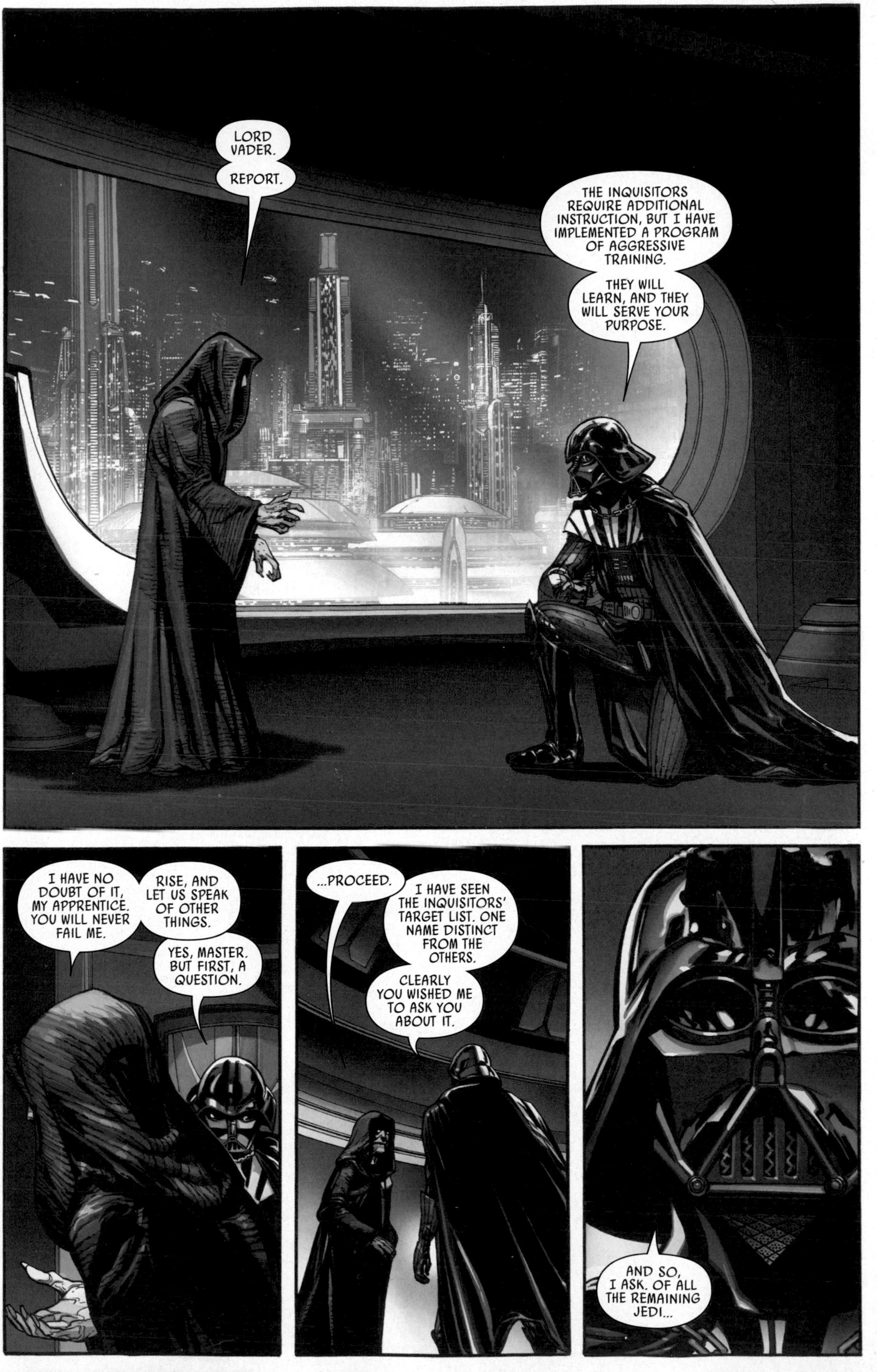

LORD VADER.
REPORT.
THE INQUISITORS REQUIRE ADDITIONAL INSTRUCTION, BUT I HAVE IMPLEMENTED A PROGRAM OF AGGRESSIVE TRAINING.
THEY WILL LEARN, AND THEY WILL SERVE YOUR PURPOSE.
I HAVE NO DOUBT OF IT, MY APPRENTICE. YOU WILL NEVER FAIL ME.
RISE, AND LET US SPEAK OF OTHER THINGS.
YES, MASTER. BUT FIRST, A QUESTION.
...PROCEED.
I HAVE SEEN THE INQUISITORS' TARGET LIST. ONE NAME DISTINCT FROM THE OTHERS.
CLEARLY YOU WISHED ME TO ASK YOU ABOUT IT.
AND SO, I ASK. OF ALL THE REMAINING JEDI...

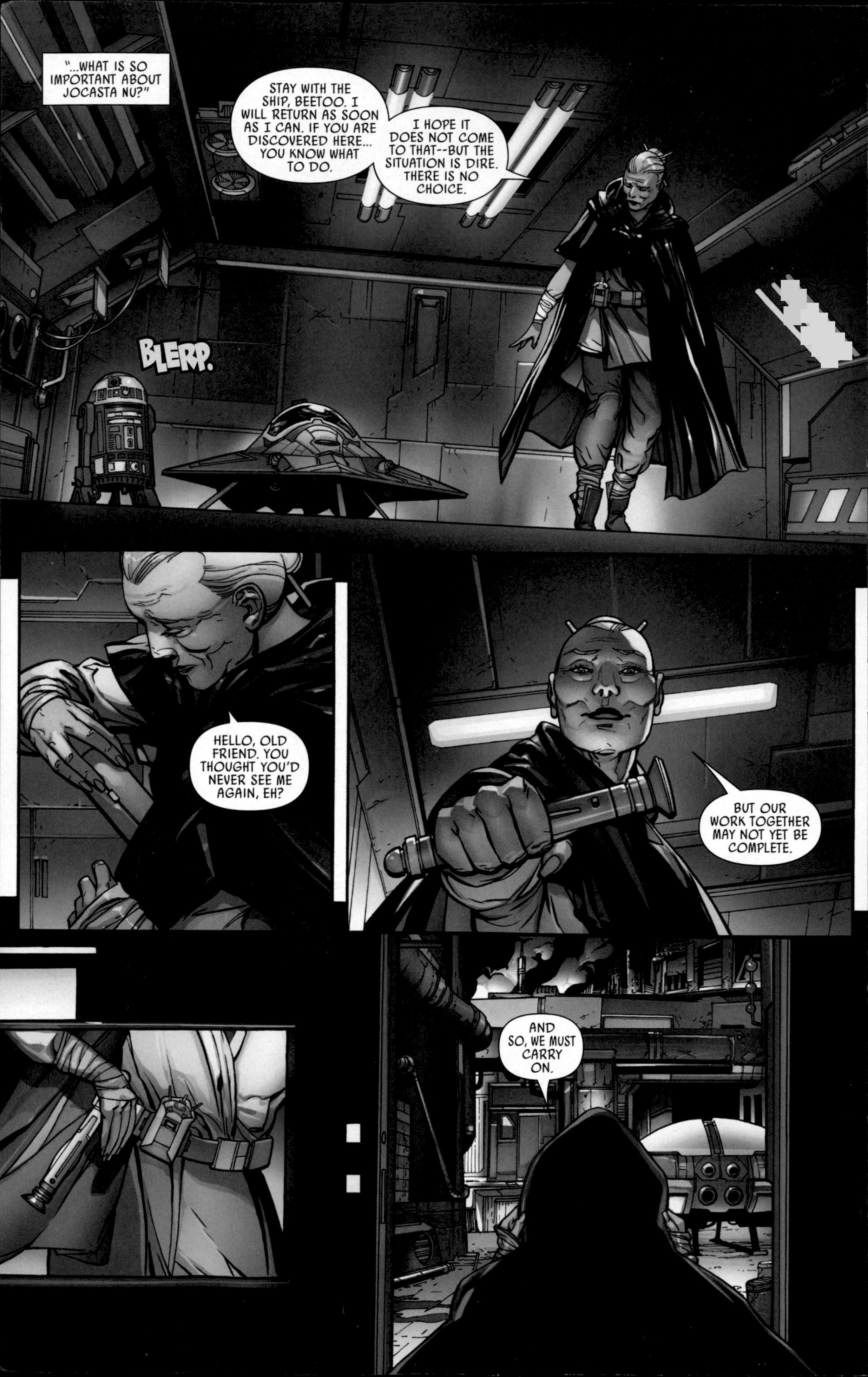
"...WHAT IS SO IMPORTANT ABOUT JOCASTA NU?"
STAY WITH THE SHIP, BEETOO. I WILL RETURN AS SOON AS I CAN. IF YOU ARE DISCOVERED HERE... YOU KNOW WHAT TO DO.
I HOPE IT DOES NOT COME TO THAT--BUT THE SITUATION IS DIRE. THERE IS NO CHOICE.
BLERP.
HELLO, OLD FRIEND. YOU THOUGHT YOU'D NEVER SEE ME AGAIN, EH?
BUT OUR WORK TOGETHER MAY NOT YET BE COMPLETE.
AND SO, WE MUST CARRY ON.

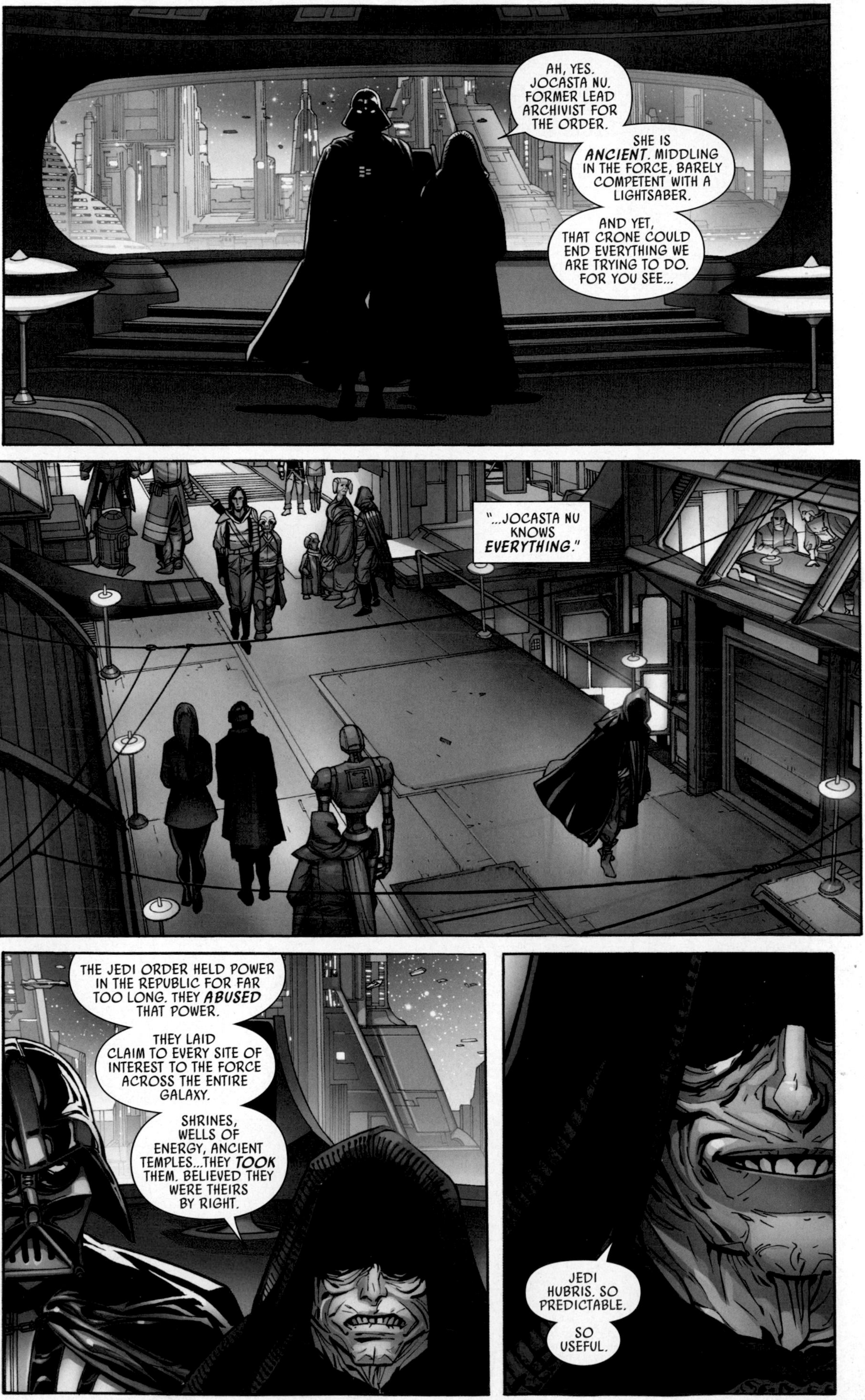
AH, YES. JOCASTA NU. FORMER LEAD ARCHIVIST FOR THE ORDER.
SHE IS ANCIENT. MIDDLING IN THE FORCE, BARELY COMPETENT WITH A LIGHTSABER.
AND YET, THAT CRONE COULD END EVERYTHING WE ARE TRYING TO DO. FOR YOU SEE...
"...JOCASTA NU KNOWS EVERYTHING."
THE JEDI ORDER HELD POWER IN THE REPUBLIC FOR FAR TOO LONG. THEY ABUSED THAT POWER.
THEY LAID CLAIM TO EVERY SITE OF INTEREST TO THE FORCE ACROSS THE ENTIRE GALAXY.
SHRINES, WELLS OF ENERGY, ANCIENT TEMPLES...THEY TOOK THEM. BELIEVED THEY WERE THEIRS BY RIGHT.
JEDI HUBRIS. SO PREDICTABLE.
SO USEFUL.

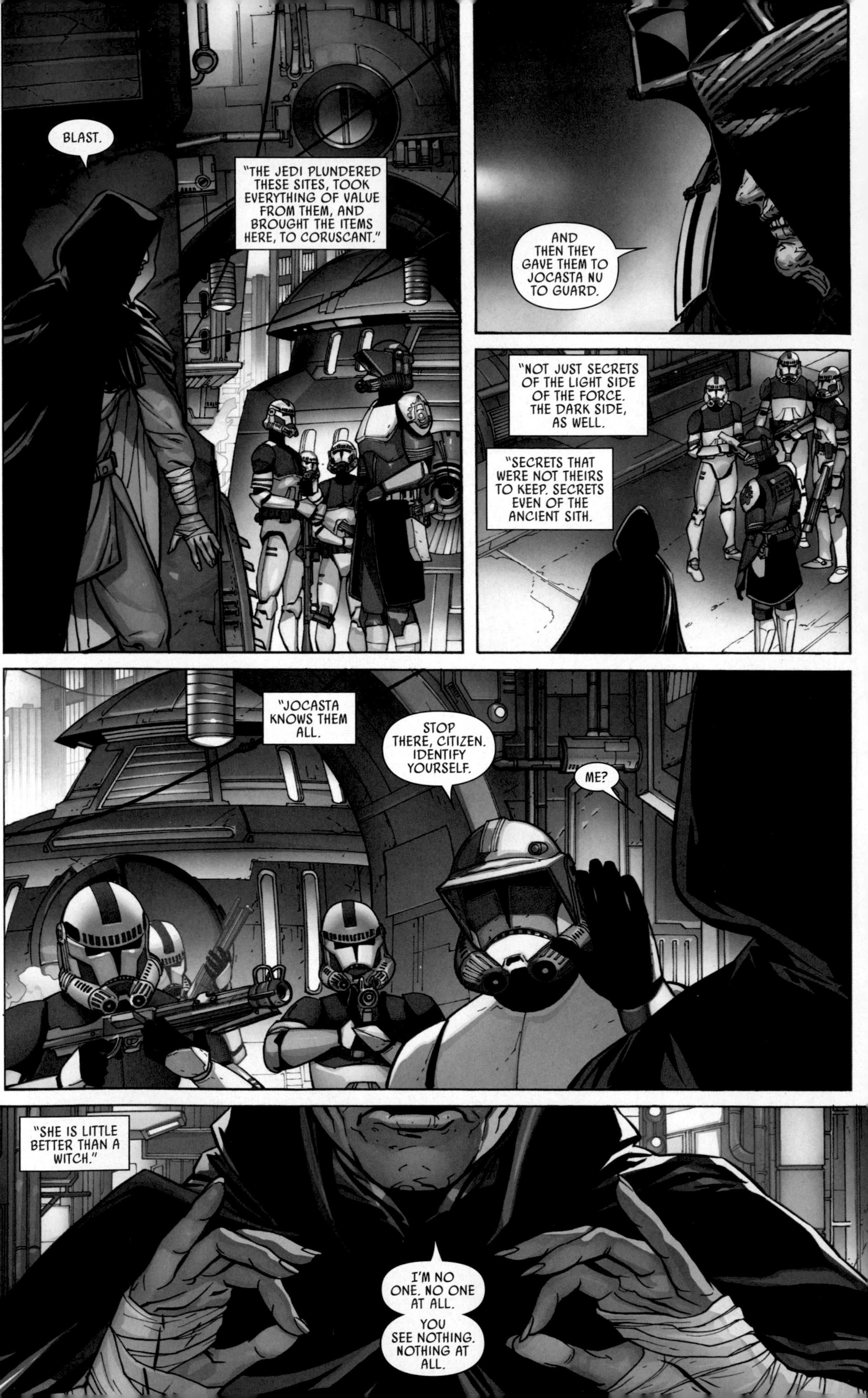
BLAST.
"THE JEDI PLUNDERED THESE SITES, TOOK EVERYTHING OF VALUE FROM THEM, AND BROUGHT THE ITEMS HERE, TO CORUSCANT."
AND THEN THEY GAVE THEM TO JOCASTA NU TO GUARD.
"NOT JUST SECRETS OF THE LIGHT SIDE OF THE FORCE. THE DARK SIDE, AS WELL.
"SECRETS THAT WERE NOT THEIRS TO KEEP. SECRETS EVEN OF THE ANCIENT SITH.
"JOCASTA KNOWS THEM ALL.
STOP THERE, CITIZEN. IDENTIFY YOURSELF.
ME?
"SHE IS LITTLE BETTER THAN A WITCH."
I'M NO ONE. NO ONE AT ALL.
YOU SEE NOTHING. NOTHING AT ALL.

SHE IS NO ONE. NO ONE AT ALL.

WE SEE NOTHING. NOTHING AT ALL.

I UNDERSTAND, MY MASTER. I WILL SEE TO HER DEATH PERSONALLY.

AH...YES. I SENSE YOUR EAGERNESS. THE IDEA OF HUNTING ANOTHER JEDI, EVEN ONE SO FEEBLE AS JOCASTA... IT CALLS TO YOU. YOU *NEED* IT.

BUT YOU WILL SET THESE DESIRES ASIDE.

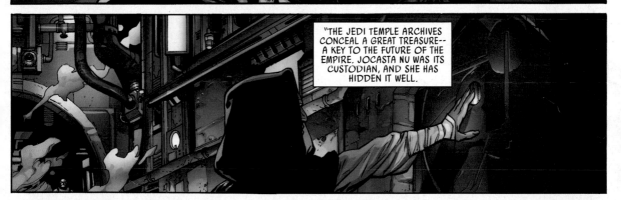

"THE JEDI TEMPLE ARCHIVES CONCEAL A GREAT TREASURE-- A KEY TO THE FUTURE OF THE EMPIRE. JOCASTA NU WAS ITS CUSTODIAN, AND SHE HAS HIDDEN IT WELL.

SSSK!

"I REQUIRE THIS TREASURE. YOU WILL FIND JOCASTA NU, YOU WILL BRING HER TO ME, AND SHE WILL TELL ME WHAT I WISH TO KNOW."

YOU DID NOT TELL THIS TO THE INQUISITORS.

OF COURSE NOT! THERE IS RISK IN JOCASTA FALLING INTO ANY HANDS BUT OURS. HER KNOWLEDGE COULD EASILY BE USED AGAINST US.

THE GRAND INQUISITOR AND THE REST SHOULD BE AWARE OF THE WOMAN--THEY CAN HELP YOU FIND HER, IF YOU WISH--BUT THEY NEED NOT KNOW HER IMPORTANCE.

THE INQUISITORS WILL BE USEFUL, BUT THEY ARE NOT SITH.

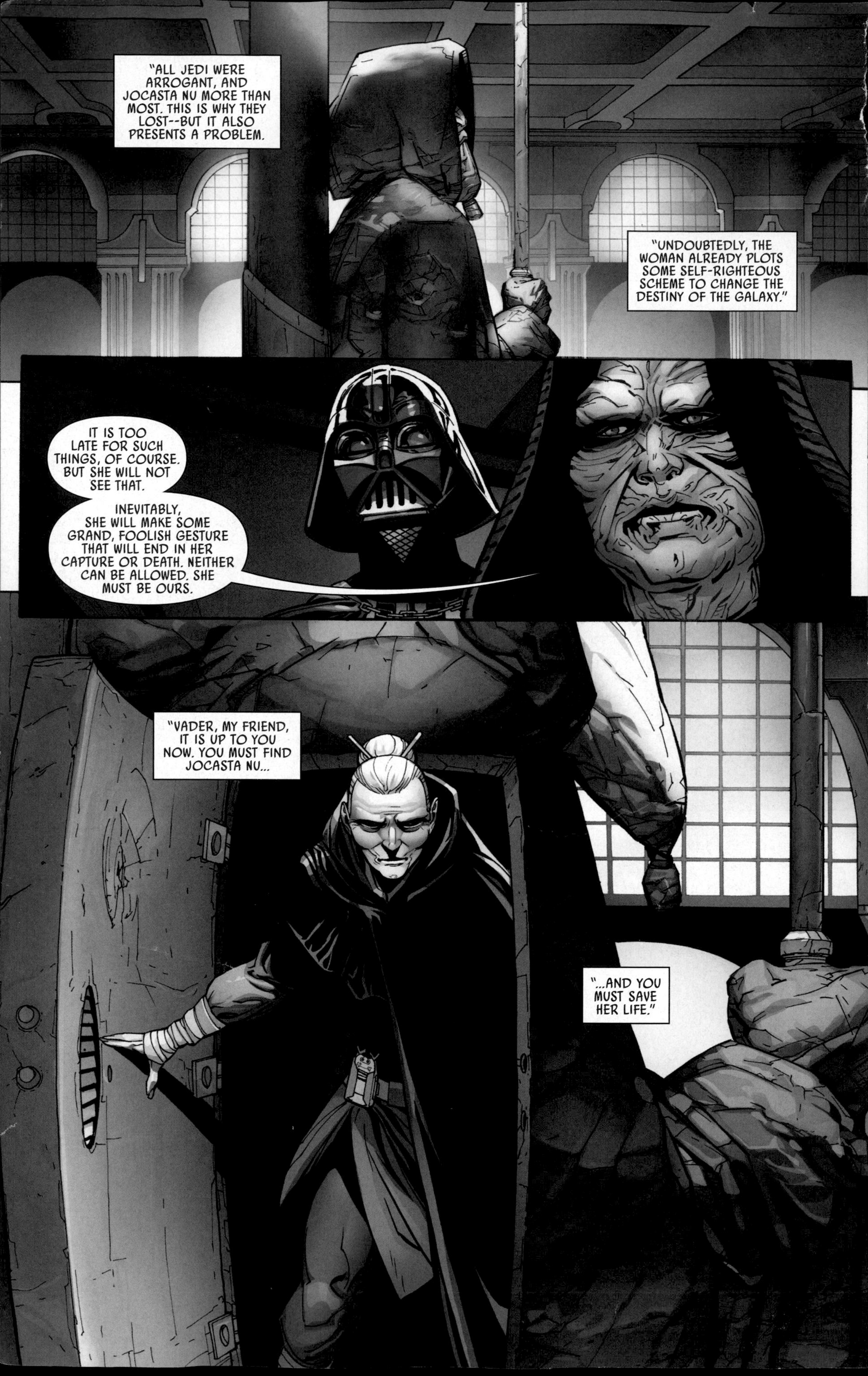
"ALL JEDI WERE ARROGANT, AND JOCASTA NU MORE THAN MOST. THIS IS WHY THEY LOST--BUT IT ALSO PRESENTS A PROBLEM.
"UNDOUBTEDLY, THE WOMAN ALREADY PLOTS SOME SELF-RIGHTEOUS SCHEME TO CHANGE THE DESTINY OF THE GALAXY."
IT IS TOO LATE FOR SUCH THINGS, OF COURSE. BUT SHE WILL NOT SEE THAT.
INEVITABLY, SHE WILL MAKE SOME GRAND, FOOLISH GESTURE THAT WILL END IN HER CAPTURE OR DEATH. NEITHER CAN BE ALLOWED. SHE MUST BE OURS.
"VADER, MY FRIEND, IT IS UP TO YOU NOW. YOU MUST FIND JOCASTA NU...
"...AND YOU MUST SAVE HER LIFE."

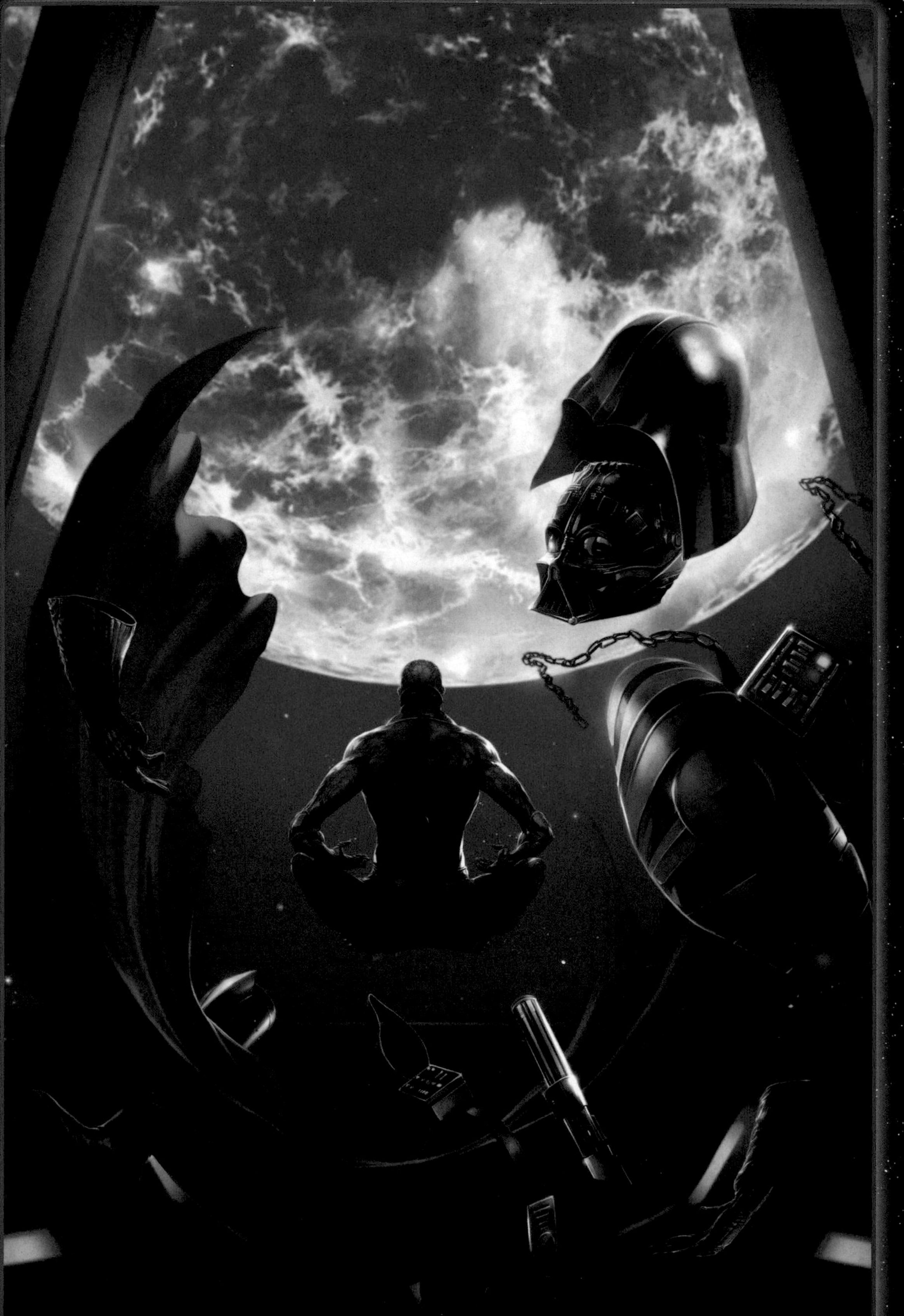

8

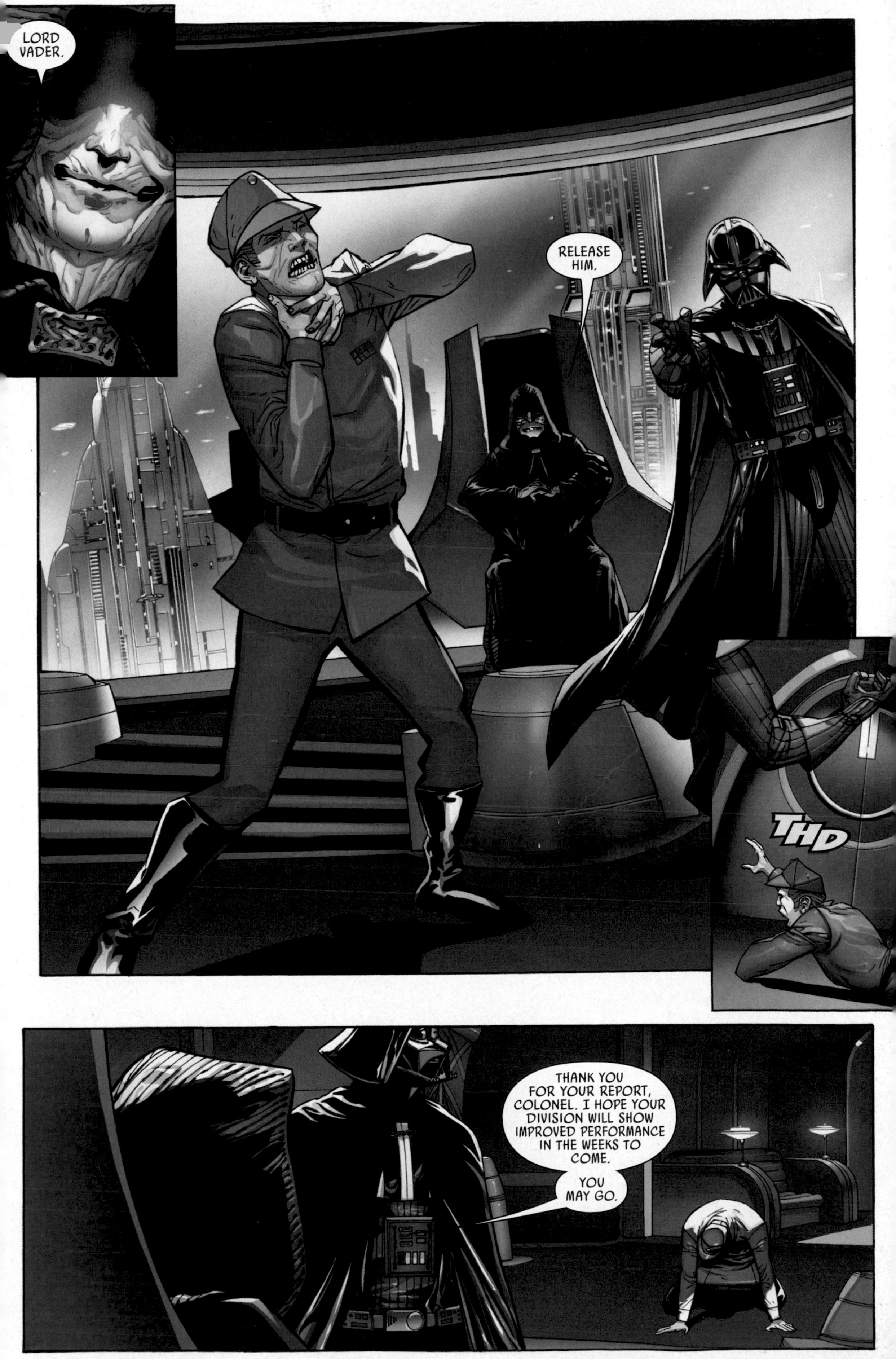
LORD VADER.
RELEASE HIM.
THD
THANK YOU FOR YOUR REPORT, COLONEL. I HOPE YOUR DIVISION WILL SHOW IMPROVED PERFORMANCE IN THE WEEKS TO COME.
YOU MAY GO.

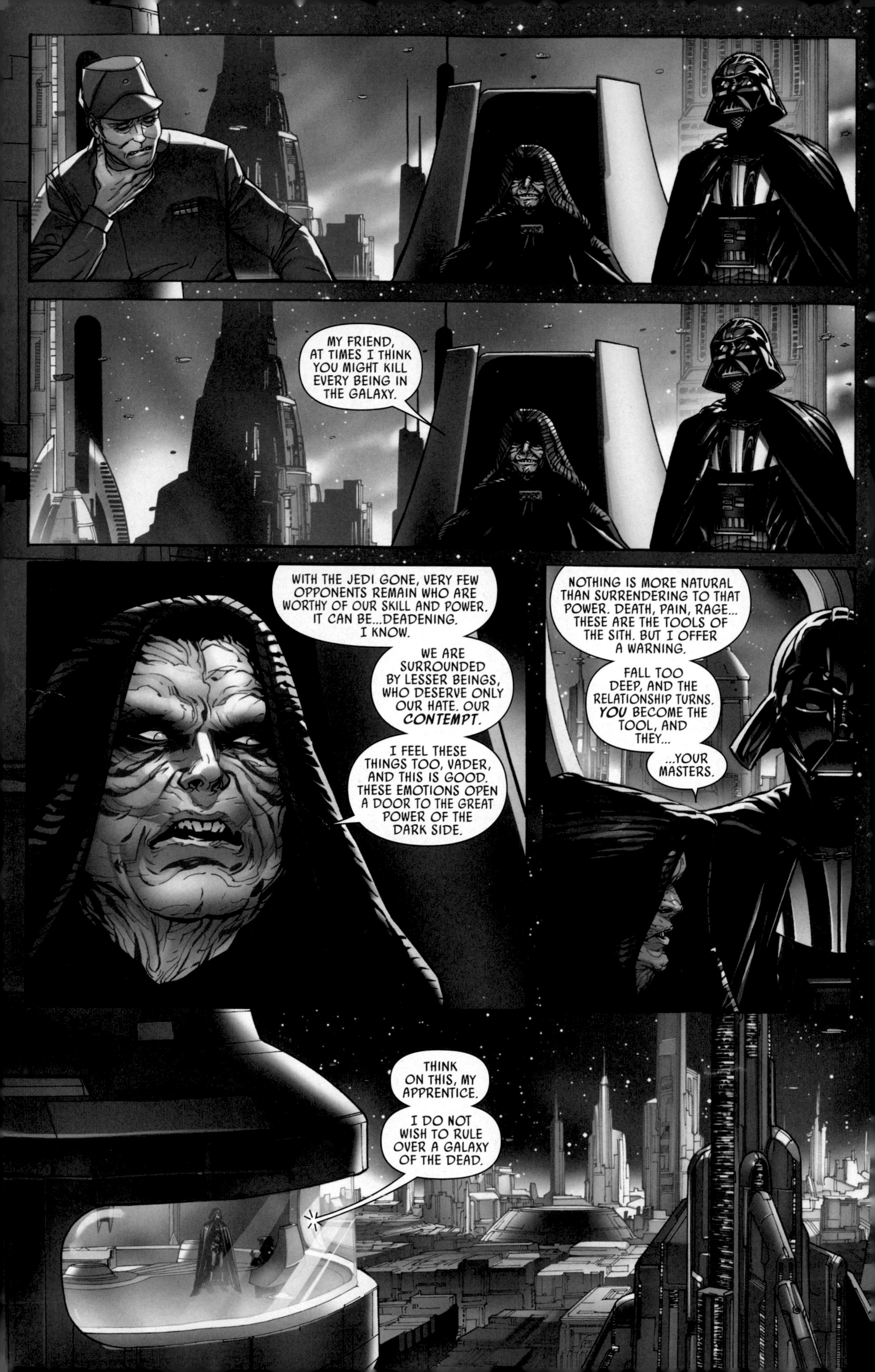
MY FRIEND, AT TIMES I THINK YOU MIGHT KILL EVERY BEING IN THE GALAXY.
WITH THE JEDI GONE, VERY FEW OPPONENTS REMAIN WHO ARE WORTHY OF OUR SKILL AND POWER. IT CAN BE...DEADENING. I KNOW.
WE ARE SURROUNDED BY LESSER BEINGS, WHO DESERVE ONLY OUR HATE. OUR *CONTEMPT*.
I FEEL THESE THINGS TOO, VADER, AND THIS IS GOOD. THESE EMOTIONS OPEN A DOOR TO THE GREAT POWER OF THE DARK SIDE.
NOTHING IS MORE NATURAL THAN SURRENDERING TO THAT POWER. DEATH, PAIN, RAGE... THESE ARE THE TOOLS OF THE SITH. BUT I OFFER A WARNING.
FALL TOO DEEP, AND THE RELATIONSHIP TURNS. *YOU* BECOME THE TOOL, AND THEY...
...YOUR MASTERS.
THINK ON THIS, MY APPRENTICE.
I DO NOT WISH TO RULE OVER A GALAXY OF THE DEAD.

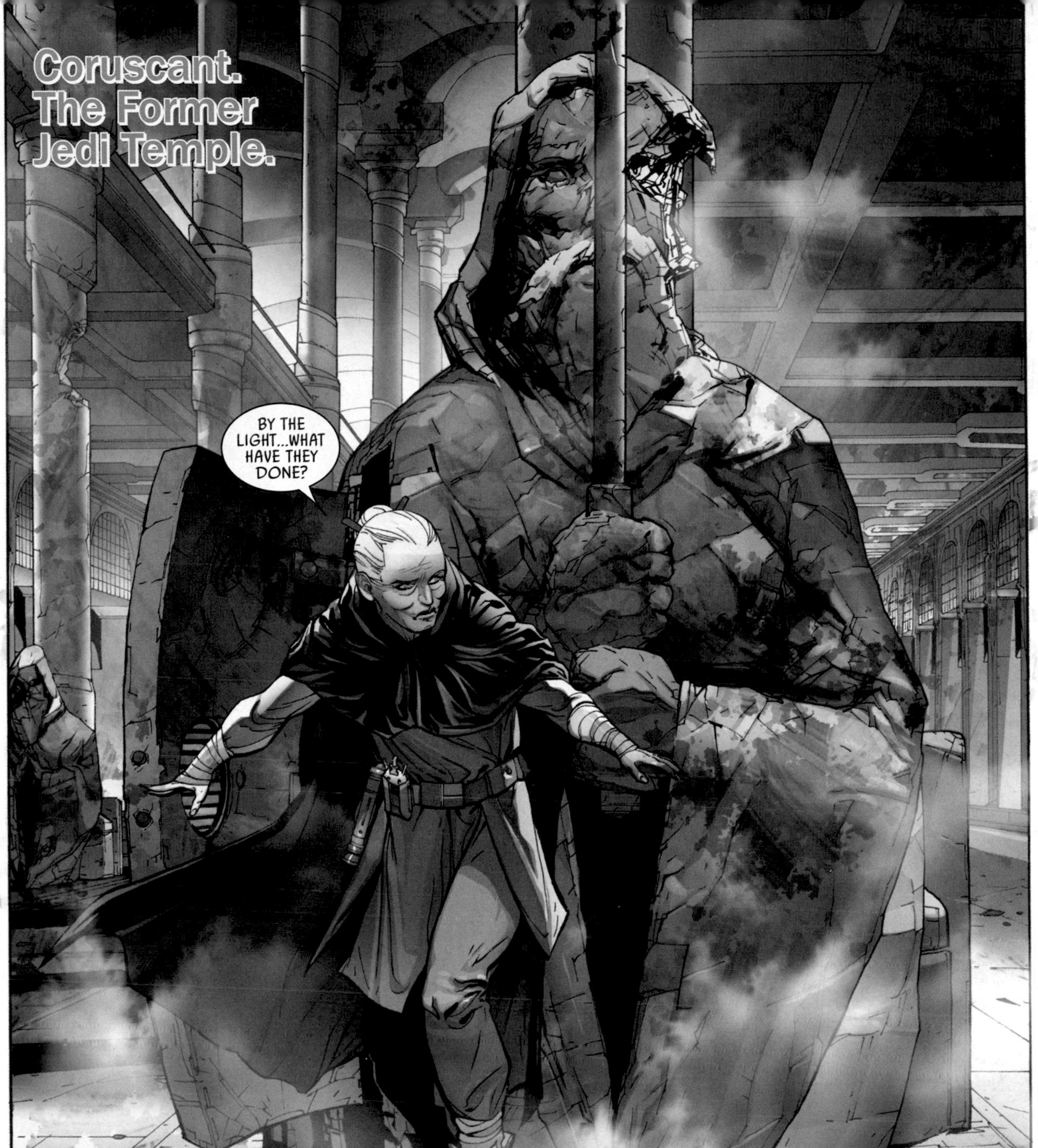
Coruscant.
The Former
Jedi Temple.
BY THE LIGHT...WHAT HAVE THEY DONE?
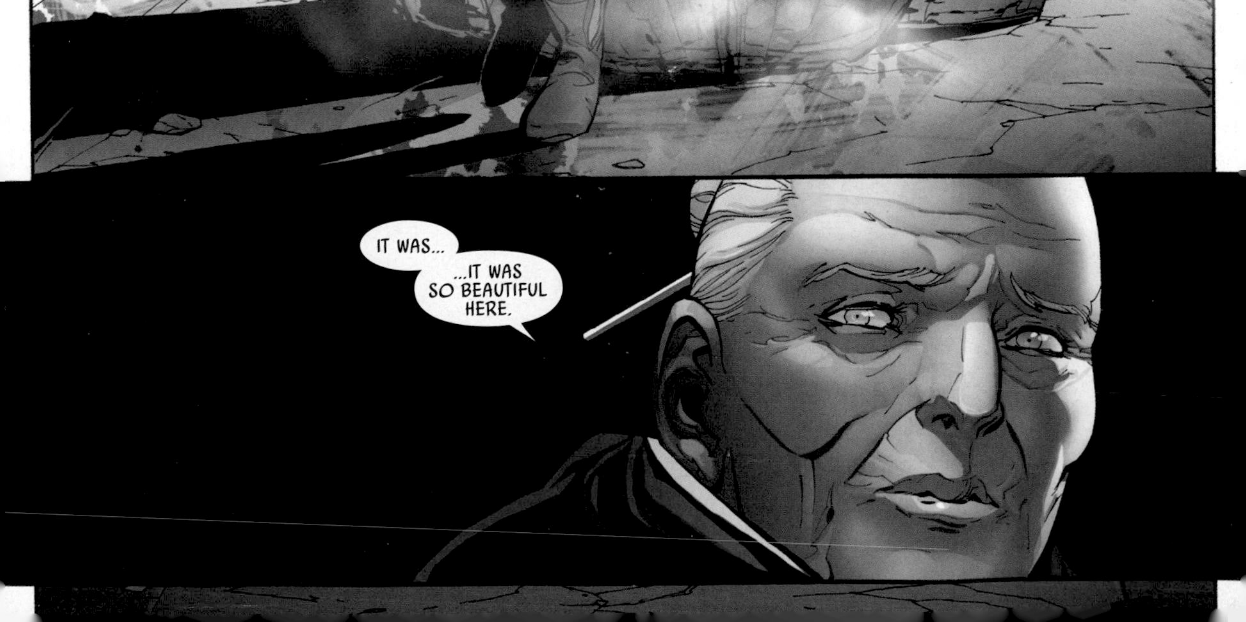
IT WAS...
...IT WAS SO BEAUTIFUL HERE.

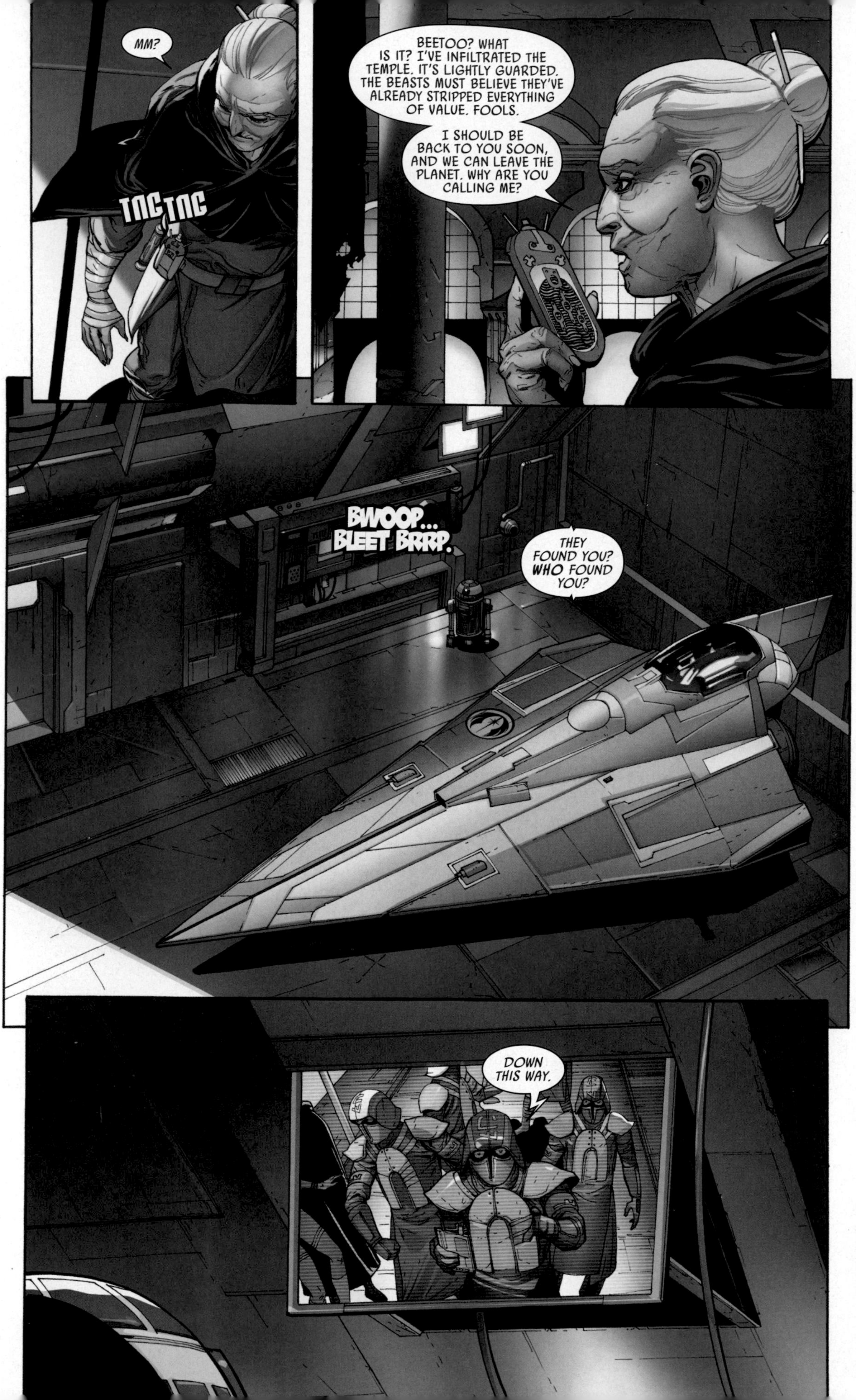
MM?
TNC TNC
BEETOO? WHAT IS IT? I'VE INFILTRATED THE TEMPLE. IT'S LIGHTLY GUARDED. THE BEASTS MUST BELIEVE THEY'VE ALREADY STRIPPED EVERYTHING OF VALUE. FOOLS.
I SHOULD BE BACK TO YOU SOON, AND WE CAN LEAVE THE PLANET. WHY ARE YOU CALLING ME?
BWOOP... BLEET BRRP.
THEY FOUND YOU? WHO FOUND YOU?
DOWN THIS WAY.

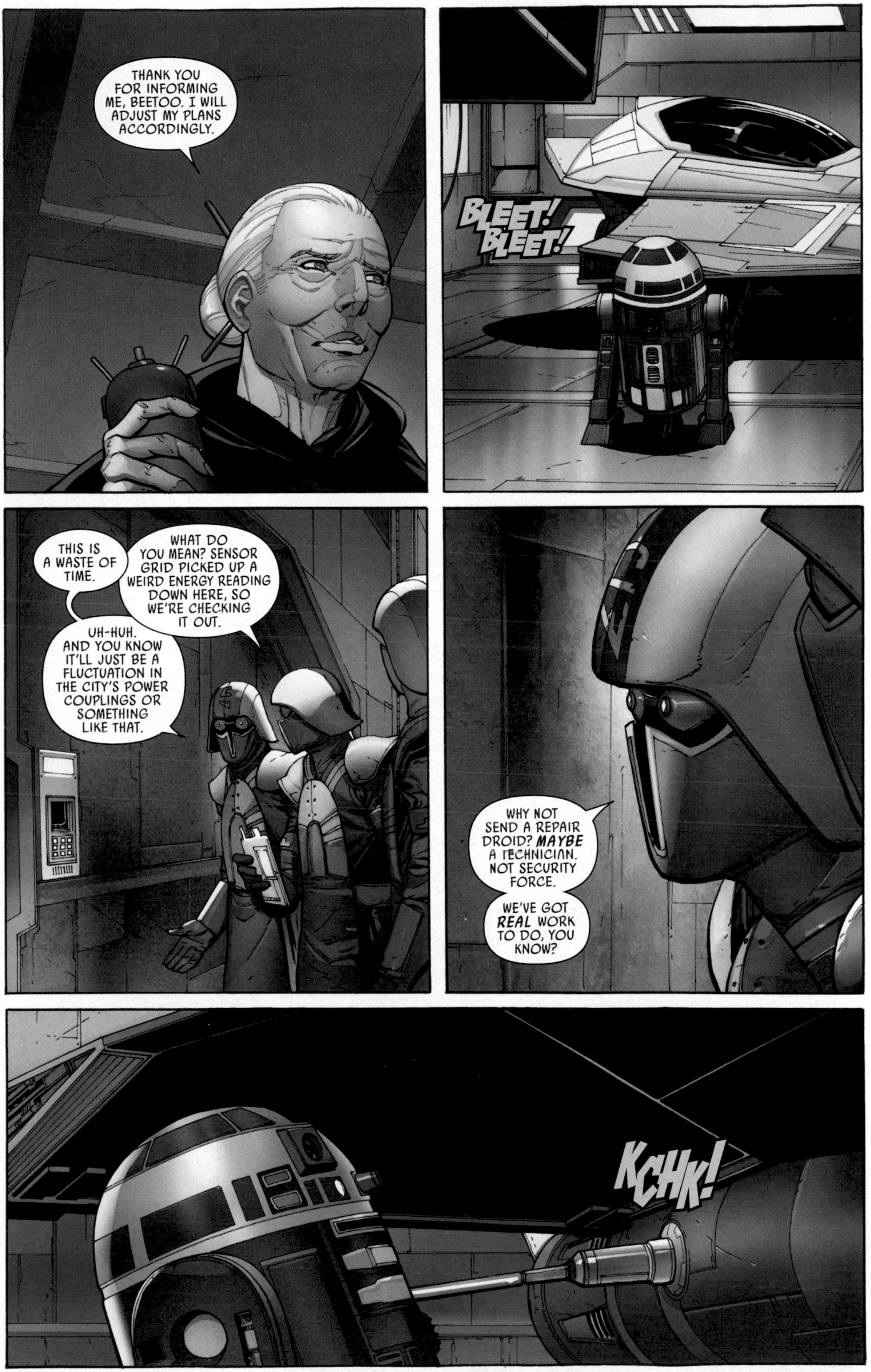
THANK YOU FOR INFORMING ME, BEETOO. I WILL ADJUST MY PLANS ACCORDINGLY.
BLEET! BLEET!
THIS IS A WASTE OF TIME.
WHAT DO YOU MEAN? SENSOR GRID PICKED UP A WEIRD ENERGY READING DOWN HERE, SO WE'RE CHECKING IT OUT.
UH-HUH. AND YOU KNOW IT'LL JUST BE A FLUCTUATION IN THE CITY'S POWER COUPLINGS OR SOMETHING LIKE THAT.
WHY NOT SEND A REPAIR DROID? MAYBE A TECHNICIAN. NOT SECURITY FORCE.
WE'VE GOT REAL WORK TO DO, YOU KNOW?
KCHK!

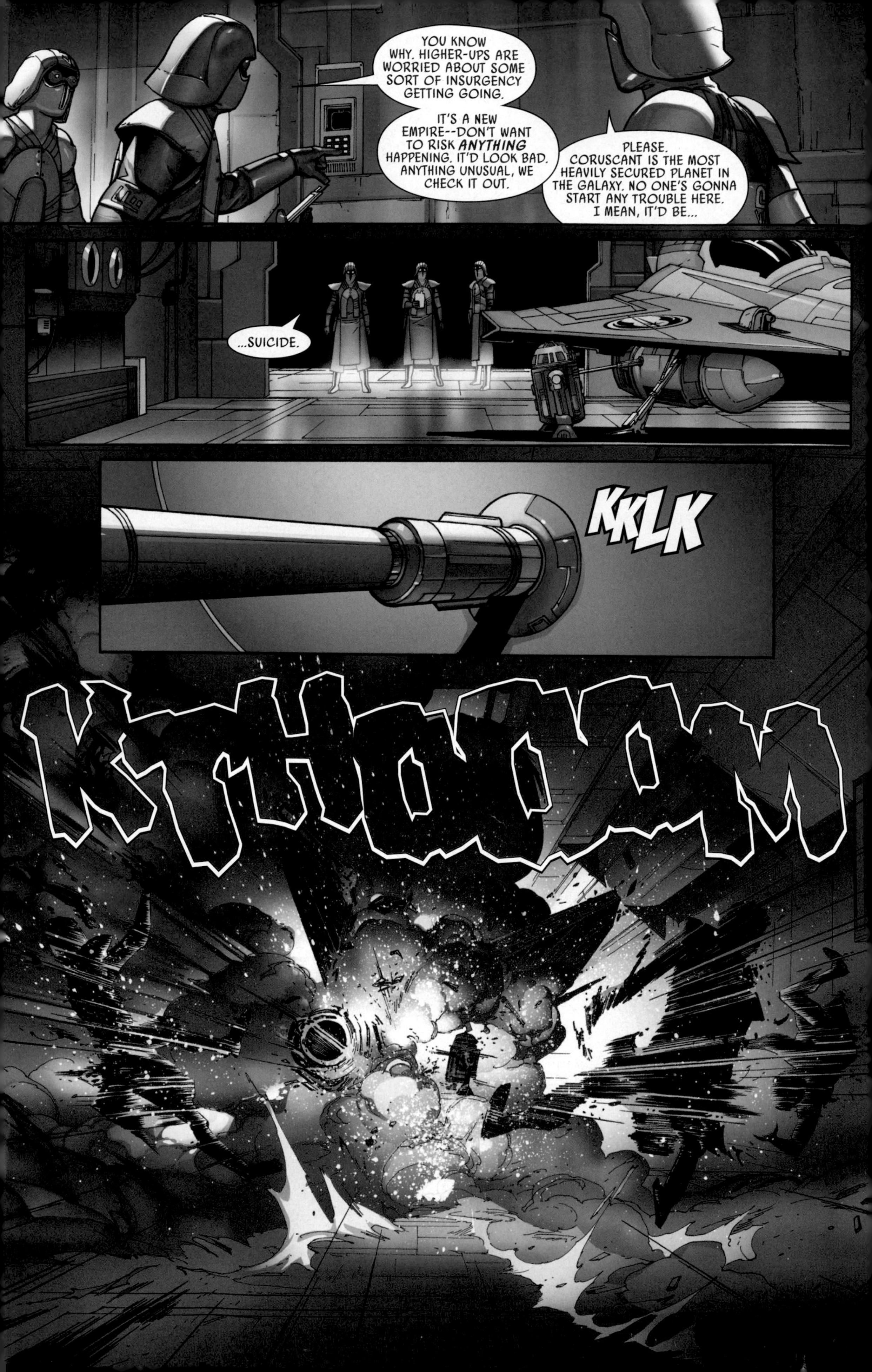
YOU KNOW WHY. HIGHER-UPS ARE WORRIED ABOUT SOME SORT OF INSURGENCY GETTING GOING.
IT'S A NEW EMPIRE--DON'T WANT TO RISK ANYTHING HAPPENING. IT'D LOOK BAD. ANYTHING UNUSUAL, WE CHECK IT OUT.
PLEASE. CORUSCANT IS THE MOST HEAVILY SECURED PLANET IN THE GALAXY. NO ONE'S GONNA START ANY TROUBLE HERE. I MEAN, IT'D BE...
...SUICIDE.
KKLK
KTHOOOM

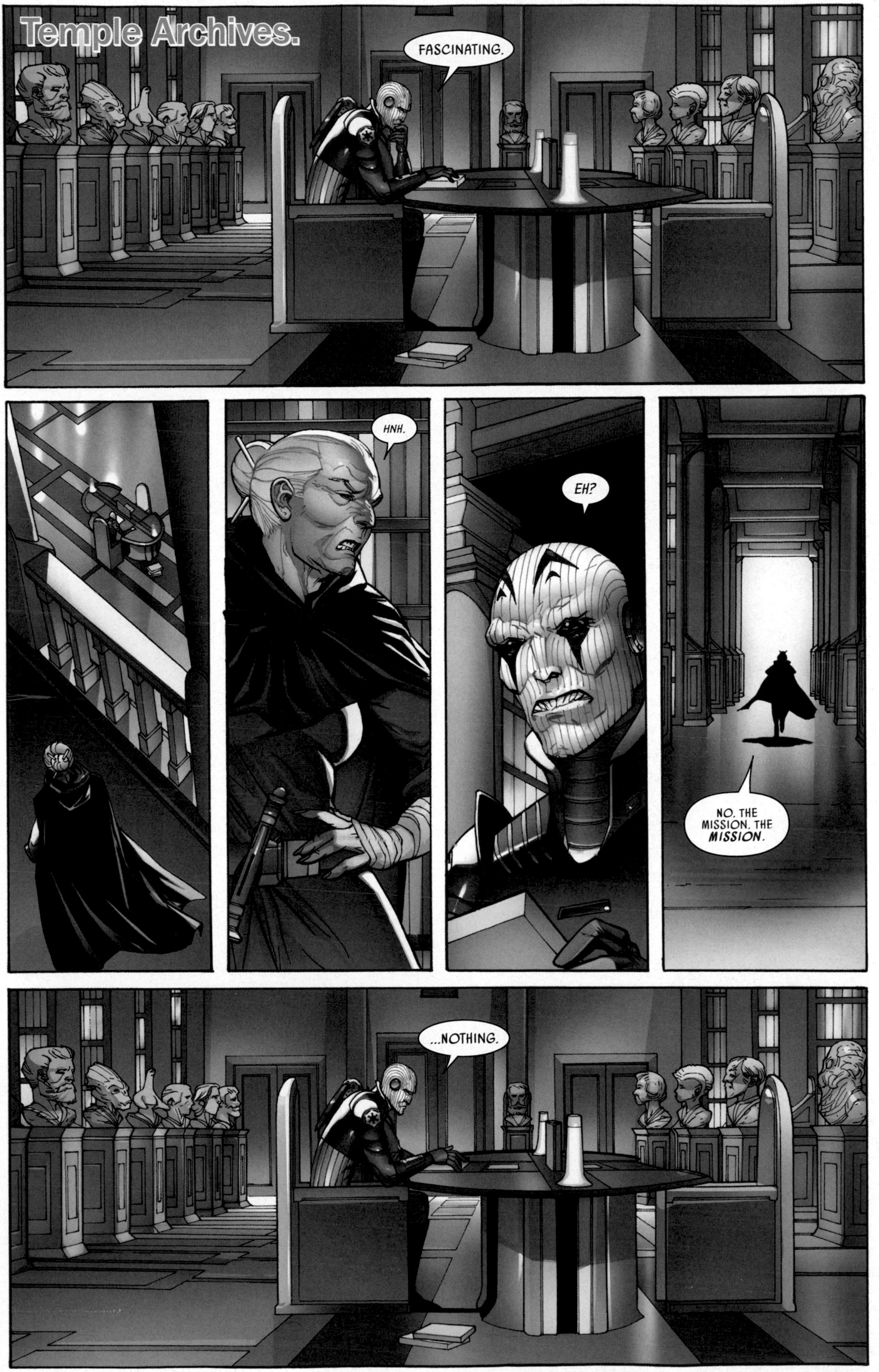
Temple Archives.
FASCINATING.
HNH.
EH?
NO. THE MISSION. THE MISSION.
...NOTHING.

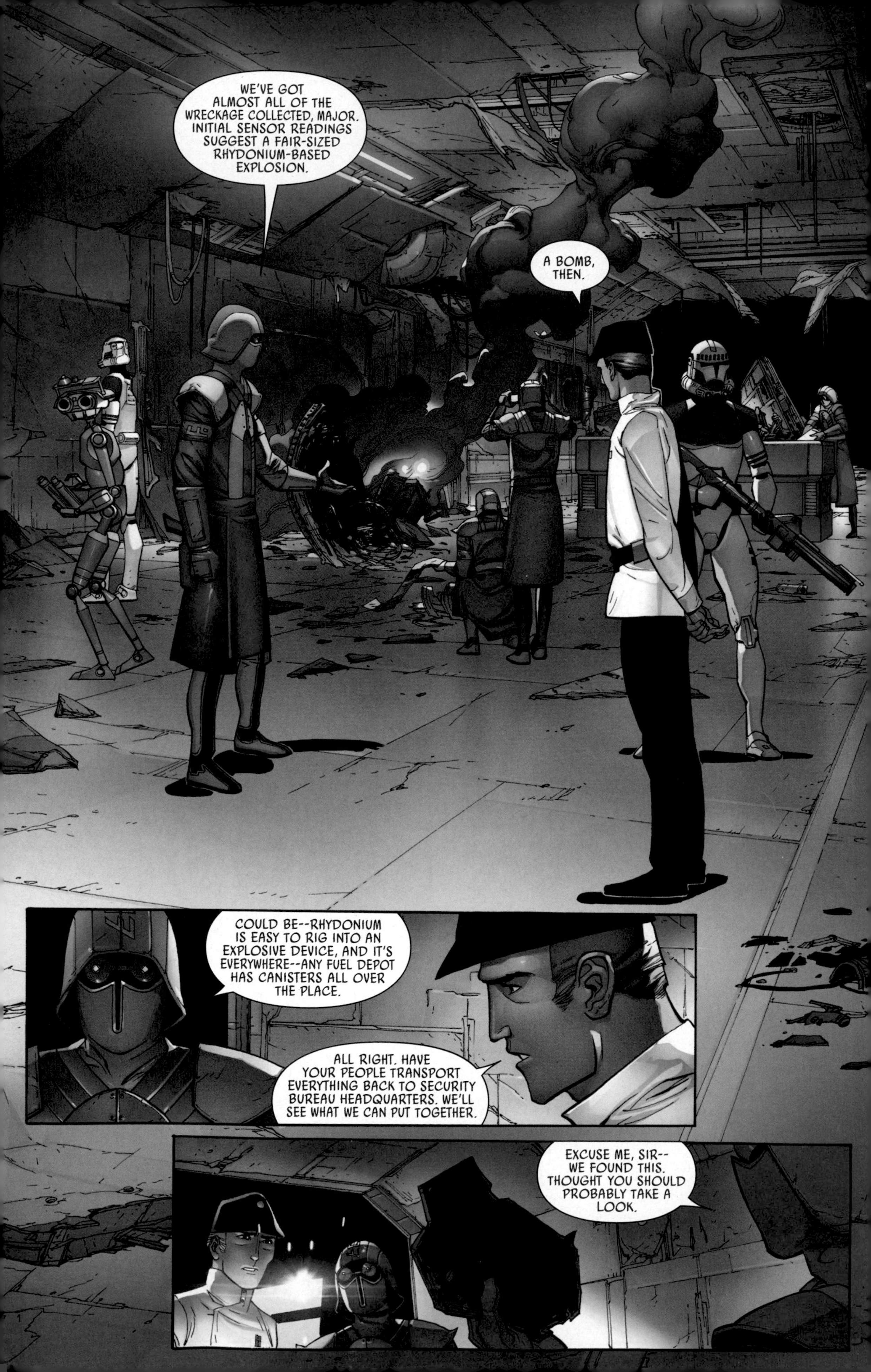
WE'VE GOT ALMOST ALL OF THE WRECKAGE COLLECTED, MAJOR. INITIAL SENSOR READINGS SUGGEST A FAIR-SIZED RHYDONIUM-BASED EXPLOSION.
A BOMB, THEN.
COULD BE--RHYDONIUM IS EASY TO RIG INTO AN EXPLOSIVE DEVICE, AND IT'S EVERYWHERE--ANY FUEL DEPOT HAS CANISTERS ALL OVER THE PLACE.
ALL RIGHT. HAVE YOUR PEOPLE TRANSPORT EVERYTHING BACK TO SECURITY BUREAU HEADQUARTERS. WE'LL SEE WHAT WE CAN PUT TOGETHER.
EXCUSE ME, SIR--WE FOUND THIS. THOUGHT YOU SHOULD PROBABLY TAKE A LOOK.

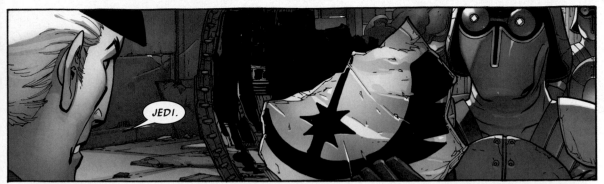

JEDI.

IT CAN'T BE REAL, SIR. THE JEDI ARE GONE. WE'VE SEEN GRAFFITI HERE AND THERE EVER SINCE THE PURGE... PROBABLY JUST MORE OF THAT.

PERHAPS, BUT I STILL NEED TO CALL IT IN. NEW DIRECTIVES CAME DOWN. ANY HINT OF THE JEDI, NO MATTER HOW SMALL, MUST BE REPORTED.

THAT GOES FOR YOUR TEAMS TOO, CAPTAIN. SPREAD THE WORD AMONG YOUR PEOPLE.

OF COURSE, SIR, I WILL. BUT... REPORTED TO WHOM?

SOMEONE NEW. I'VE NEVER HEARD OF HIM. STRANGE NAME.

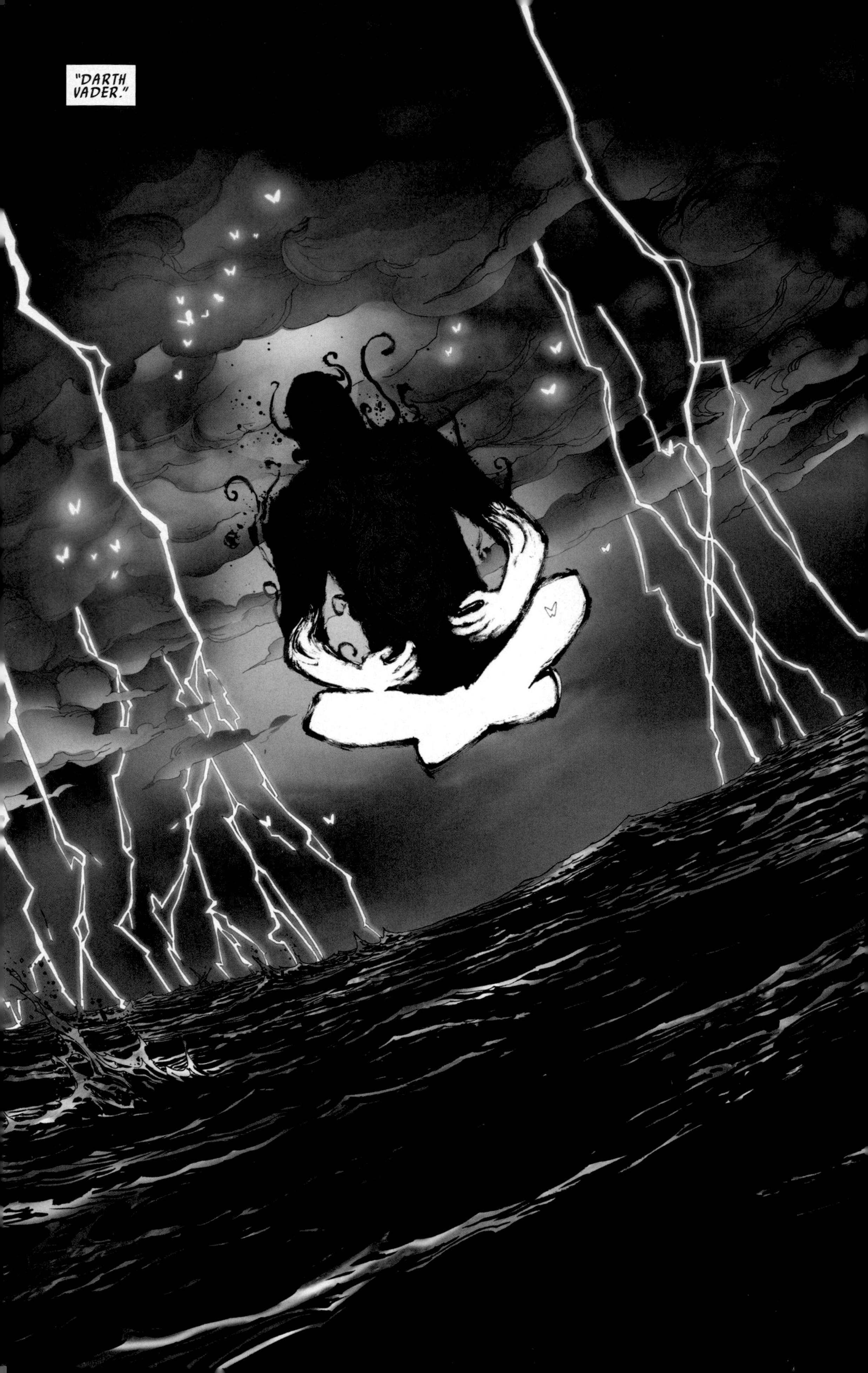
"DARTH VADER."

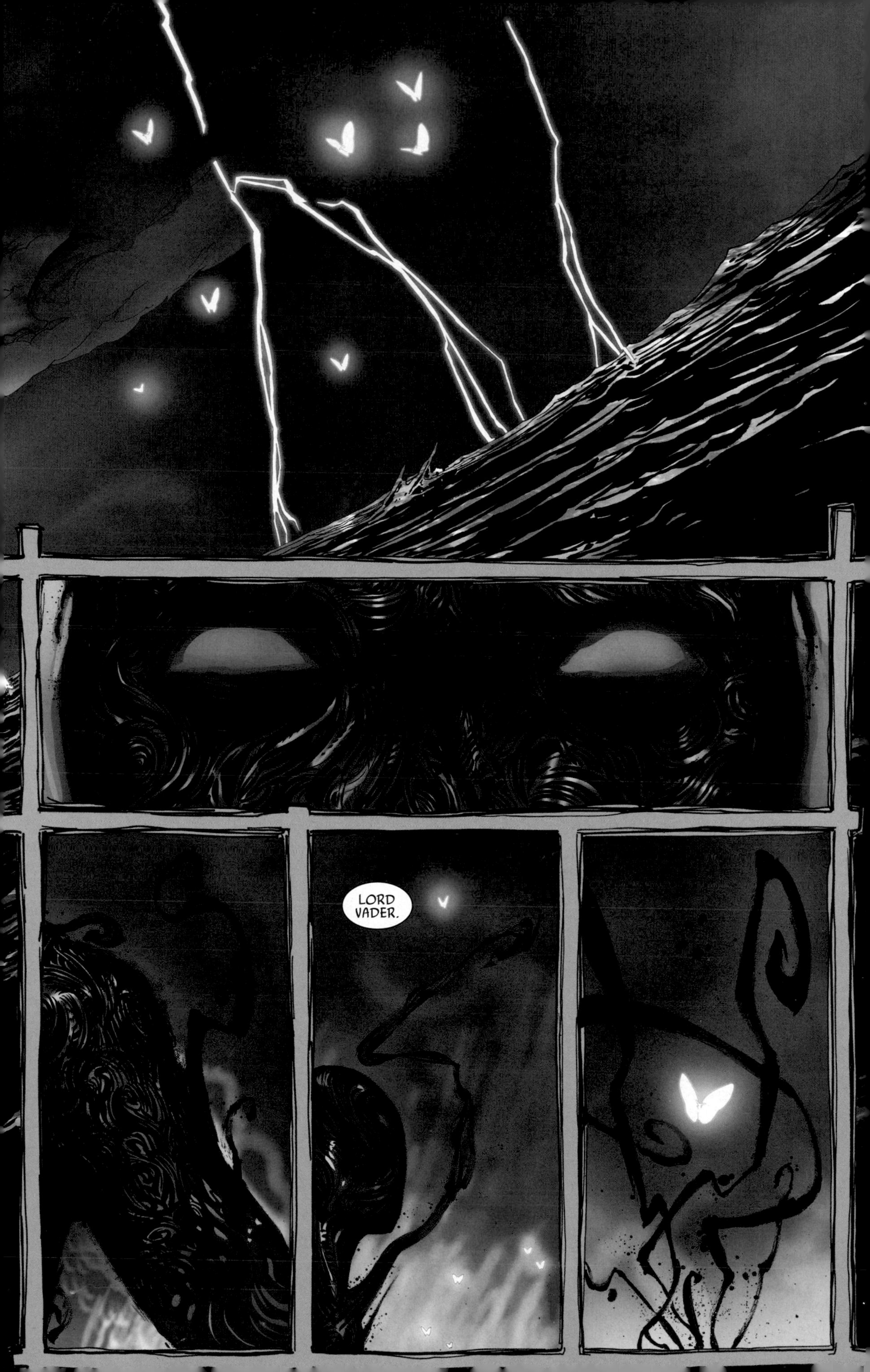
LORD VADER.

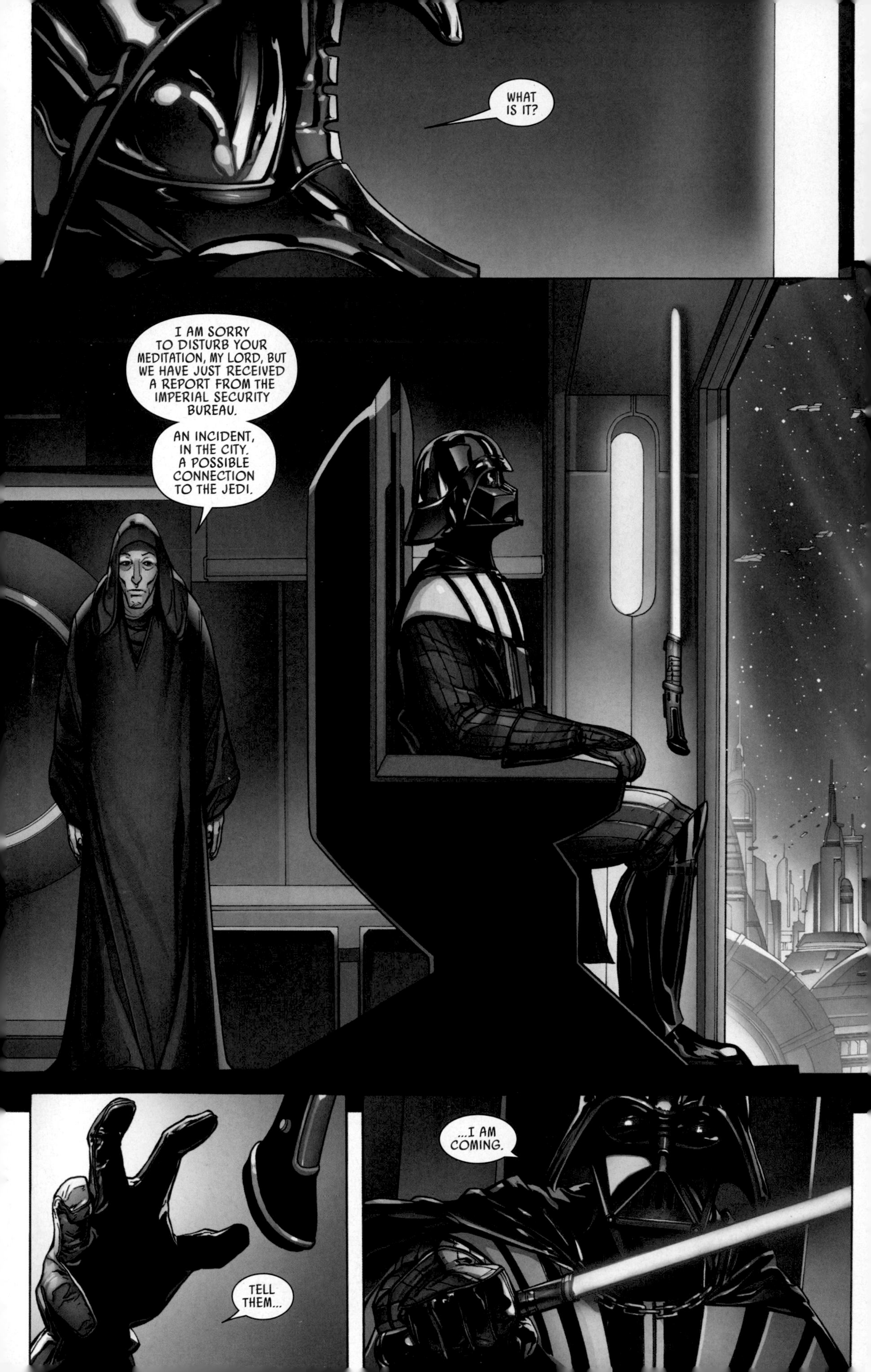
WHAT IS IT?
I AM SORRY TO DISTURB YOUR MEDITATION, MY LORD, BUT WE HAVE JUST RECEIVED A REPORT FROM THE IMPERIAL SECURITY BUREAU.
AN INCIDENT, IN THE CITY. A POSSIBLE CONNECTION TO THE JEDI.
TELL THEM...
...I AM COMING.

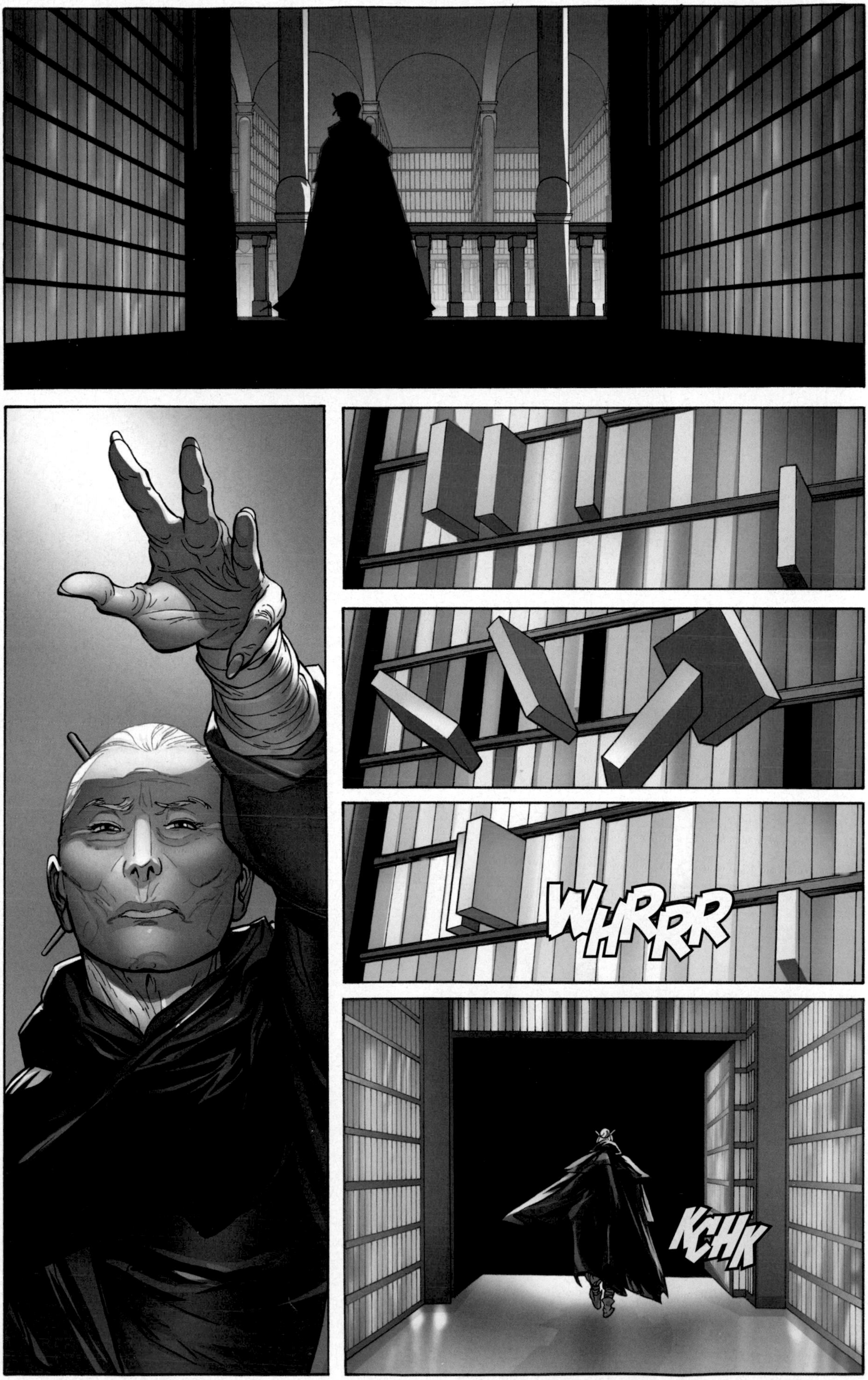
WHRRR
KCHK

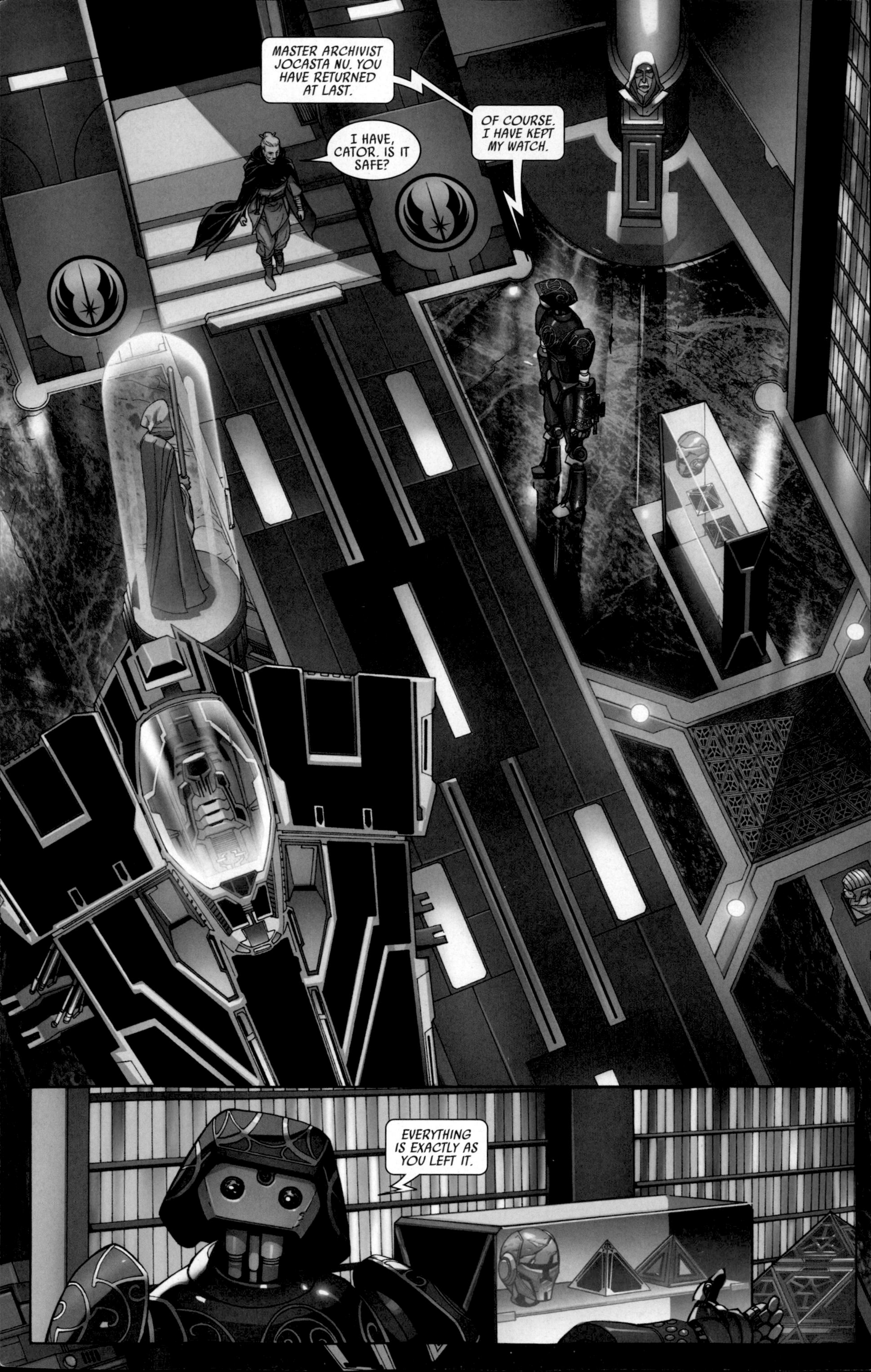
MASTER ARCHIVIST JOCASTA NU. YOU HAVE RETURNED AT LAST.
I HAVE, CATOR. IS IT SAFE?
OF COURSE. I HAVE KEPT MY WATCH.
EVERYTHING IS EXACTLY AS YOU LEFT IT.

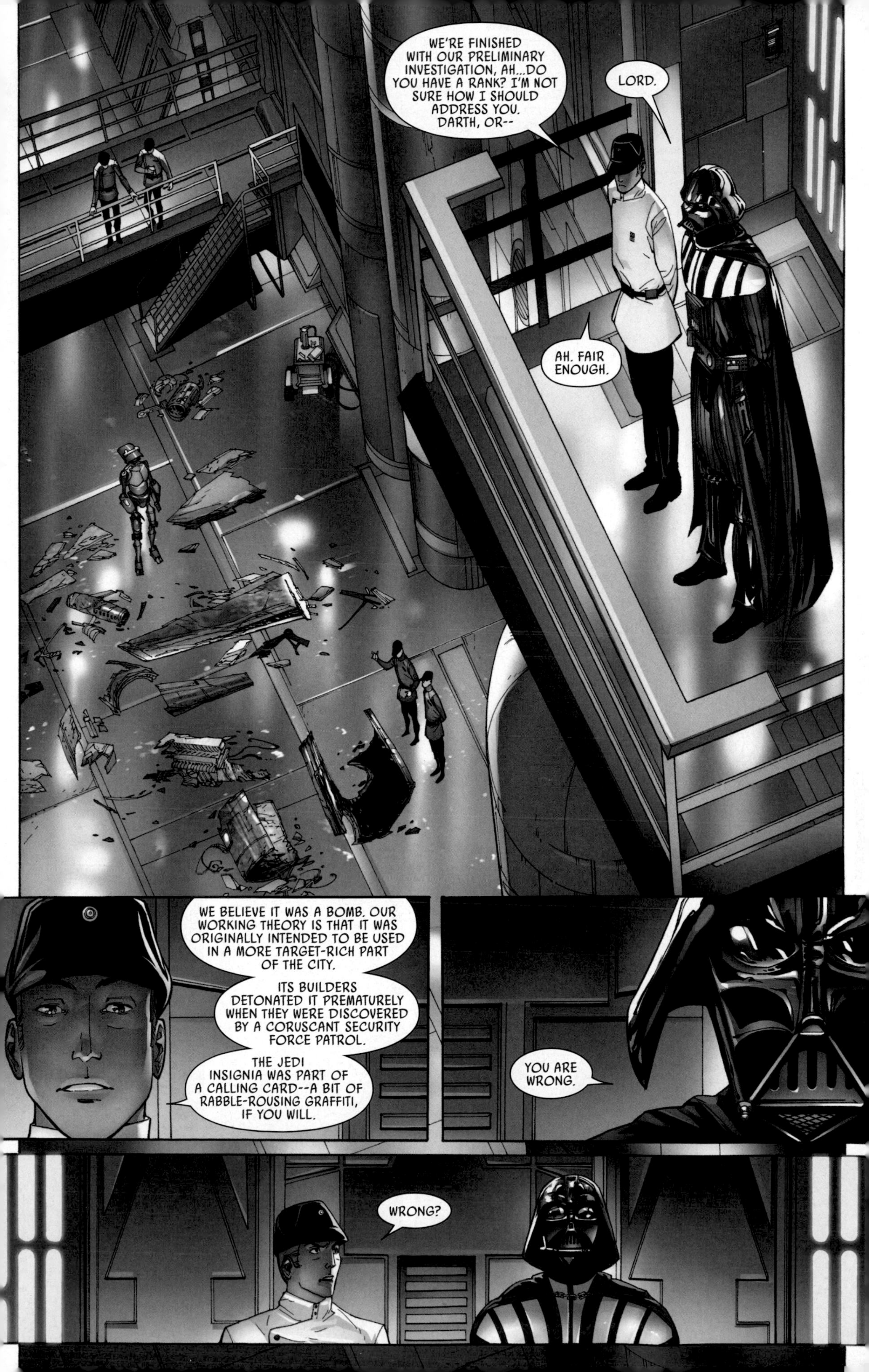
WE'RE FINISHED WITH OUR PRELIMINARY INVESTIGATION, AH...DO YOU HAVE A RANK? I'M NOT SURE HOW I SHOULD ADDRESS YOU. DARTH, OR--
LORD.
AH. FAIR ENOUGH.
WE BELIEVE IT WAS A BOMB. OUR WORKING THEORY IS THAT IT WAS ORIGINALLY INTENDED TO BE USED IN A MORE TARGET-RICH PART OF THE CITY.
ITS BUILDERS DETONATED IT PREMATURELY WHEN THEY WERE DISCOVERED BY A CORUSCANT SECURITY FORCE PATROL.
THE JEDI INSIGNIA WAS PART OF A CALLING CARD--A BIT OF RABBLE-ROUSING GRAFFITI, IF YOU WILL.
YOU ARE WRONG.
WRONG?

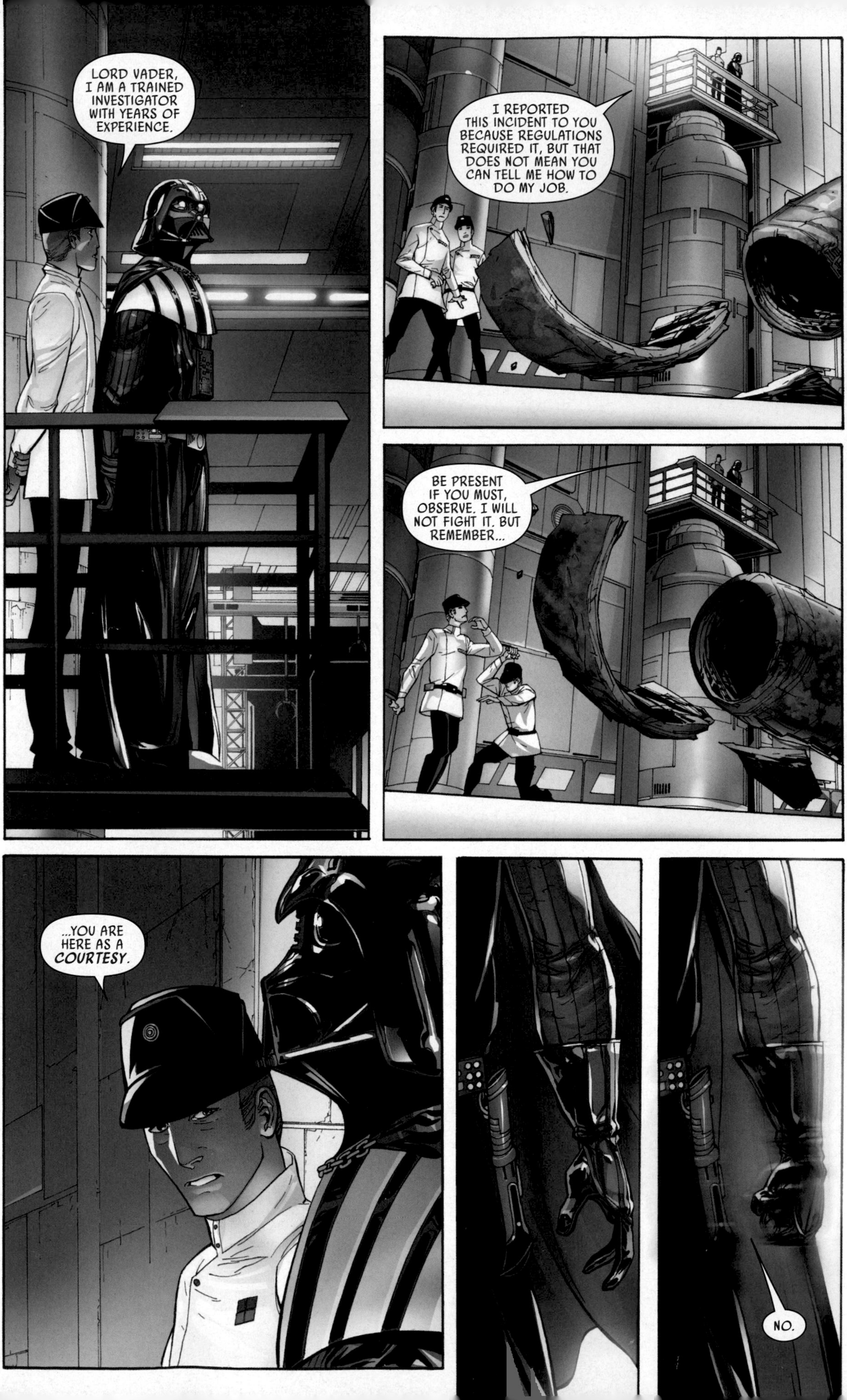
LORD VADER, I AM A TRAINED INVESTIGATOR WITH YEARS OF EXPERIENCE.
I REPORTED THIS INCIDENT TO YOU BECAUSE REGULATIONS REQUIRED IT, BUT THAT DOES NOT MEAN YOU CAN TELL ME HOW TO DO MY JOB.
BE PRESENT IF YOU MUST, OBSERVE. I WILL NOT FIGHT IT. BUT REMEMBER...
...YOU ARE HERE AS A COURTESY.
NO.

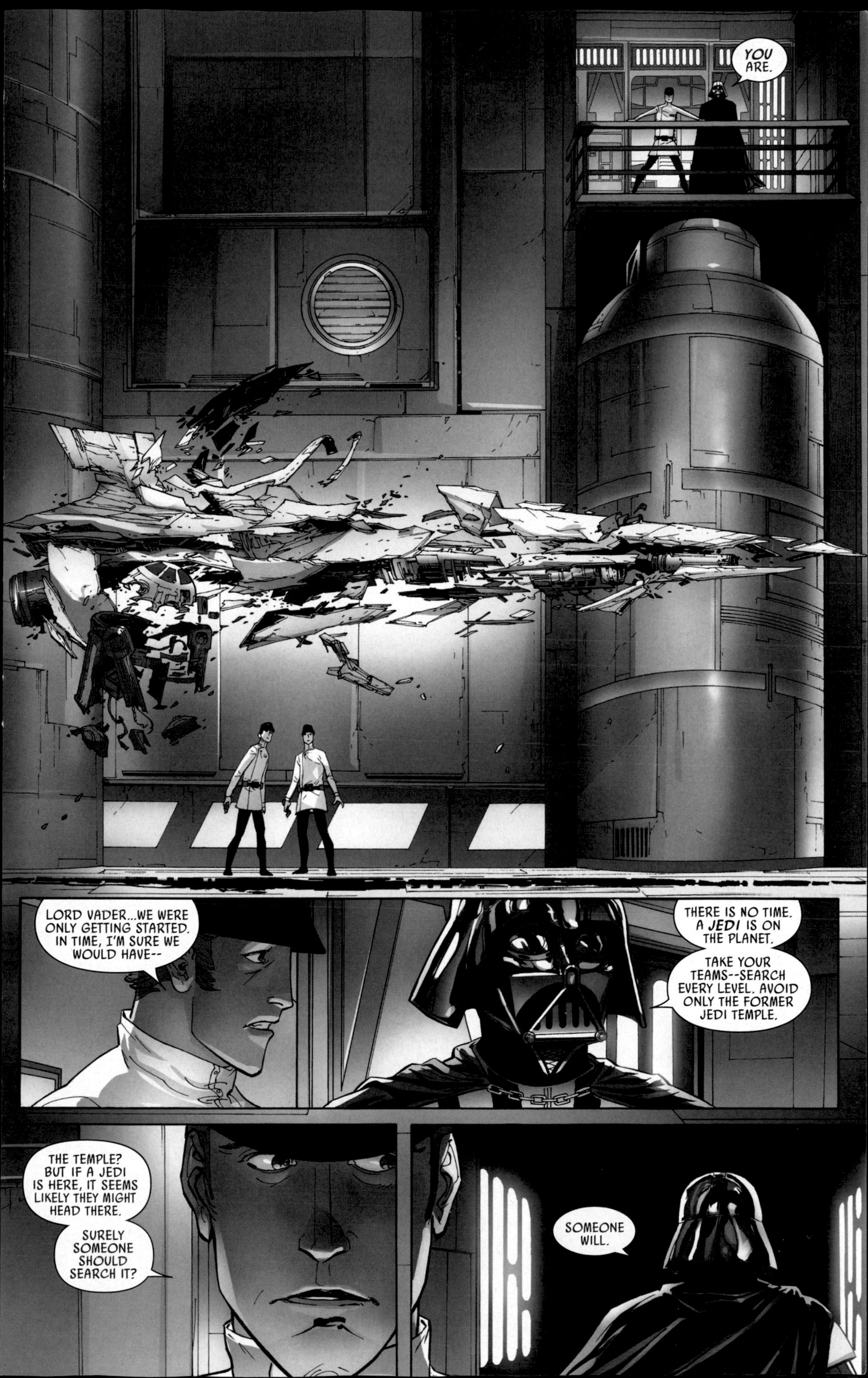
YOU ARE.
LORD VADER...WE WERE ONLY GETTING STARTED. IN TIME, I'M SURE WE WOULD HAVE--
THERE IS NO TIME. A JEDI IS ON THE PLANET.
TAKE YOUR TEAMS--SEARCH EVERY LEVEL. AVOID ONLY THE FORMER JEDI TEMPLE.
THE TEMPLE? BUT IF A JEDI IS HERE, IT SEEMS LIKELY THEY MIGHT HEAD THERE.
SURELY SOMEONE SHOULD SEARCH IT?
SOMEONE WILL.

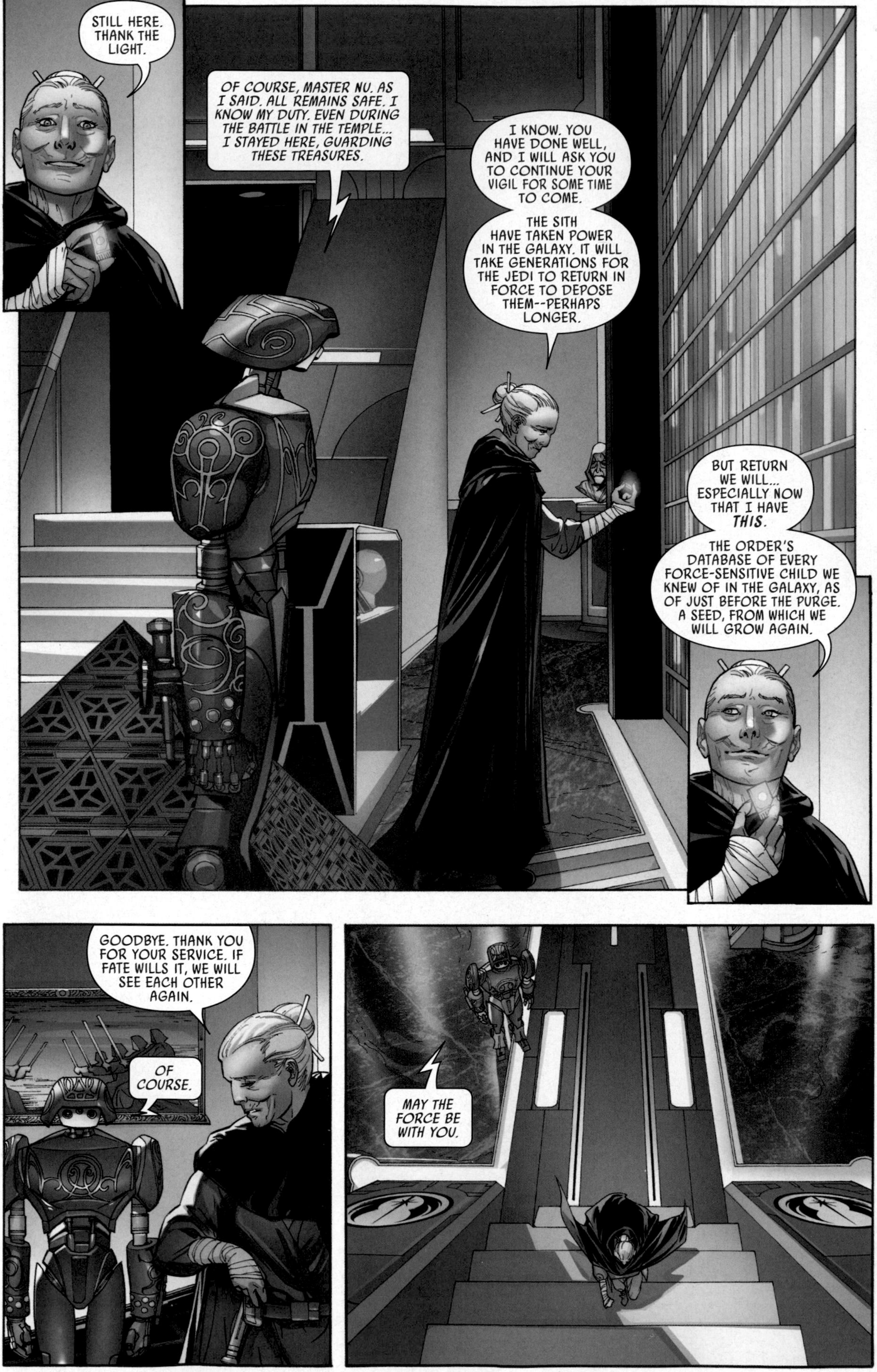
STILL HERE. THANK THE LIGHT.
OF COURSE, MASTER NU. AS I SAID. ALL REMAINS SAFE. I KNOW MY DUTY. EVEN DURING THE BATTLE IN THE TEMPLE... I STAYED HERE, GUARDING THESE TREASURES.
I KNOW. YOU HAVE DONE WELL, AND I WILL ASK YOU TO CONTINUE YOUR VIGIL FOR SOME TIME TO COME.
THE SITH HAVE TAKEN POWER IN THE GALAXY. IT WILL TAKE GENERATIONS FOR THE JEDI TO RETURN IN FORCE TO DEPOSE THEM--PERHAPS LONGER.
BUT RETURN WE WILL... ESPECIALLY NOW THAT I HAVE *THIS*.
THE ORDER'S DATABASE OF EVERY FORCE-SENSITIVE CHILD WE KNEW OF IN THE GALAXY, AS OF JUST BEFORE THE PURGE. A SEED, FROM WHICH WE WILL GROW AGAIN.
GOODBYE. THANK YOU FOR YOUR SERVICE. IF FATE WILLS IT, WE WILL SEE EACH OTHER AGAIN.
OF COURSE.
MAY THE FORCE BE WITH YOU.

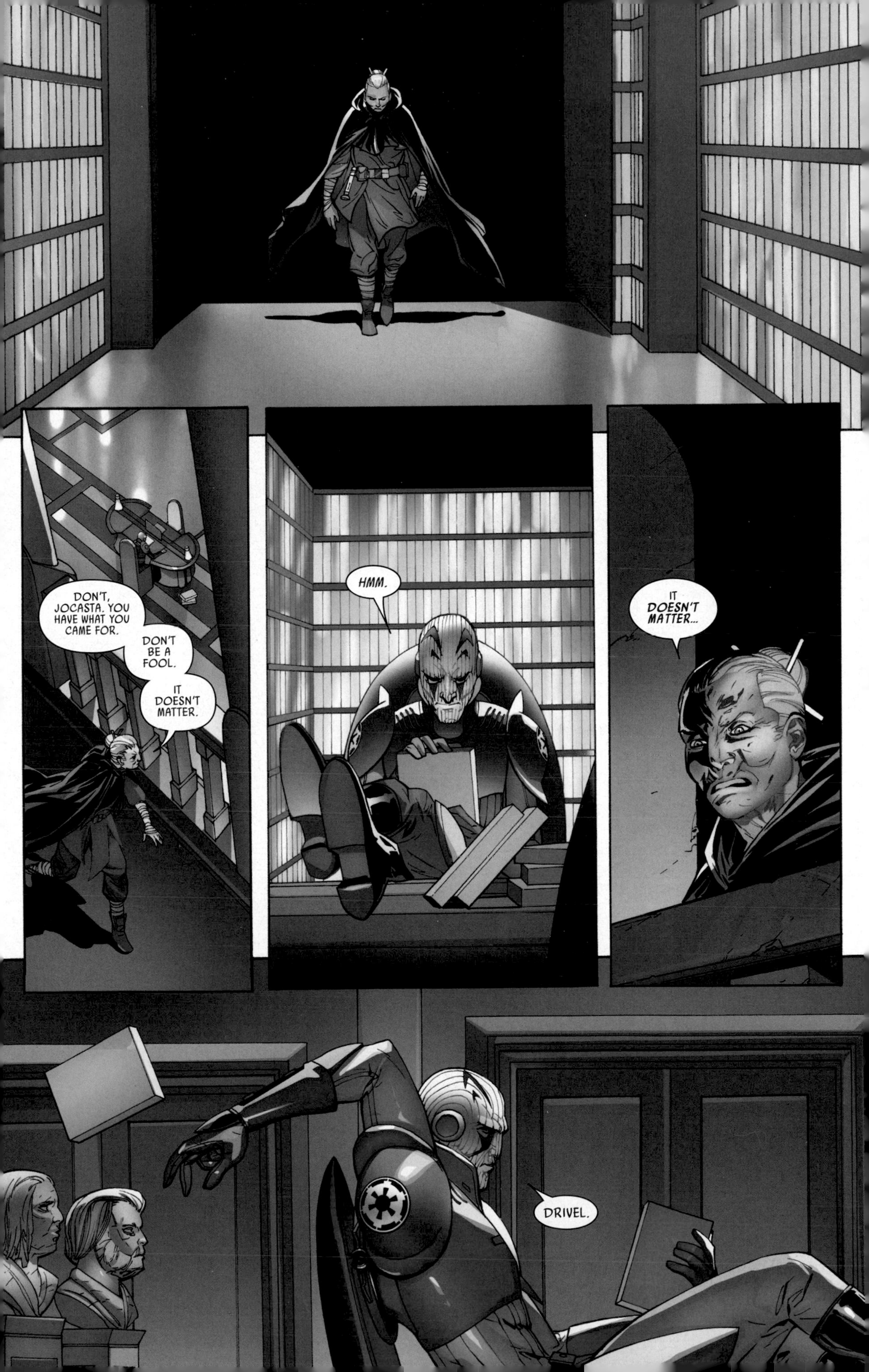
DON'T, JOCASTA. YOU HAVE WHAT YOU CAME FOR.
DON'T BE A FOOL.
IT DOESN'T MATTER.
HMM.
IT DOESN'T MATTER...
DRIVEL.

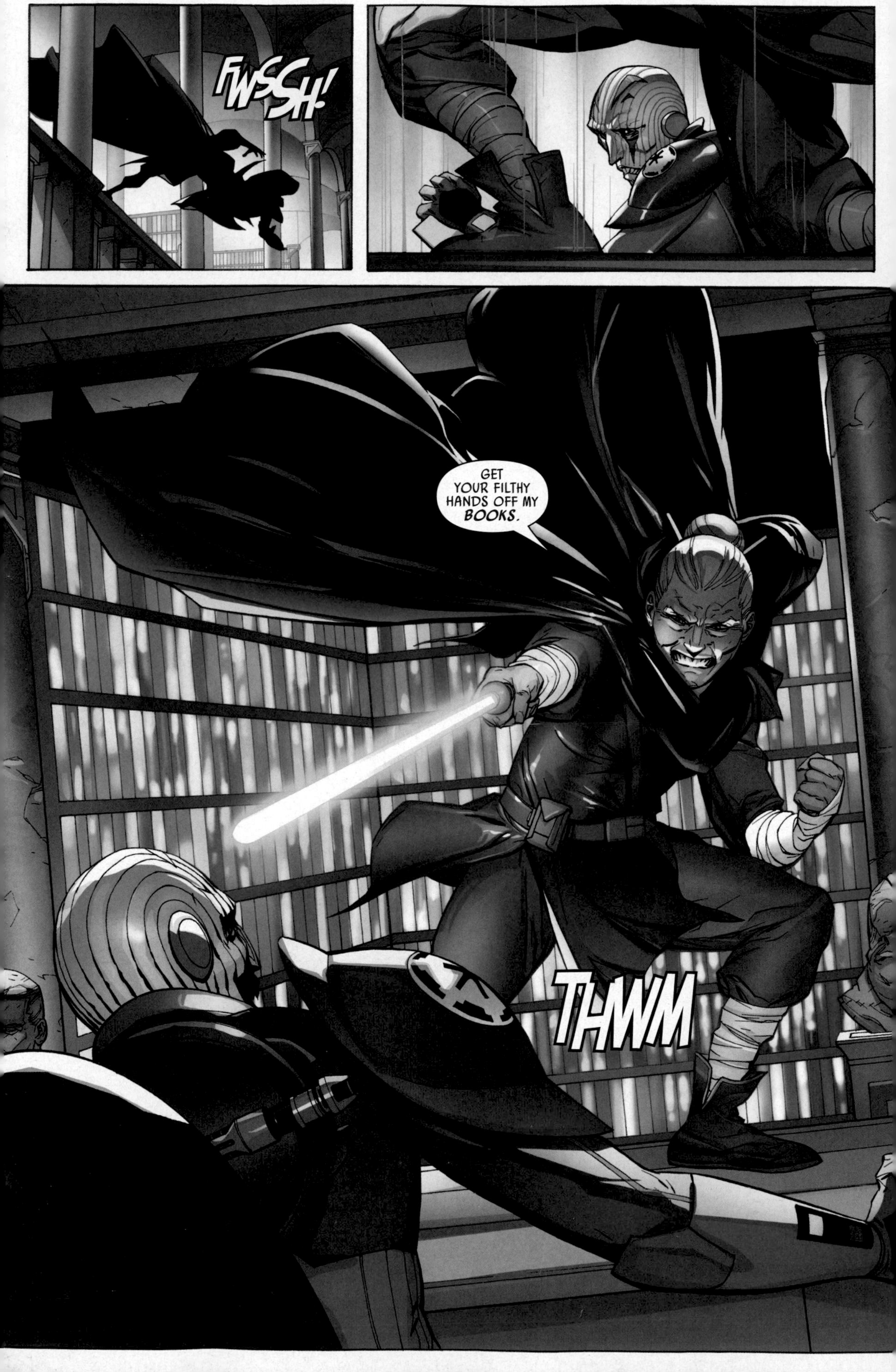
FWSSH!
GET YOUR FILTHY HANDS OFF MY BOOKS.
THWM

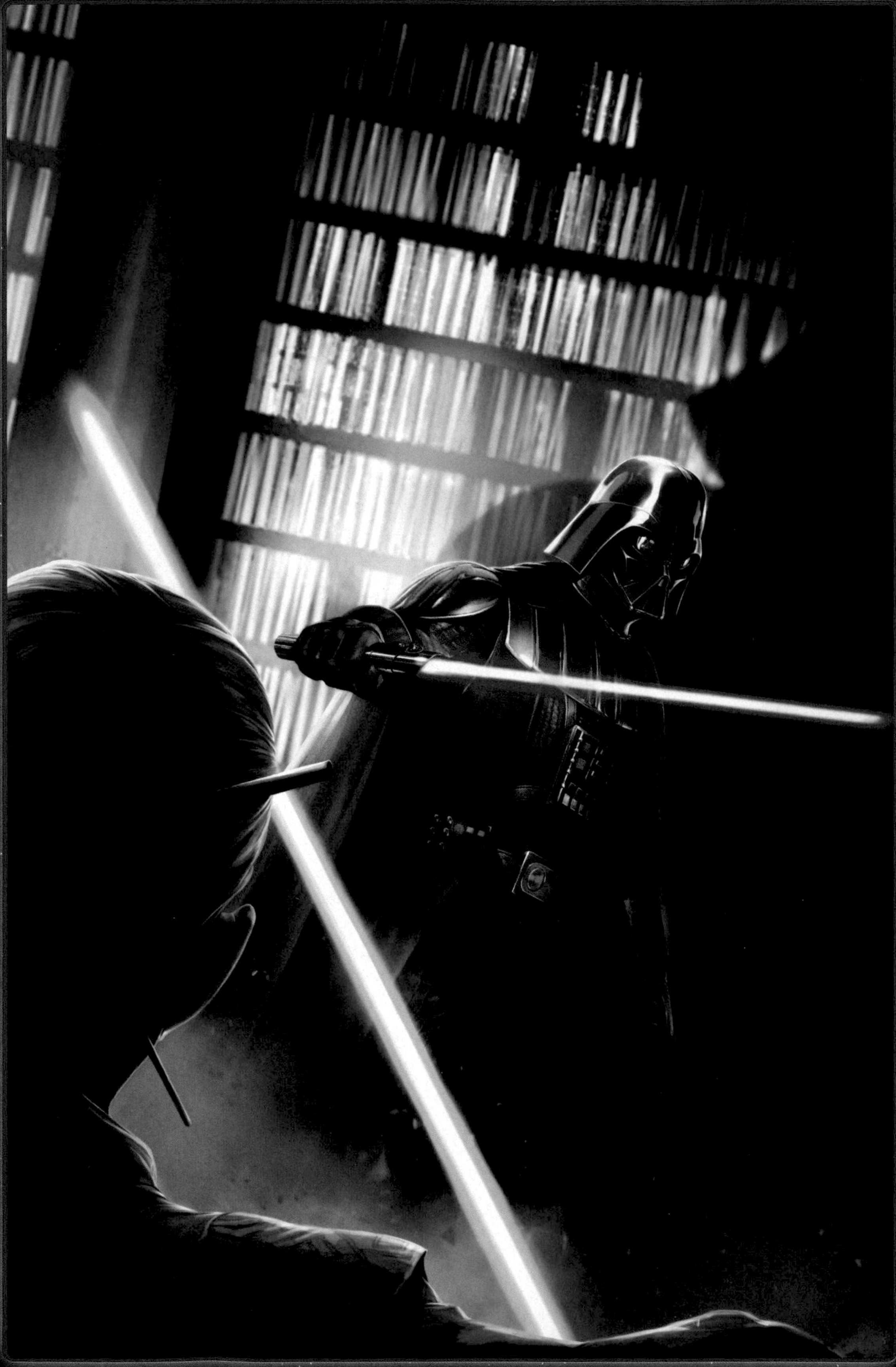

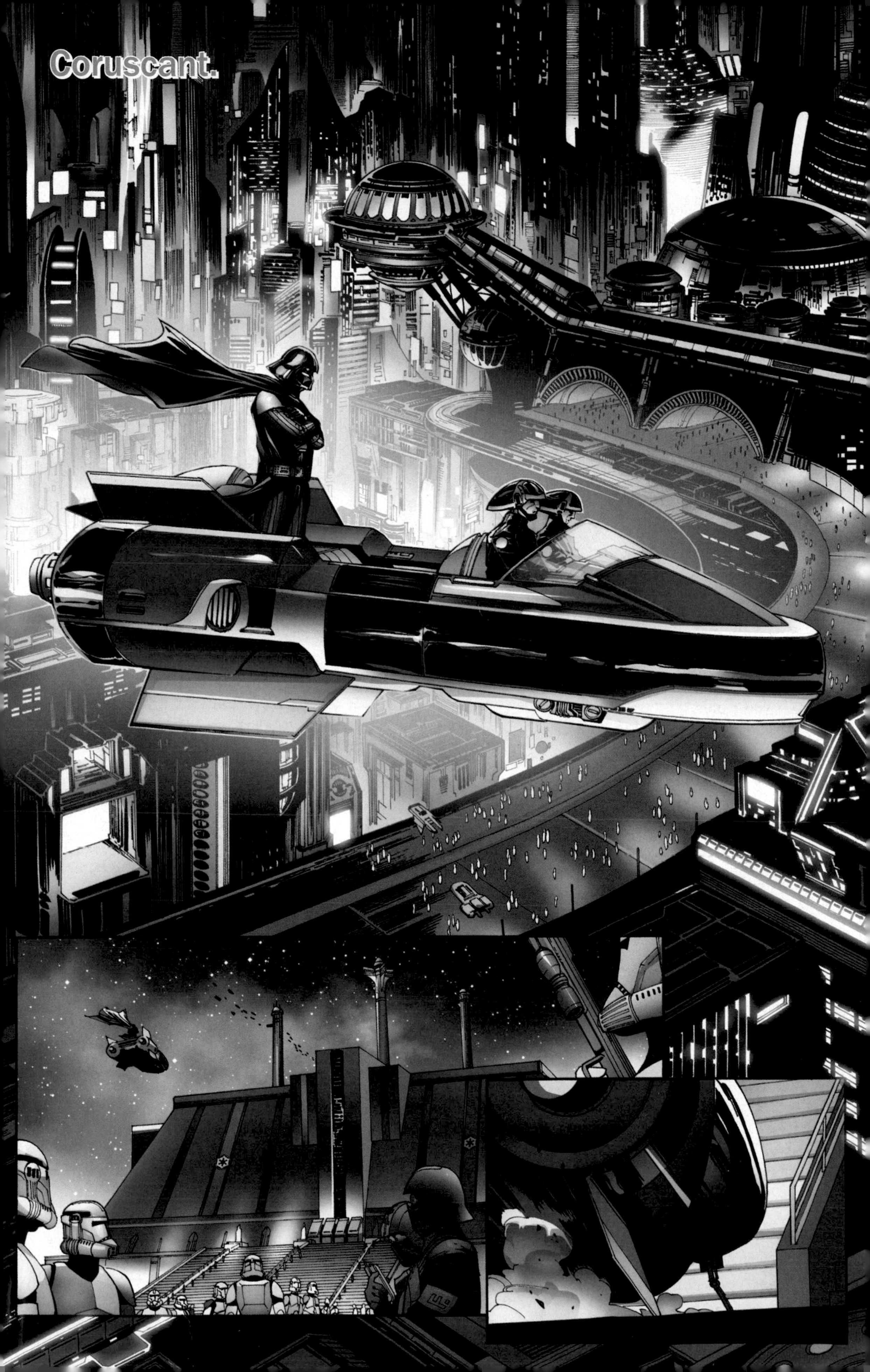
Coruscant.

THE TEMPLE IS SEALED, LORD VADER.

WHAT ARE YOUR ORDERS?

UNLESS AUTHORIZED BY EITHER THE EMPEROR OR ME--NO ONE ENTERS, NO ONE LEAVES.

DON'T WORRY. WE'VE GOT TWO FULL COMPANIES HERE, PLUS A BIG CONTINGENT OF CORUSCANT SECURITY FORCE. THE WHOLE PLACE IS SURROUNDED.

NO ONE'S GETTING PAST US.

SEE THAT THEY DO NOT.

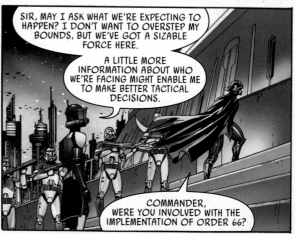

SIR, MAY I ASK WHAT WE'RE EXPECTING TO HAPPEN? I DON'T WANT TO OVERSTEP MY BOUNDS, BUT WE'VE GOT A SIZABLE FORCE HERE.

A LITTLE MORE INFORMATION ABOUT WHO WE'RE FACING MIGHT ENABLE ME TO MAKE BETTER TACTICAL DECISIONS.

COMMANDER, WERE YOU INVOLVED WITH THE IMPLEMENTATION OF ORDER 66?

YES. I WAS HERE ON CORUSCANT. DID MY PART-- ALL THE CLONES DID. SHUT THOSE JEDI AGITATORS DOWN COLD.

IT SEEMS, COMMANDER...

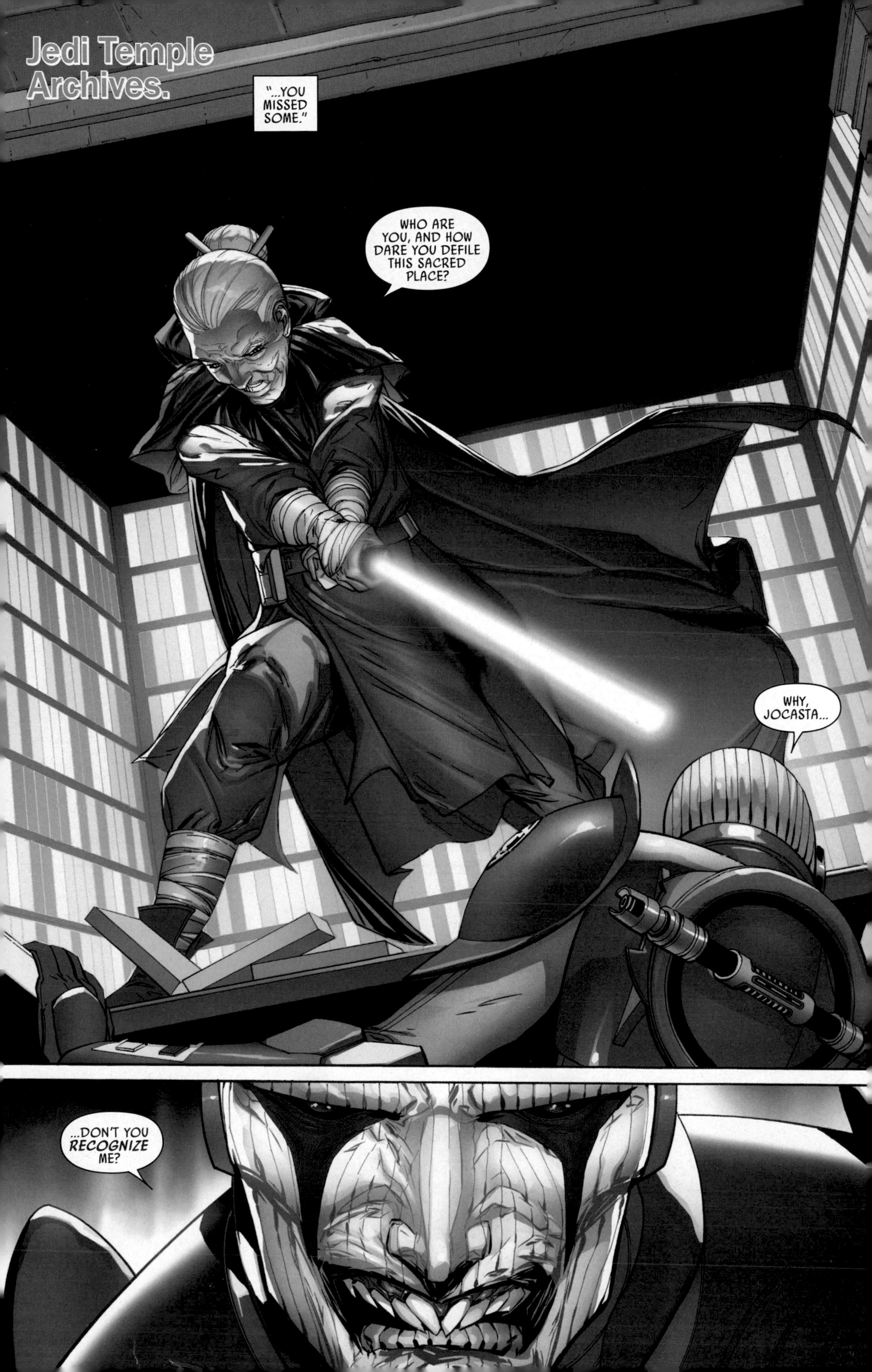
Jedi Temple Archives.
"...YOU MISSED SOME."
WHO ARE YOU, AND HOW DARE YOU DEFILE THIS SACRED PLACE?
WHY, JOCASTA...
...DON'T YOU RECOGNIZE ME?

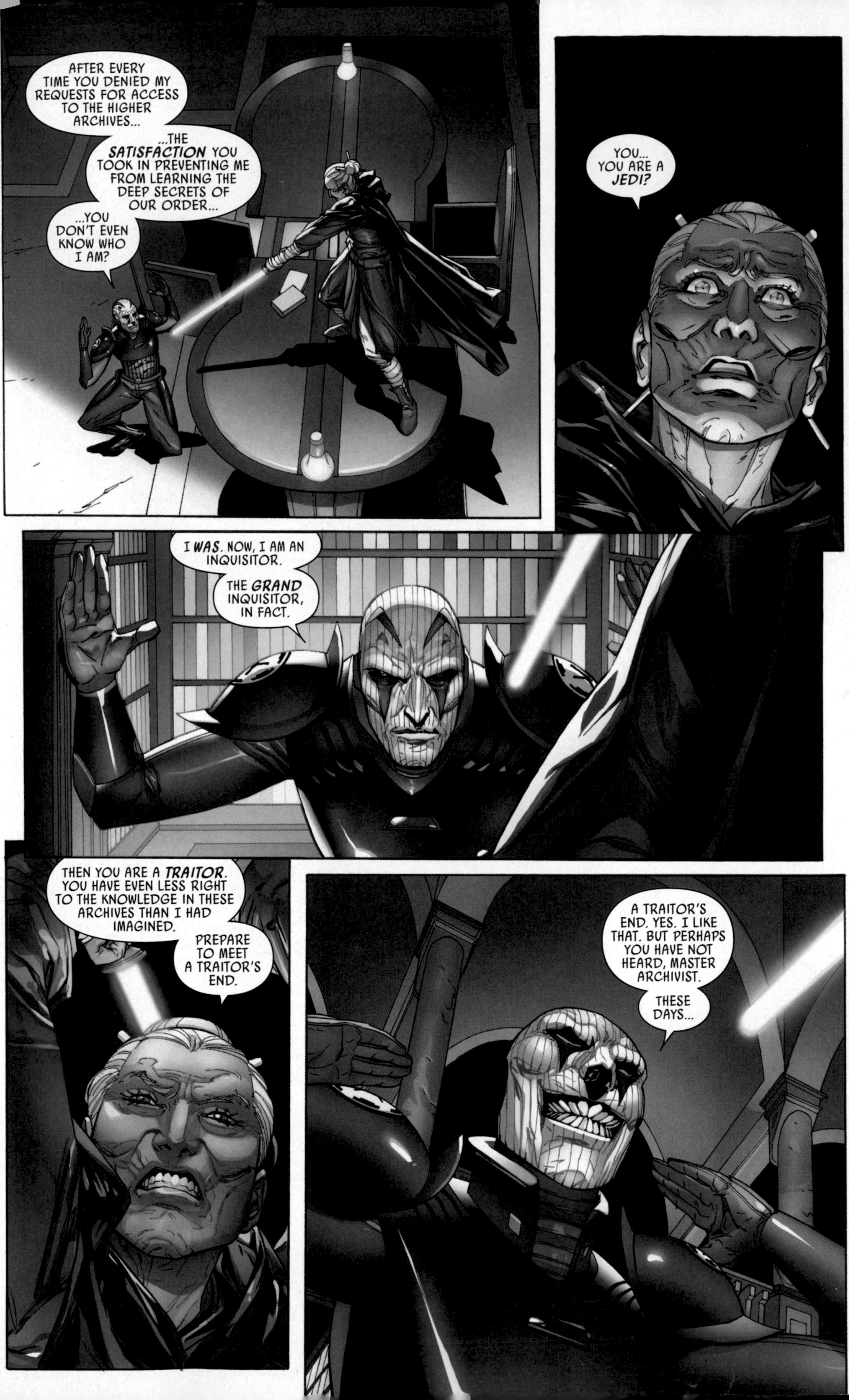
AFTER EVERY TIME YOU DENIED MY REQUESTS FOR ACCESS TO THE HIGHER ARCHIVES...
...THE SATISFACTION YOU TOOK IN PREVENTING ME FROM LEARNING THE DEEP SECRETS OF OUR ORDER...
...YOU DON'T EVEN KNOW WHO I AM?
YOU... YOU ARE A JEDI?
I WAS. NOW, I AM AN INQUISITOR.
THE GRAND INQUISITOR, IN FACT.
THEN YOU ARE A TRAITOR. YOU HAVE EVEN LESS RIGHT TO THE KNOWLEDGE IN THESE ARCHIVES THAN I HAD IMAGINED.
PREPARE TO MEET A TRAITOR'S END.
A TRAITOR'S END. YES. I LIKE THAT. BUT PERHAPS YOU HAVE NOT HEARD, MASTER ARCHIVIST.
THESE DAYS...

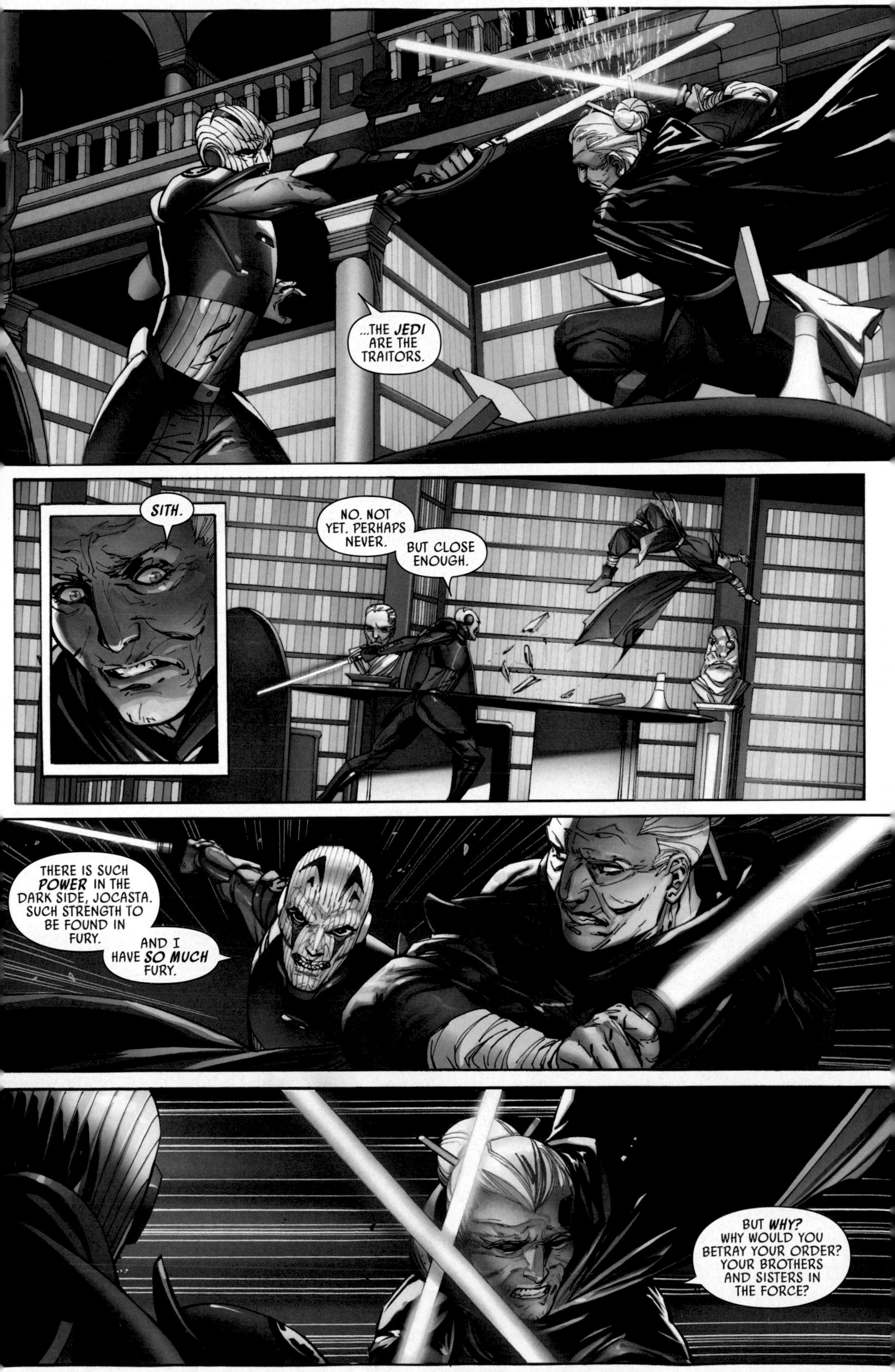
...THE JEDI ARE THE TRAITORS.
SITH.
NO. NOT YET. PERHAPS NEVER.
BUT CLOSE ENOUGH.
THERE IS SUCH POWER IN THE DARK SIDE, JOCASTA. SUCH STRENGTH TO BE FOUND IN FURY.
AND I HAVE SO MUCH FURY.
BUT WHY? WHY WOULD YOU BETRAY YOUR ORDER? YOUR BROTHERS AND SISTERS IN THE FORCE?

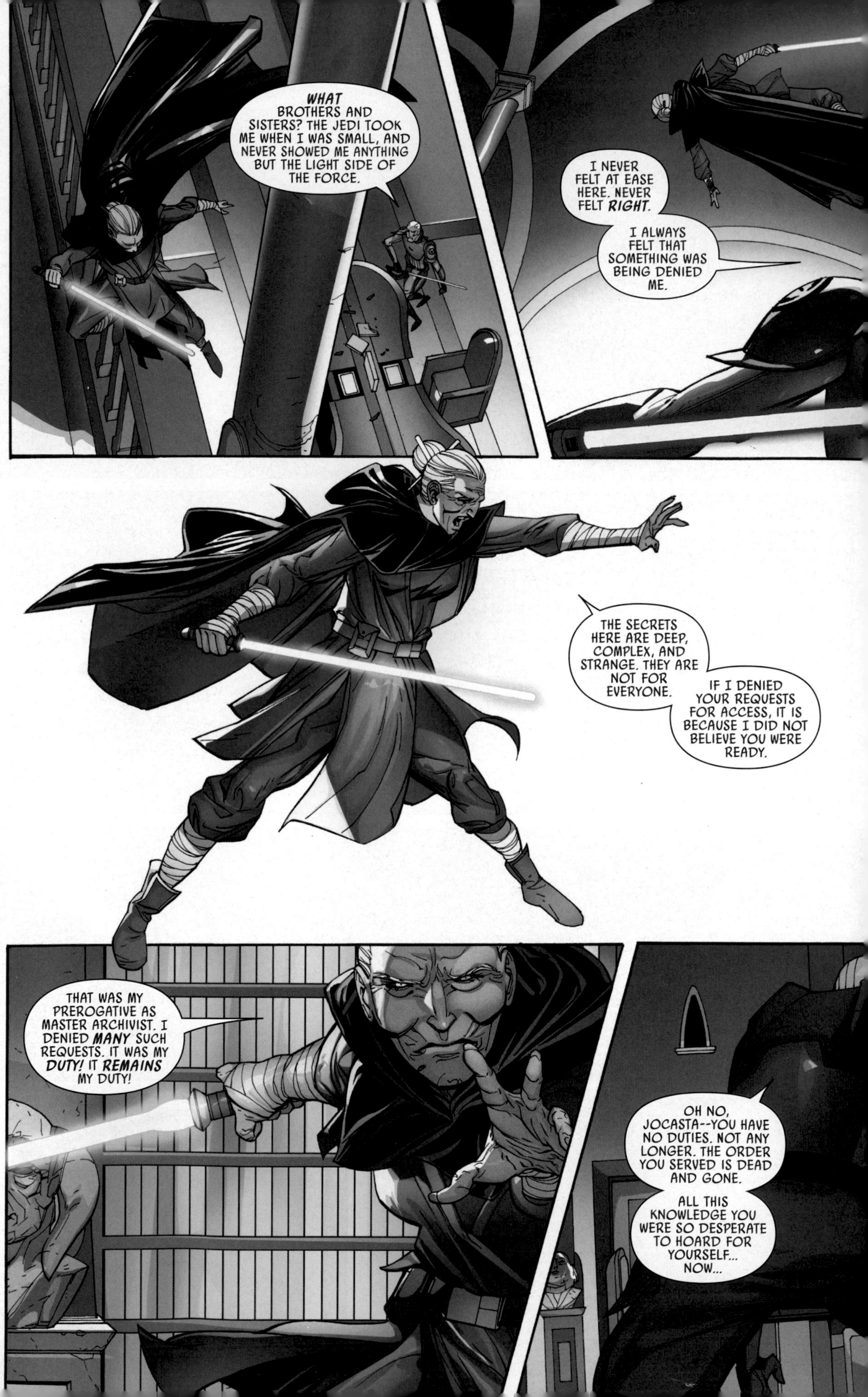
WHAT BROTHERS AND SISTERS? THE JEDI TOOK ME WHEN I WAS SMALL, AND NEVER SHOWED ME ANYTHING BUT THE LIGHT SIDE OF THE FORCE.
I NEVER FELT AT EASE HERE. NEVER FELT RIGHT.
I ALWAYS FELT THAT SOMETHING WAS BEING DENIED ME.
THE SECRETS HERE ARE DEEP, COMPLEX, AND STRANGE. THEY ARE NOT FOR EVERYONE.
IF I DENIED YOUR REQUESTS FOR ACCESS, IT IS BECAUSE I DID NOT BELIEVE YOU WERE READY.
THAT WAS MY PREROGATIVE AS MASTER ARCHIVIST. I DENIED MANY SUCH REQUESTS. IT WAS MY DUTY! IT REMAINS MY DUTY!
OH NO, JOCASTA--YOU HAVE NO DUTIES. NOT ANY LONGER. THE ORDER YOU SERVED IS DEAD AND GONE.
ALL THIS KNOWLEDGE YOU WERE SO DESPERATE TO HOARD FOR YOURSELF... NOW...

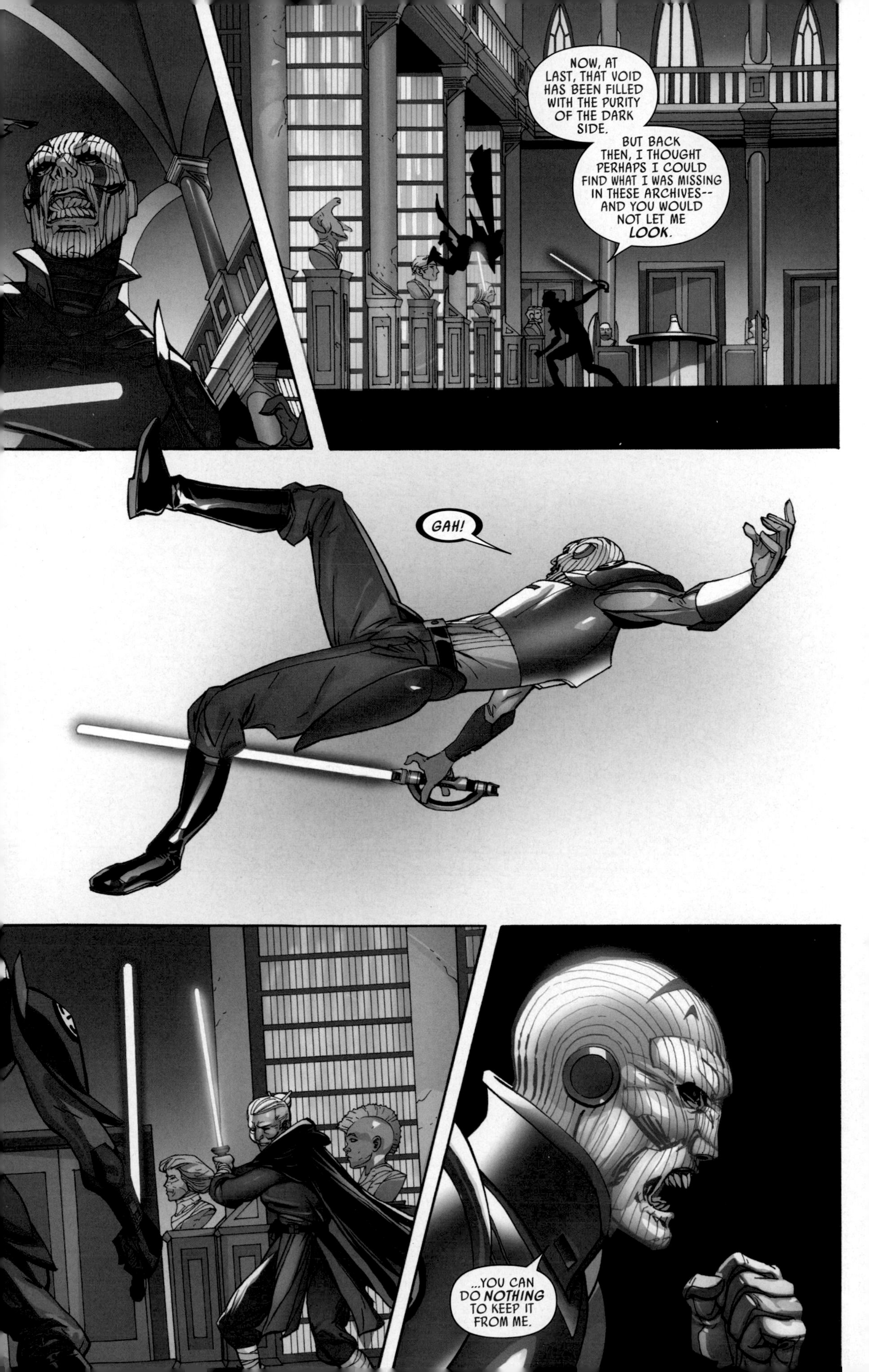
NOW, AT LAST, THAT VOID HAS BEEN FILLED WITH THE PURITY OF THE DARK SIDE.
BUT BACK THEN, I THOUGHT PERHAPS I COULD FIND WHAT I WAS MISSING IN THESE ARCHIVES-- AND YOU WOULD NOT LET ME LOOK.
GAH!
...YOU CAN DO NOTHING TO KEEP IT FROM ME.

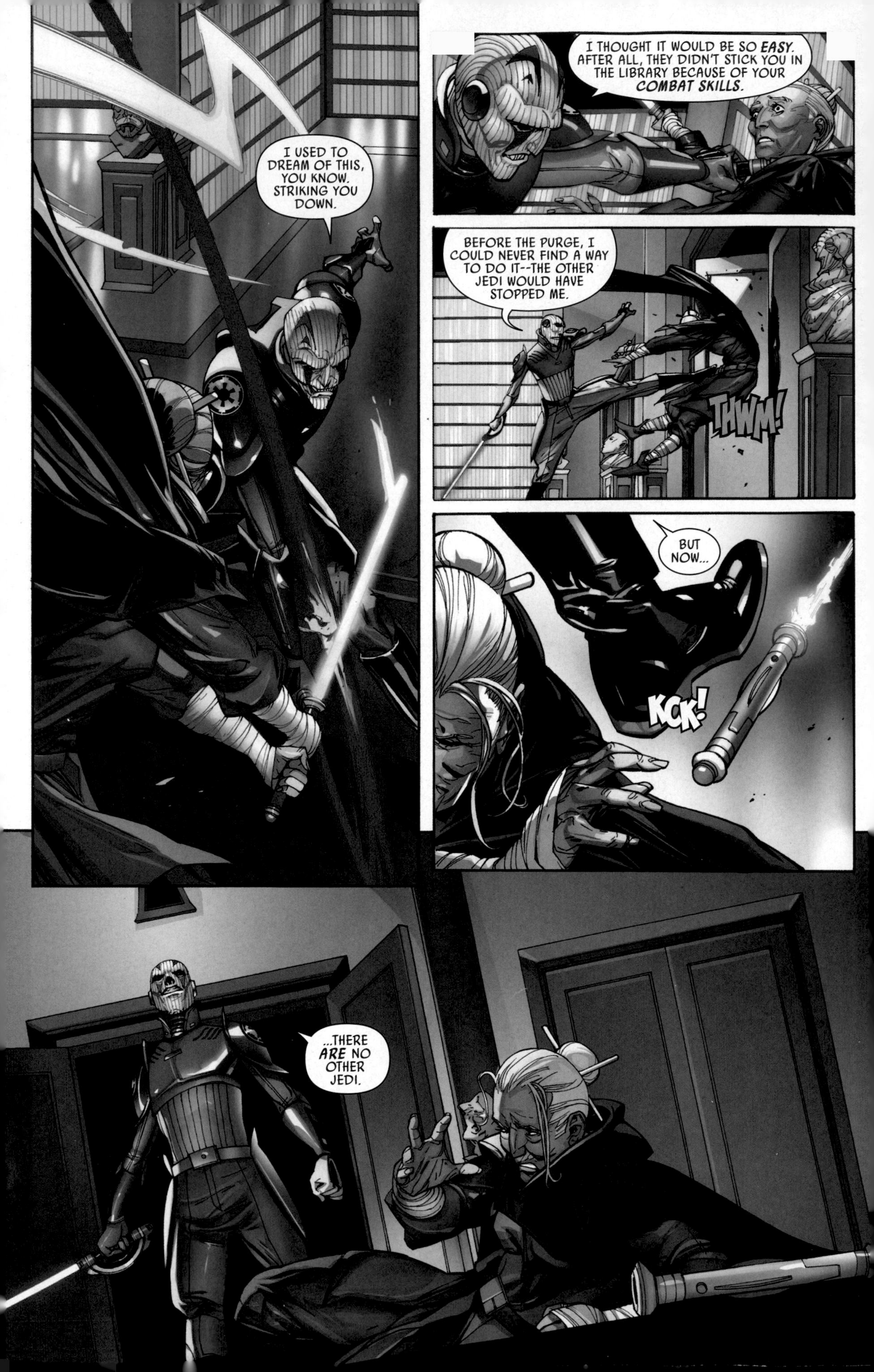
I USED TO DREAM OF THIS, YOU KNOW. STRIKING YOU DOWN.
I THOUGHT IT WOULD BE SO *EASY*. AFTER ALL, THEY DIDN'T STICK YOU IN THE LIBRARY BECAUSE OF YOUR **COMBAT SKILLS**.
BEFORE THE PURGE, I COULD NEVER FIND A WAY TO DO IT--THE OTHER JEDI WOULD HAVE STOPPED ME.
THWM!
BUT NOW...
KCK!
...THERE *ARE* NO OTHER JEDI.

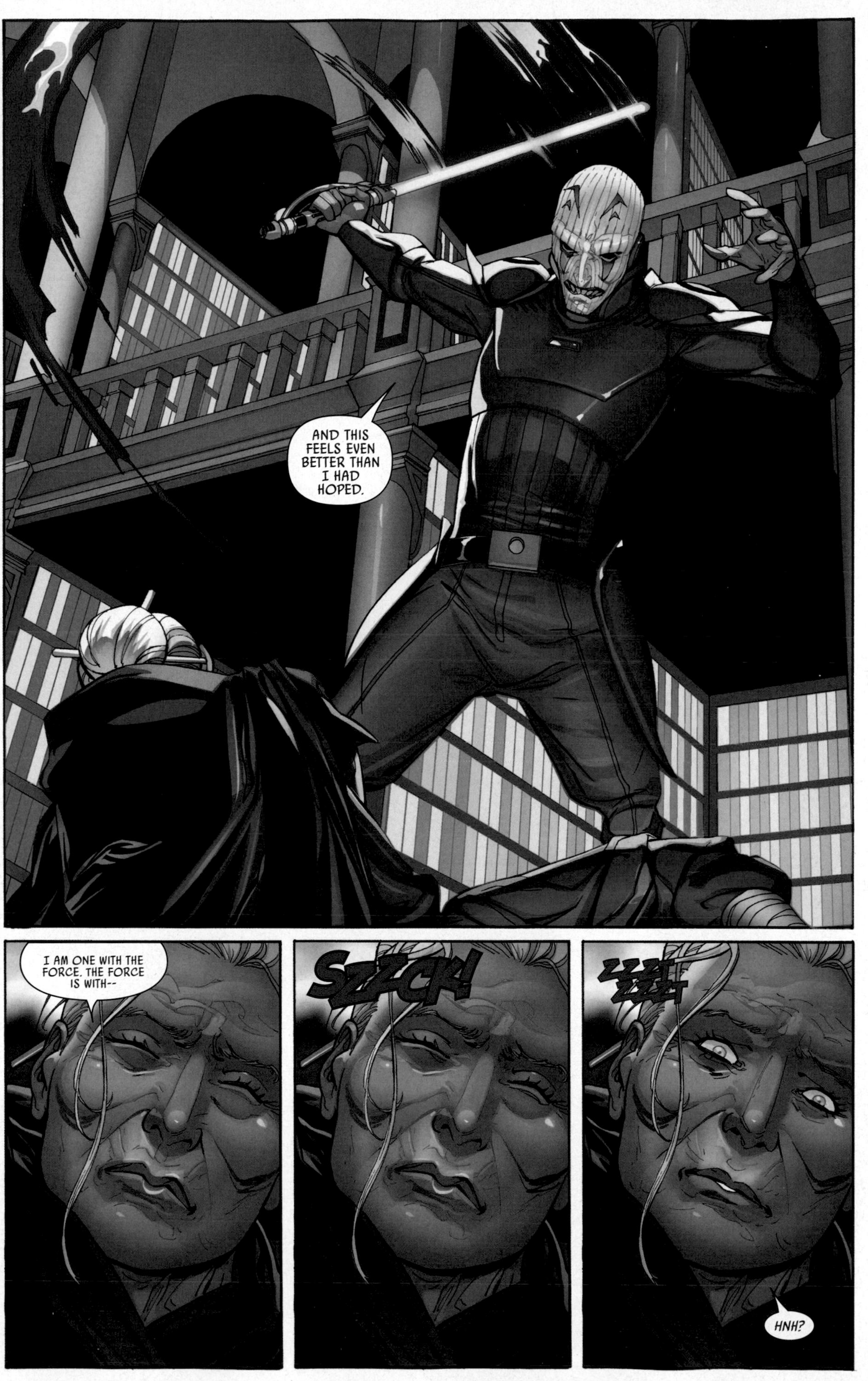
AND THIS FEELS EVEN BETTER THAN I HAD HOPED.
I AM ONE WITH THE FORCE. THE FORCE IS WITH--
SZZCK!
HNH?

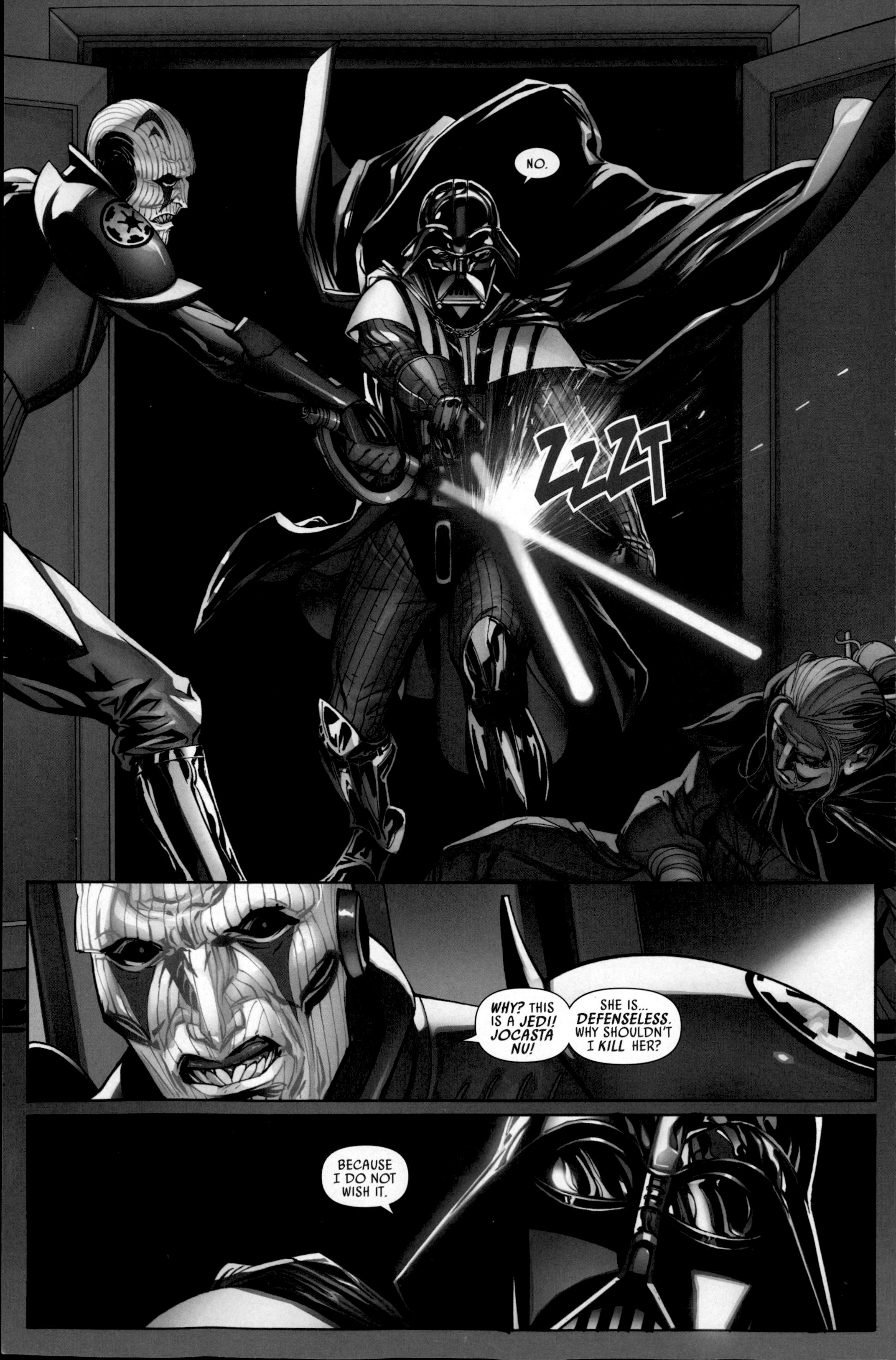
NO.
ZZZT
WHY? THIS IS A JEDI! JOCASTA NU!
SHE IS... DEFENSELESS. WHY SHOULDN'T I KILL HER?
BECAUSE I DO NOT WISH IT.

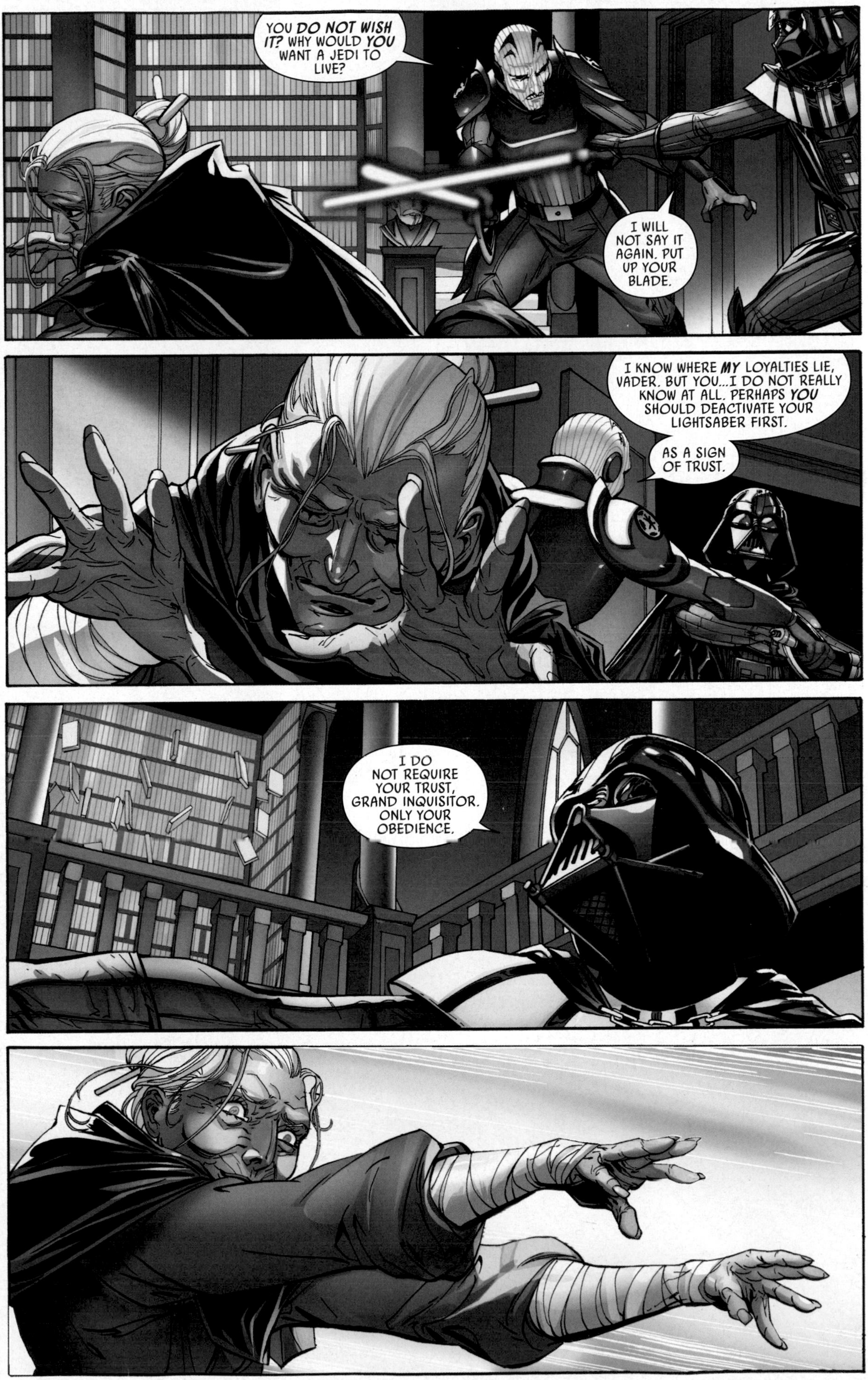
YOU DO NOT WISH IT? WHY WOULD YOU WANT A JEDI TO LIVE?
I WILL NOT SAY IT AGAIN. PUT UP YOUR BLADE.
I KNOW WHERE MY LOYALTIES LIE, VADER. BUT YOU...I DO NOT REALLY KNOW AT ALL. PERHAPS YOU SHOULD DEACTIVATE YOUR LIGHTSABER FIRST.
AS A SIGN OF TRUST.
I DO NOT REQUIRE YOUR TRUST, GRAND INQUISITOR. ONLY YOUR OBEDIENCE.

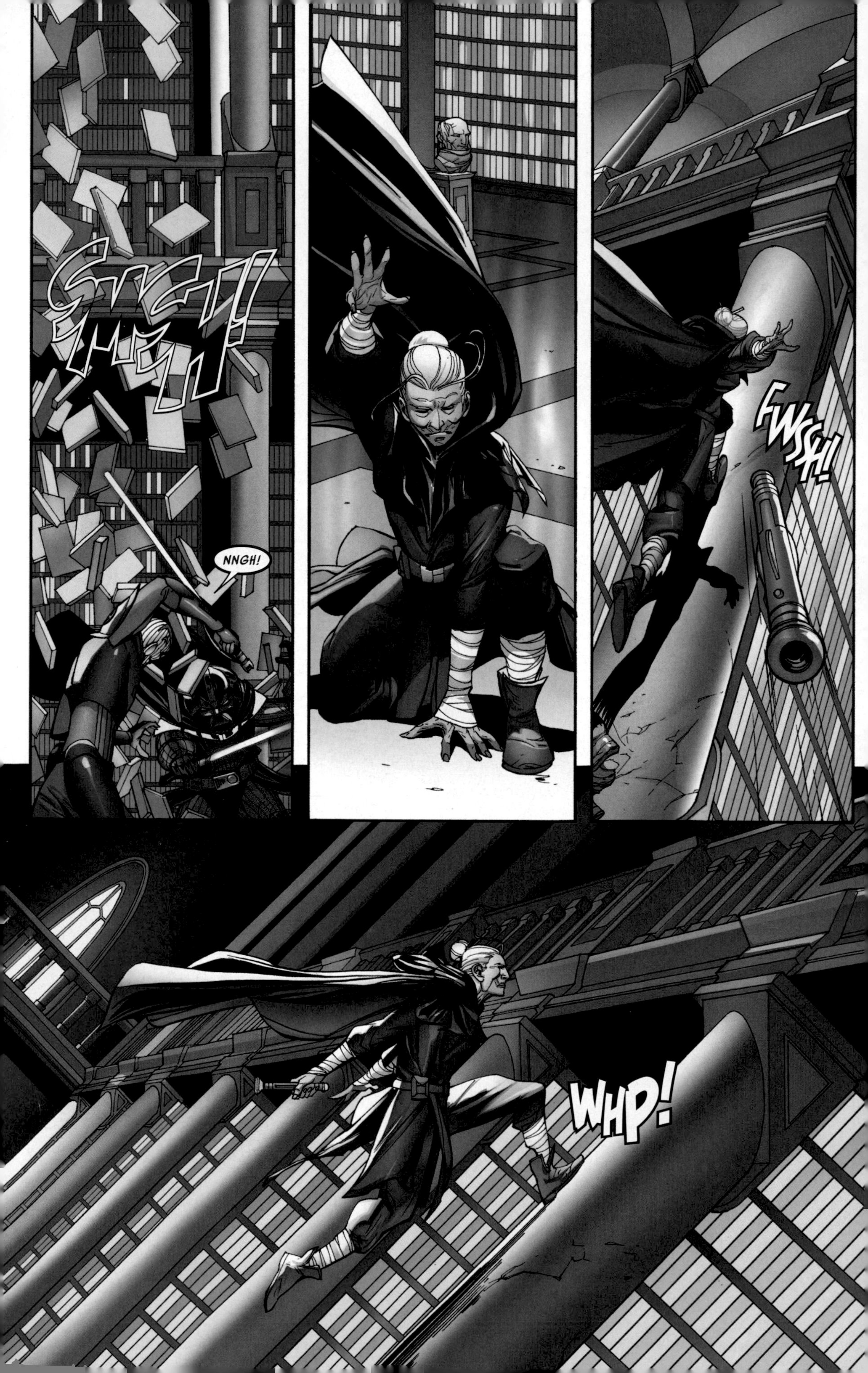
NNGH!
FWSSH!
WHP!

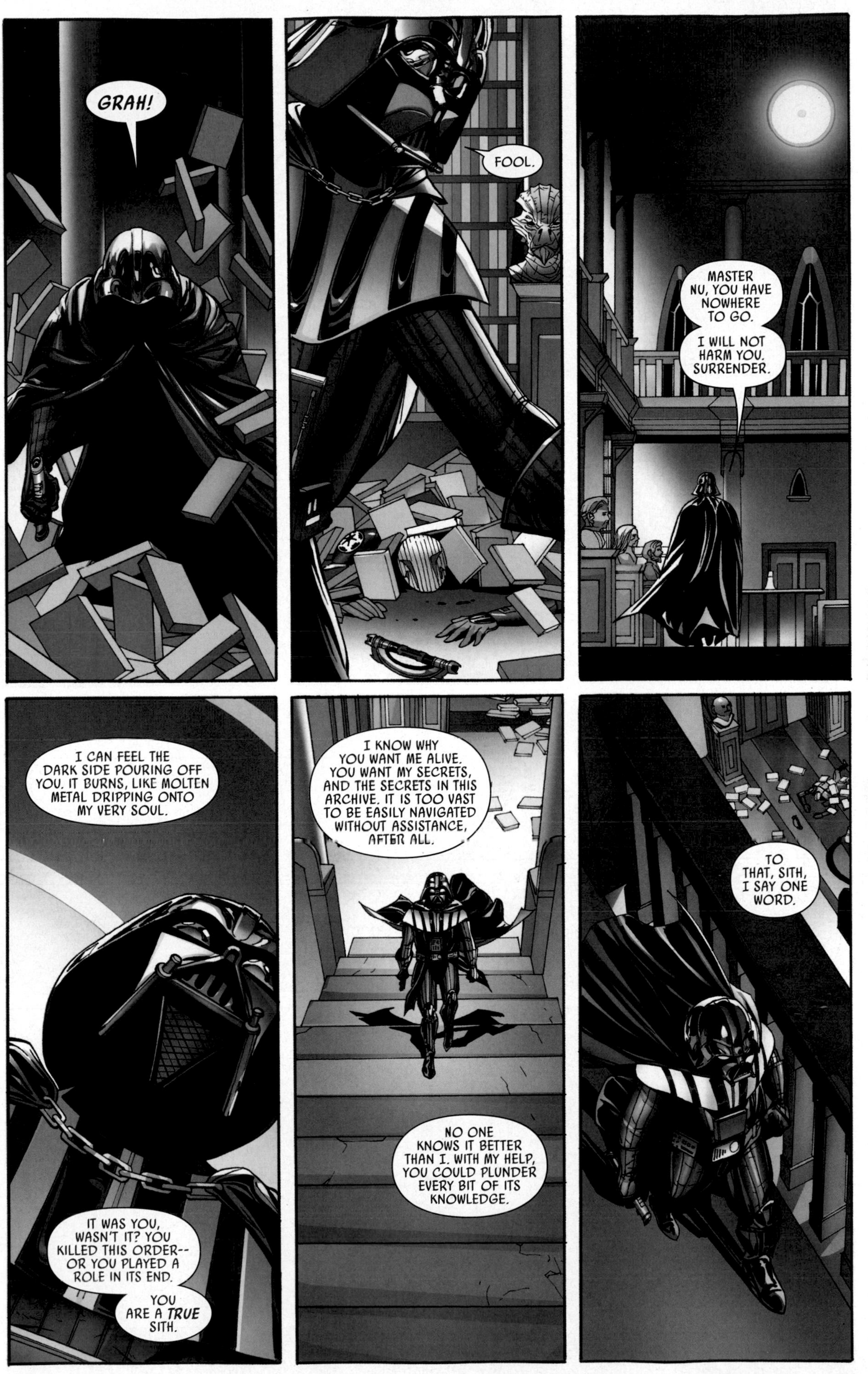
GRAH!
FOOL.
MASTER NU, YOU HAVE NOWHERE TO GO.
I WILL NOT HARM YOU. SURRENDER.
I CAN FEEL THE DARK SIDE POURING OFF YOU. IT BURNS, LIKE MOLTEN METAL DRIPPING ONTO MY VERY SOUL.
IT WAS YOU, WASN'T IT? YOU KILLED THIS ORDER-- OR YOU PLAYED A ROLE IN ITS END.
YOU ARE A *TRUE* SITH.
I KNOW WHY YOU WANT ME ALIVE. YOU WANT MY SECRETS, AND THE SECRETS IN THIS ARCHIVE. IT IS TOO VAST TO BE EASILY NAVIGATED WITHOUT ASSISTANCE, AFTER ALL.
NO ONE KNOWS IT BETTER THAN I. WITH MY HELP, YOU COULD PLUNDER EVERY BIT OF ITS KNOWLEDGE.
TO THAT, SITH, I SAY ONE WORD.

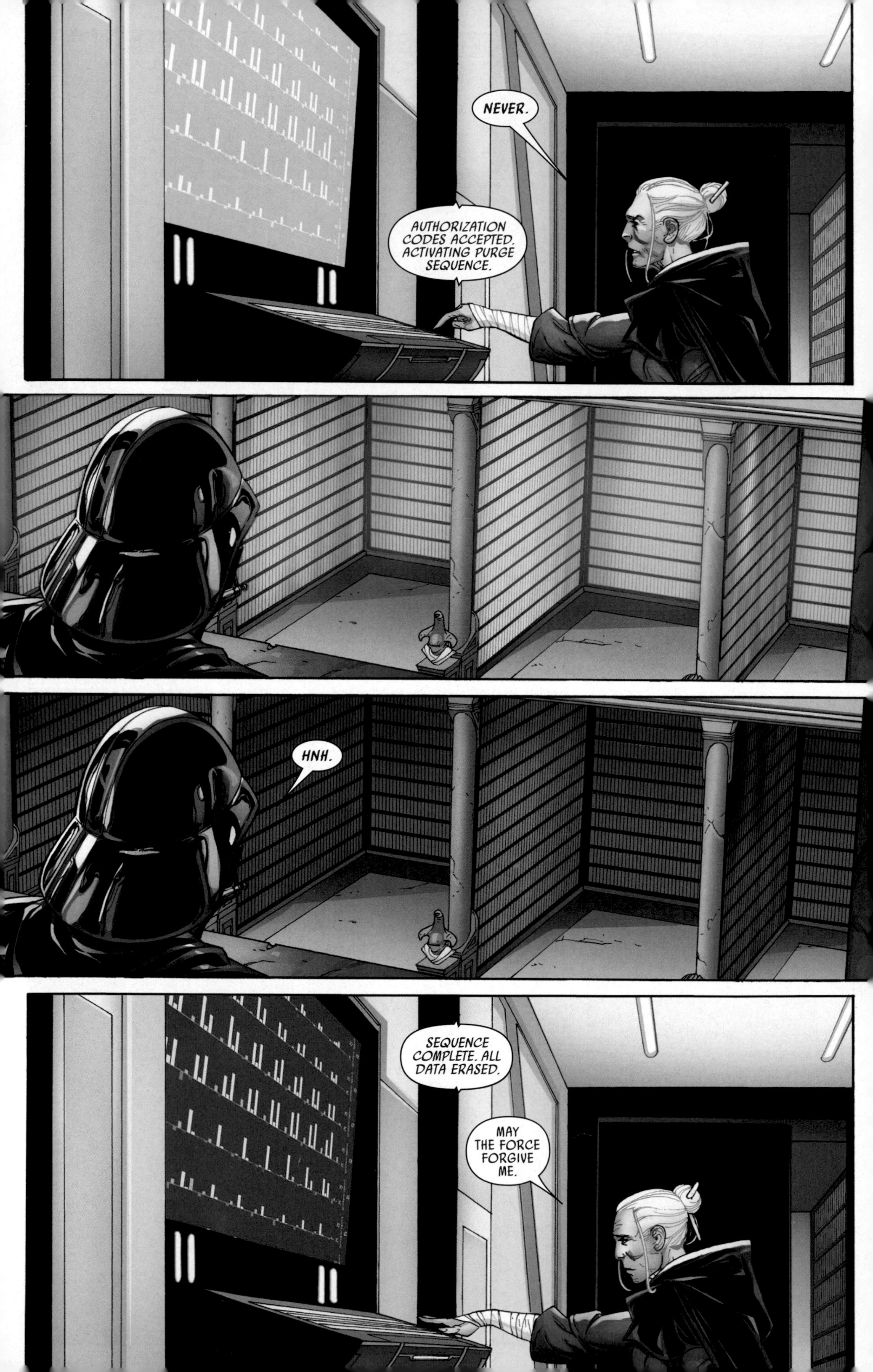
NEVER.
AUTHORIZATION CODES ACCEPTED. ACTIVATING PURGE SEQUENCE.
HNH.
SEQUENCE COMPLETE. ALL DATA ERASED.
MAY THE FORCE FORGIVE ME.

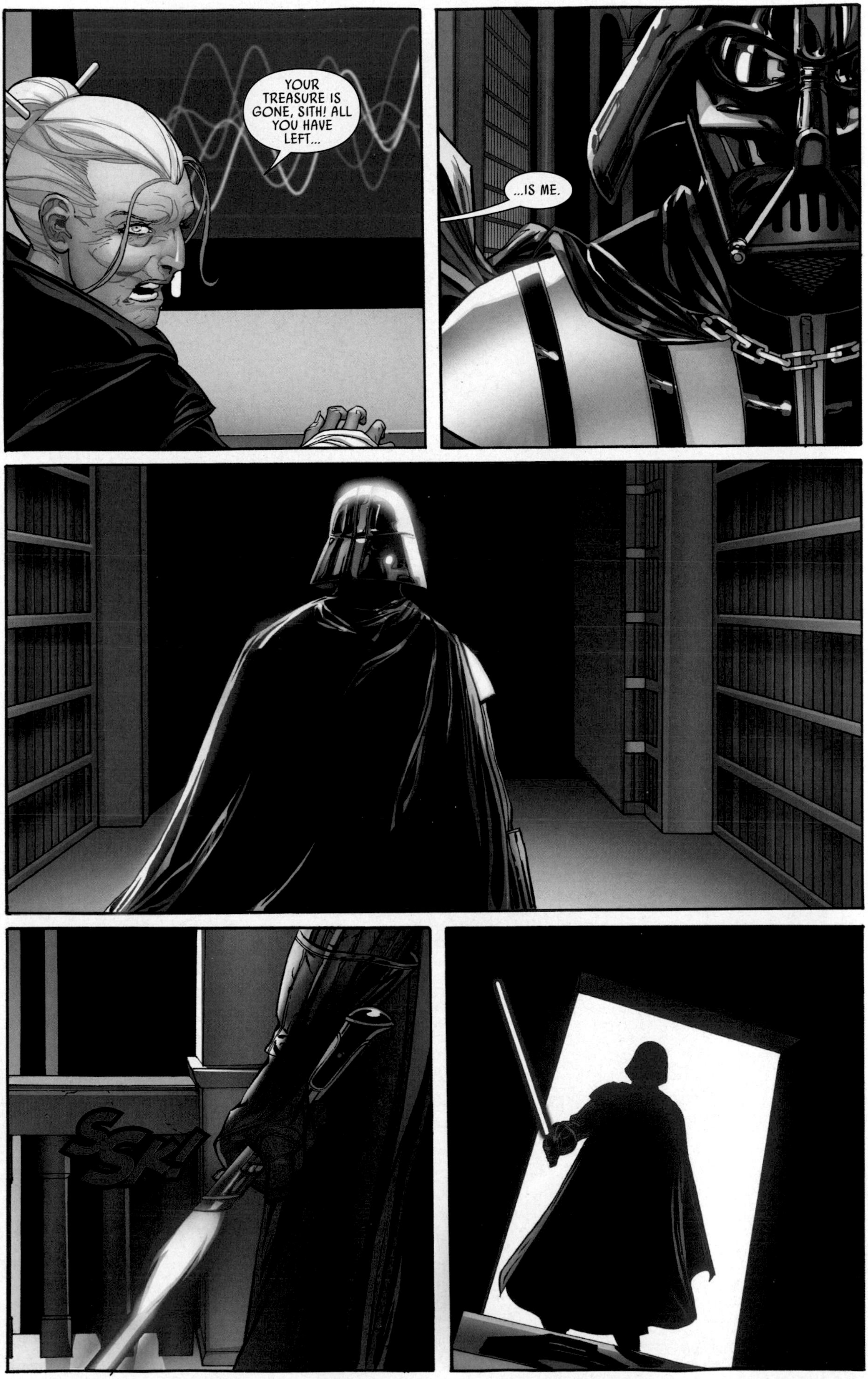
YOUR TREASURE IS GONE, SITH! ALL YOU HAVE LEFT...
...IS ME.

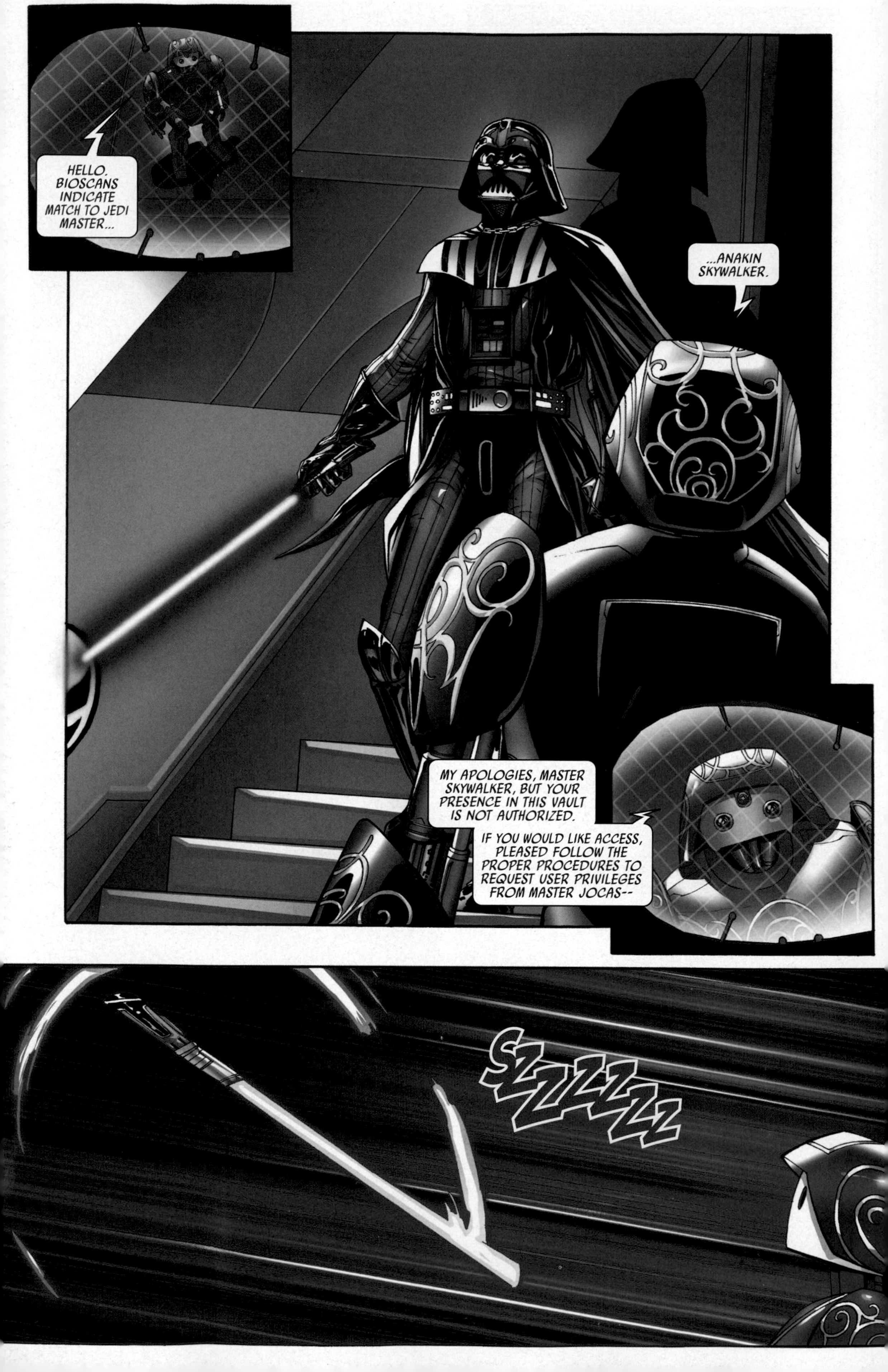
HELLO. BIOSCANS INDICATE MATCH TO JEDI MASTER...
...ANAKIN SKYWALKER.
MY APOLOGIES, MASTER SKYWALKER, BUT YOUR PRESENCE IN THIS VAULT IS NOT AUTHORIZED.
IF YOU WOULD LIKE ACCESS, PLEASED FOLLOW THE PROPER PROCEDURES TO REQUEST USER PRIVILEGES FROM MASTER JOCAS--
SZZZZZZ

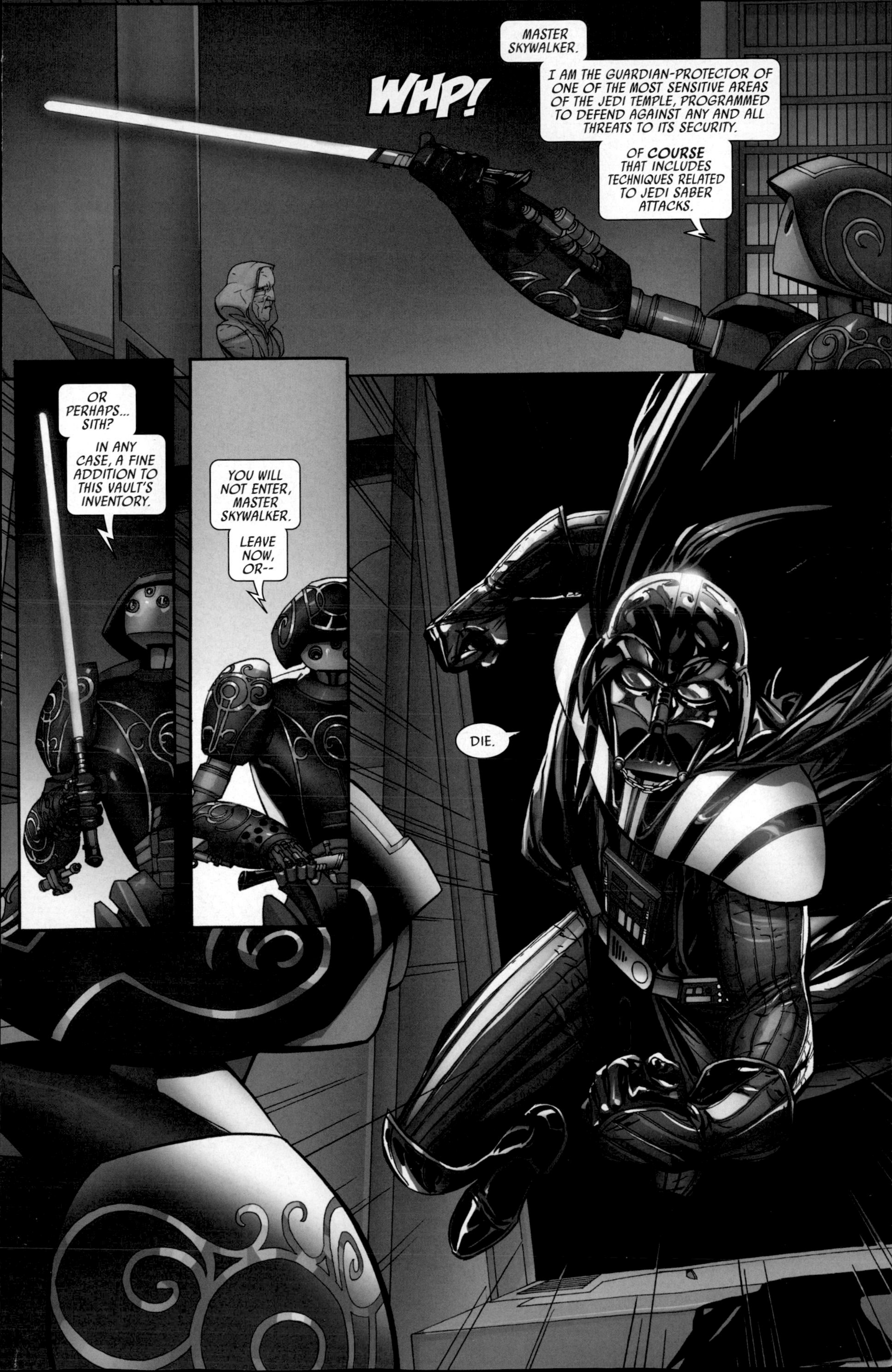
WHP!
MASTER SKYWALKER.
I AM THE GUARDIAN-PROTECTOR OF ONE OF THE MOST SENSITIVE AREAS OF THE JEDI TEMPLE, PROGRAMMED TO DEFEND AGAINST ANY AND ALL THREATS TO ITS SECURITY.
OF COURSE THAT INCLUDES TECHNIQUES RELATED TO JEDI SABER ATTACKS.
OR PERHAPS... SITH?
IN ANY CASE, A FINE ADDITION TO THIS VAULT'S INVENTORY.
YOU WILL NOT ENTER, MASTER SKYWALKER.
LEAVE NOW, OR--
DIE.

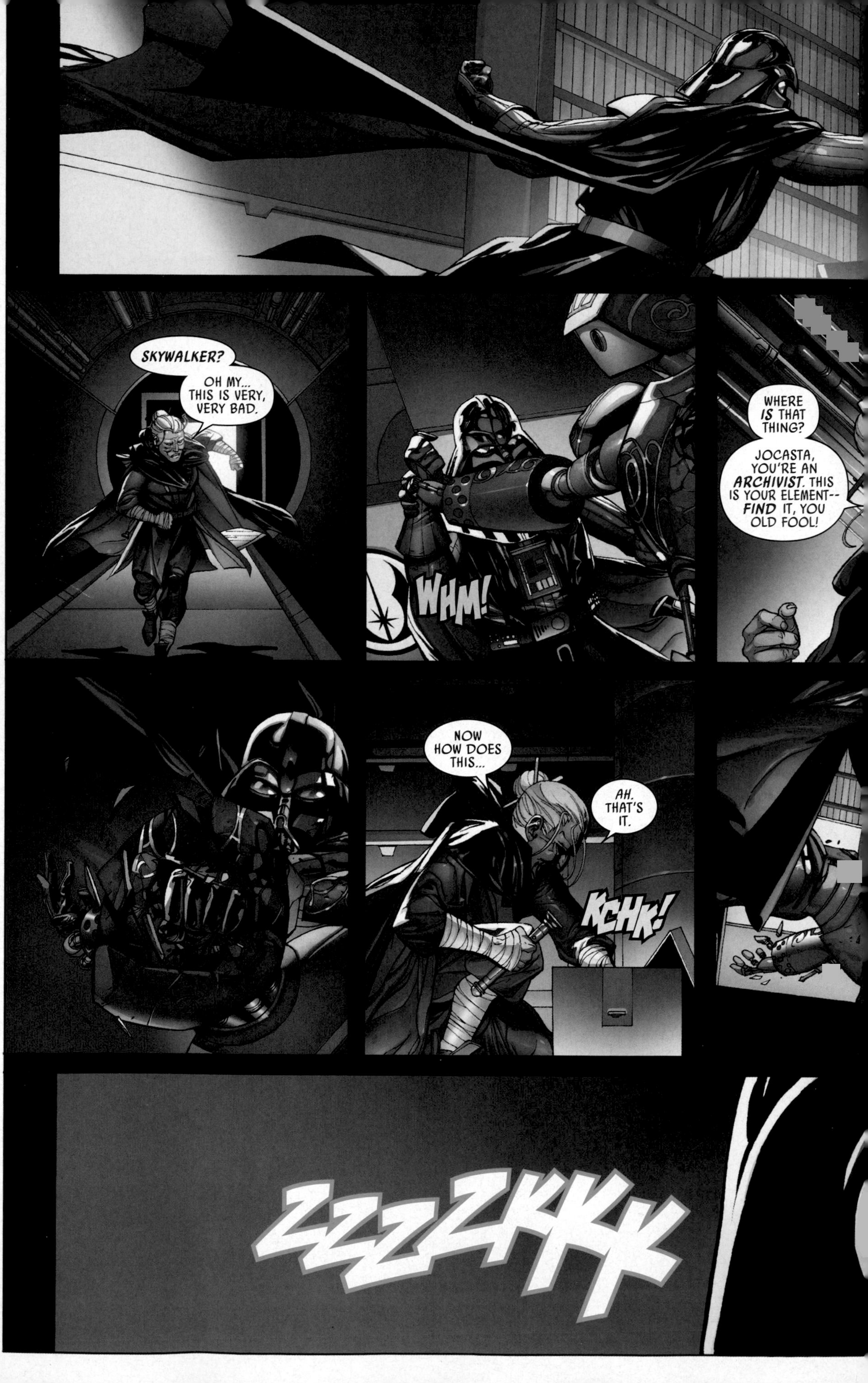
SKYWALKER?
OH MY... THIS IS VERY, VERY BAD.
WHM!
WHERE IS THAT THING?
JOCASTA, YOU'RE AN ARCHIVIST. THIS IS YOUR ELEMENT-- FIND IT, YOU OLD FOOL!
NOW HOW DOES THIS...
AH. THAT'S IT.
KCHK!
ZZZZKKK

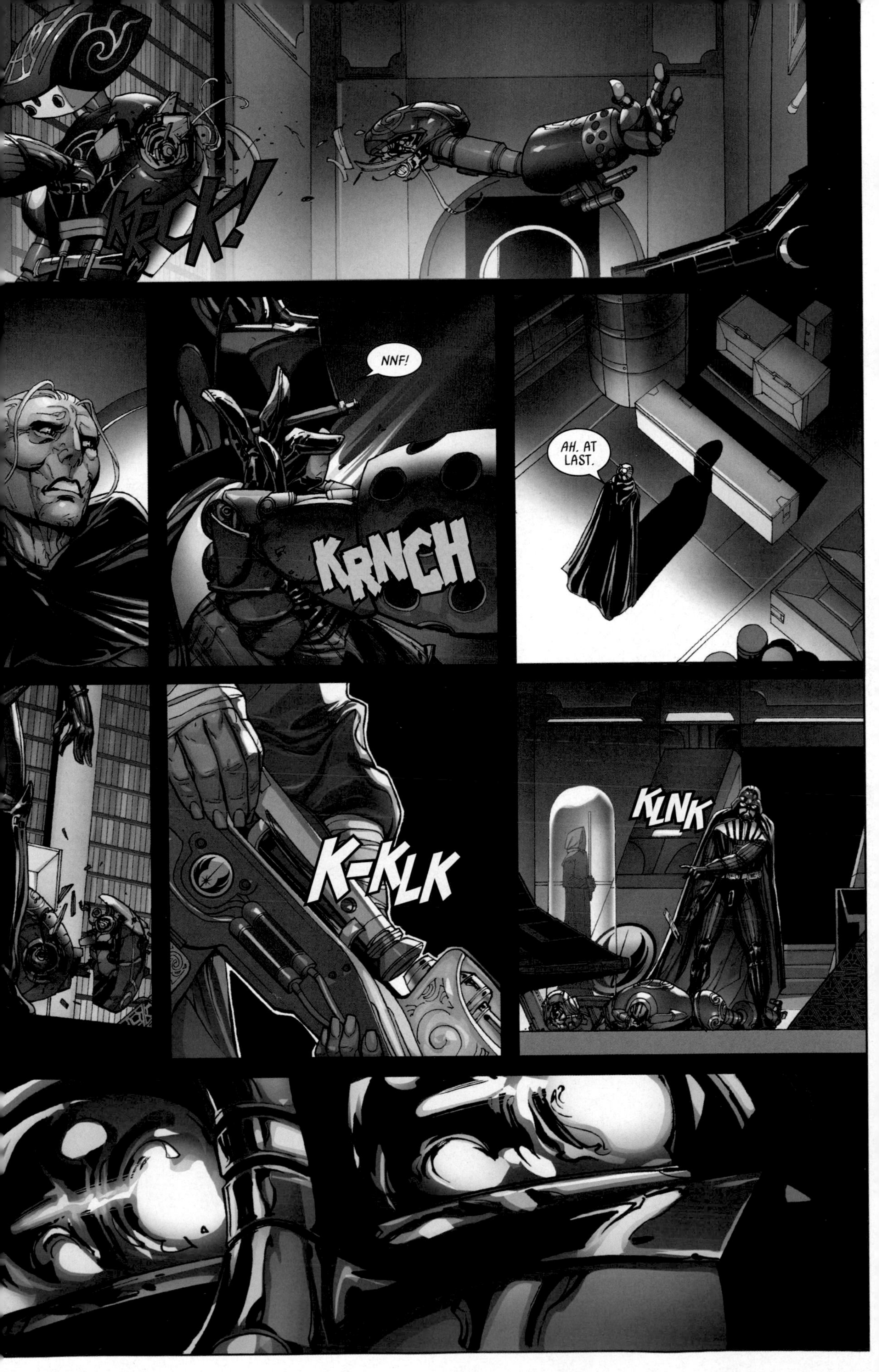

KRCK!
NNF!
KRNCH
AH. AT LAST.
K-KLK
KLNK
A?

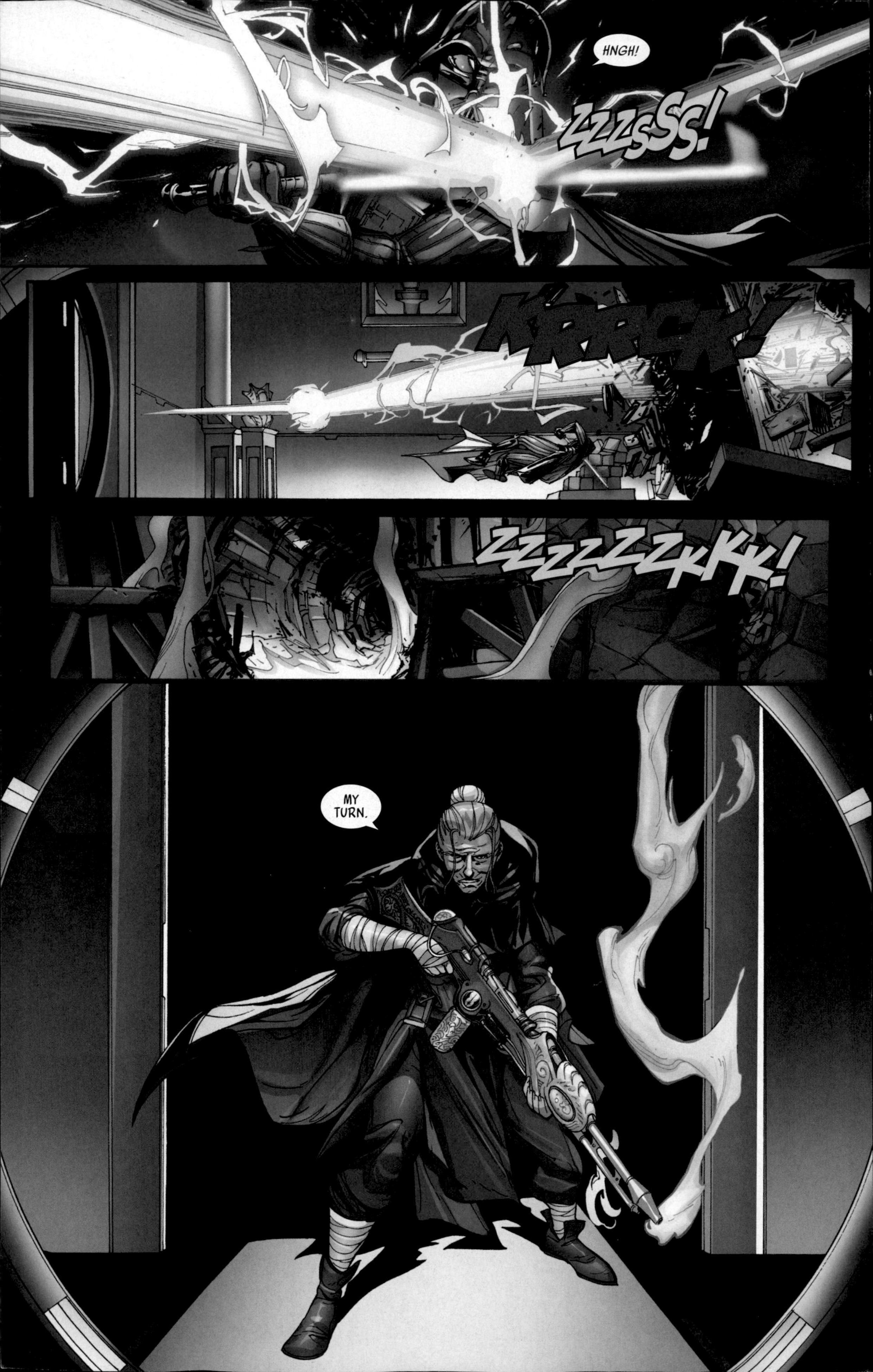
HNGH!
ZZZSSS!
KRRRCK!
ZZZZZZKKK!
MY TURN.

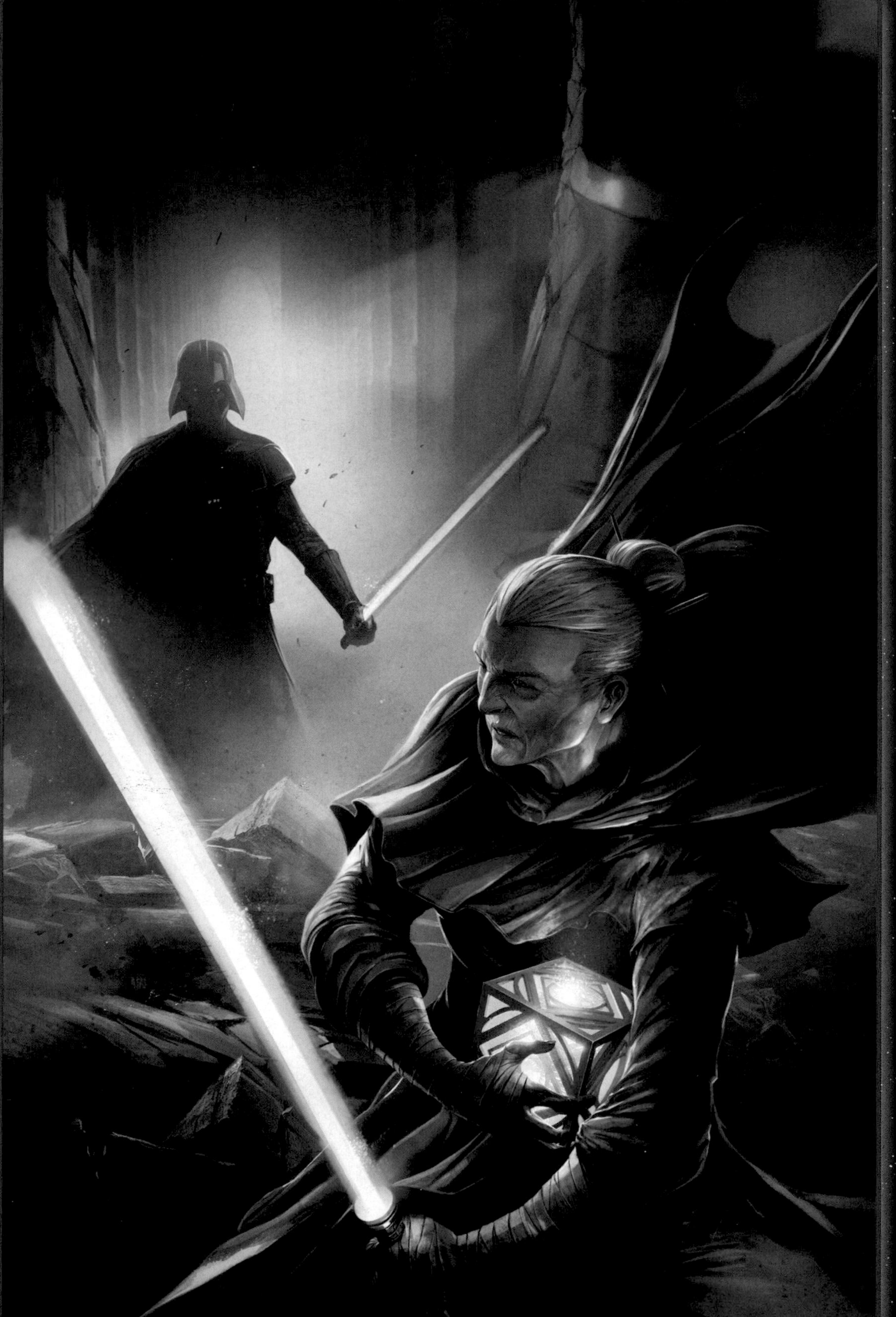

10

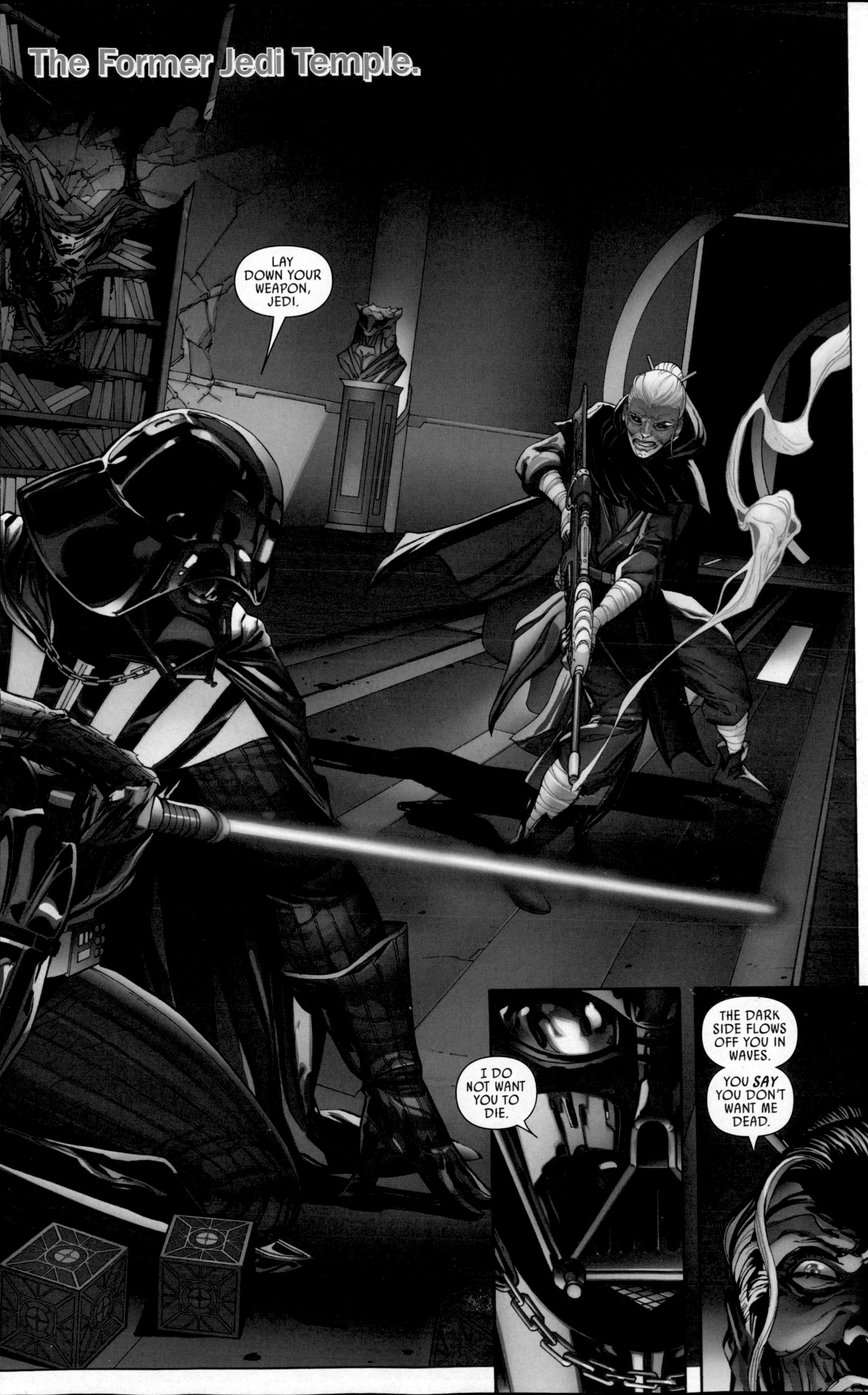
The Former Jedi Temple.
LAY DOWN YOUR WEAPON, JEDI.
I DO NOT WANT YOU TO DIE.
THE DARK SIDE FLOWS OFF YOU IN WAVES.
YOU SAY YOU DON'T WANT ME DEAD.

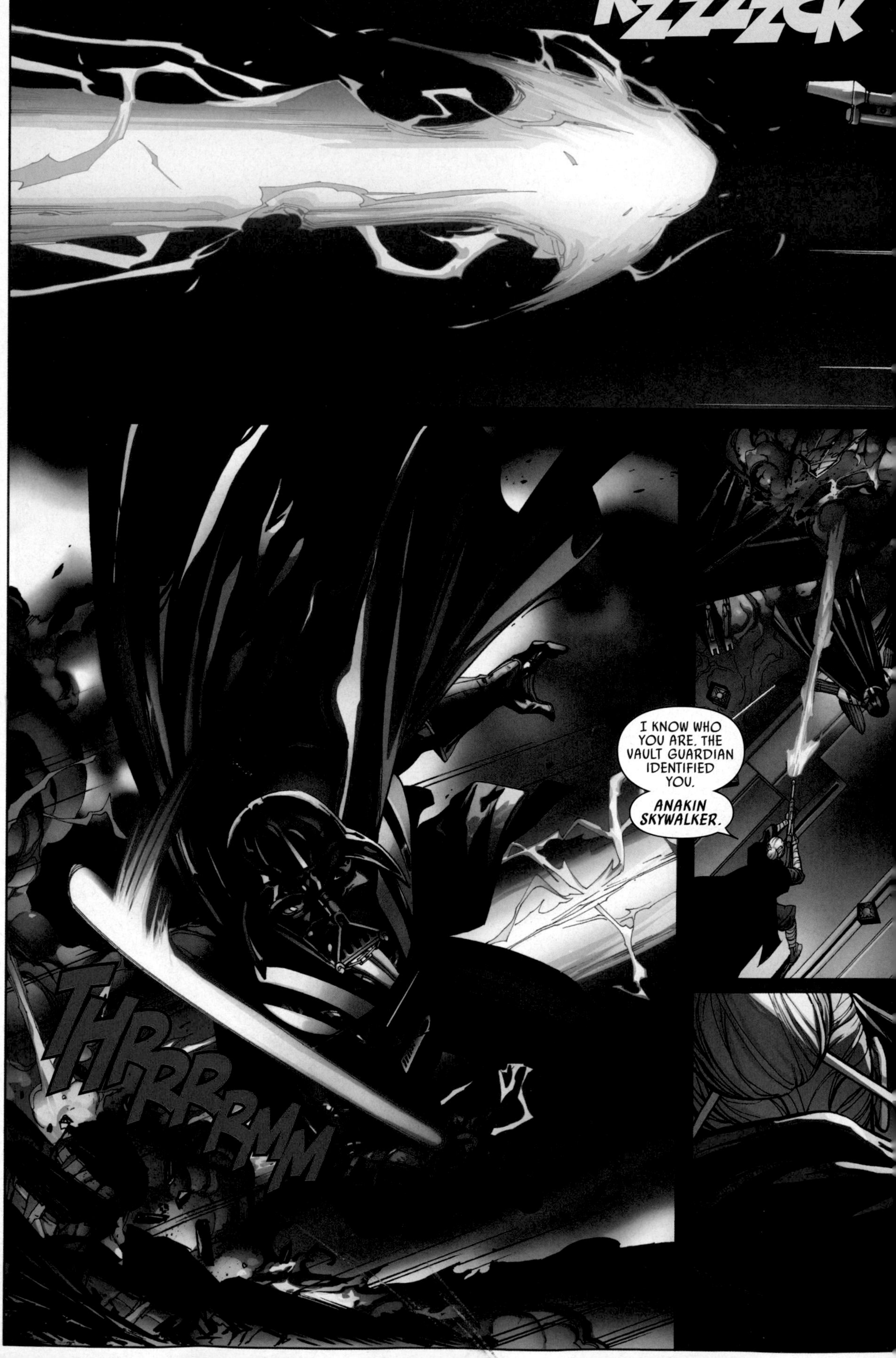

KZZZZCK
I KNOW WHO YOU ARE. THE VAULT GUARDIAN IDENTIFIED YOU.
ANAKIN SKYWALKER.
THRRRRMM

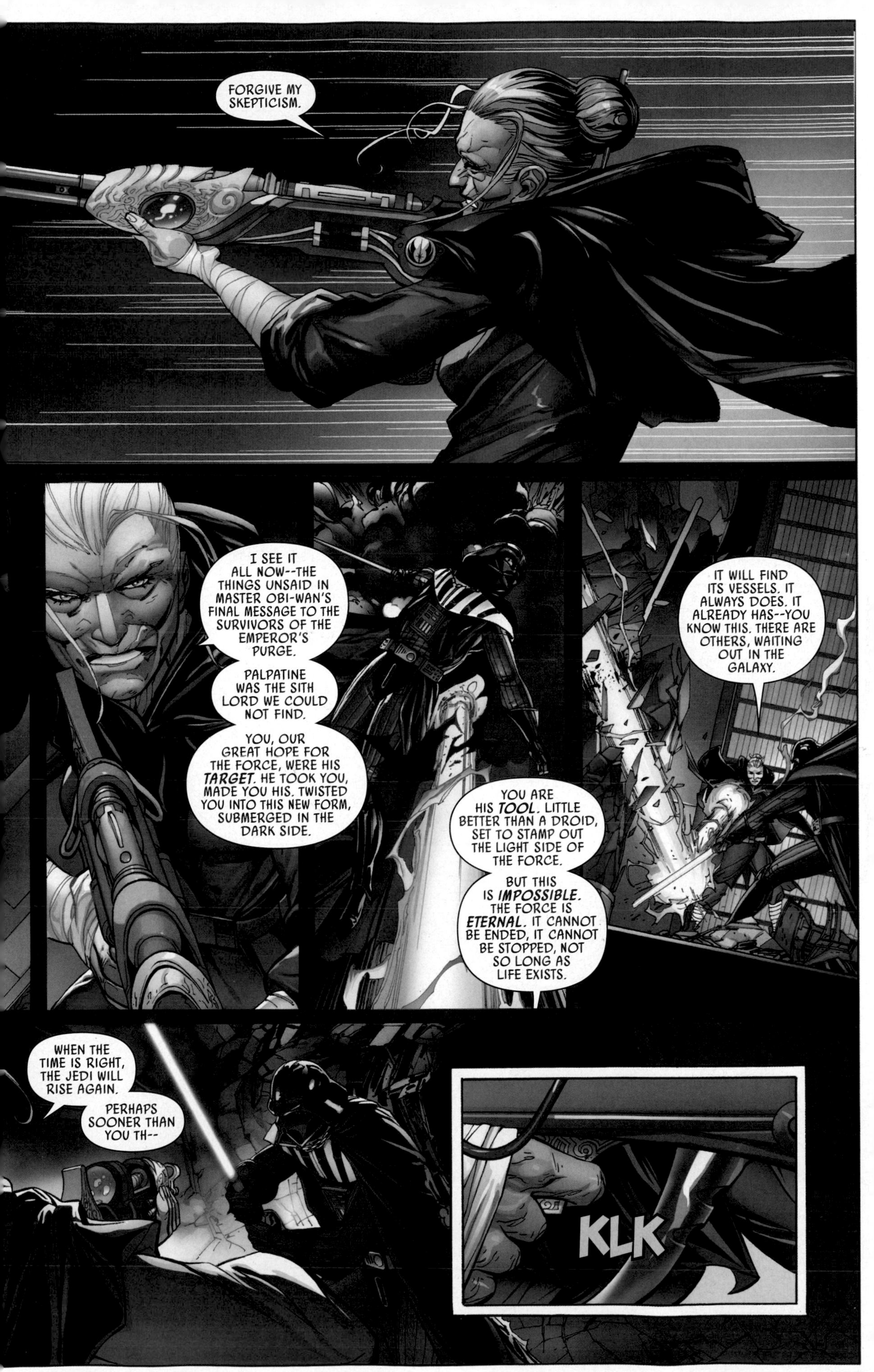
FORGIVE MY SKEPTICISM.
I SEE IT ALL NOW--THE THINGS UNSAID IN MASTER OBI-WAN'S FINAL MESSAGE TO THE SURVIVORS OF THE EMPEROR'S PURGE.
PALPATINE WAS THE SITH LORD WE COULD NOT FIND.
YOU, OUR GREAT HOPE FOR THE FORCE, WERE HIS TARGET. HE TOOK YOU, MADE YOU HIS. TWISTED YOU INTO THIS NEW FORM, SUBMERGED IN THE DARK SIDE.
YOU ARE HIS TOOL. LITTLE BETTER THAN A DROID, SET TO STAMP OUT THE LIGHT SIDE OF THE FORCE.
BUT THIS IS IMPOSSIBLE. THE FORCE IS ETERNAL. IT CANNOT BE ENDED, IT CANNOT BE STOPPED, NOT SO LONG AS LIFE EXISTS.
IT WILL FIND ITS VESSELS. IT ALWAYS DOES. IT ALREADY HAS--YOU KNOW THIS. THERE ARE OTHERS, WAITING OUT IN THE GALAXY.
WHEN THE TIME IS RIGHT, THE JEDI WILL RISE AGAIN.
PERHAPS SOONER THAN YOU TH--
KLK

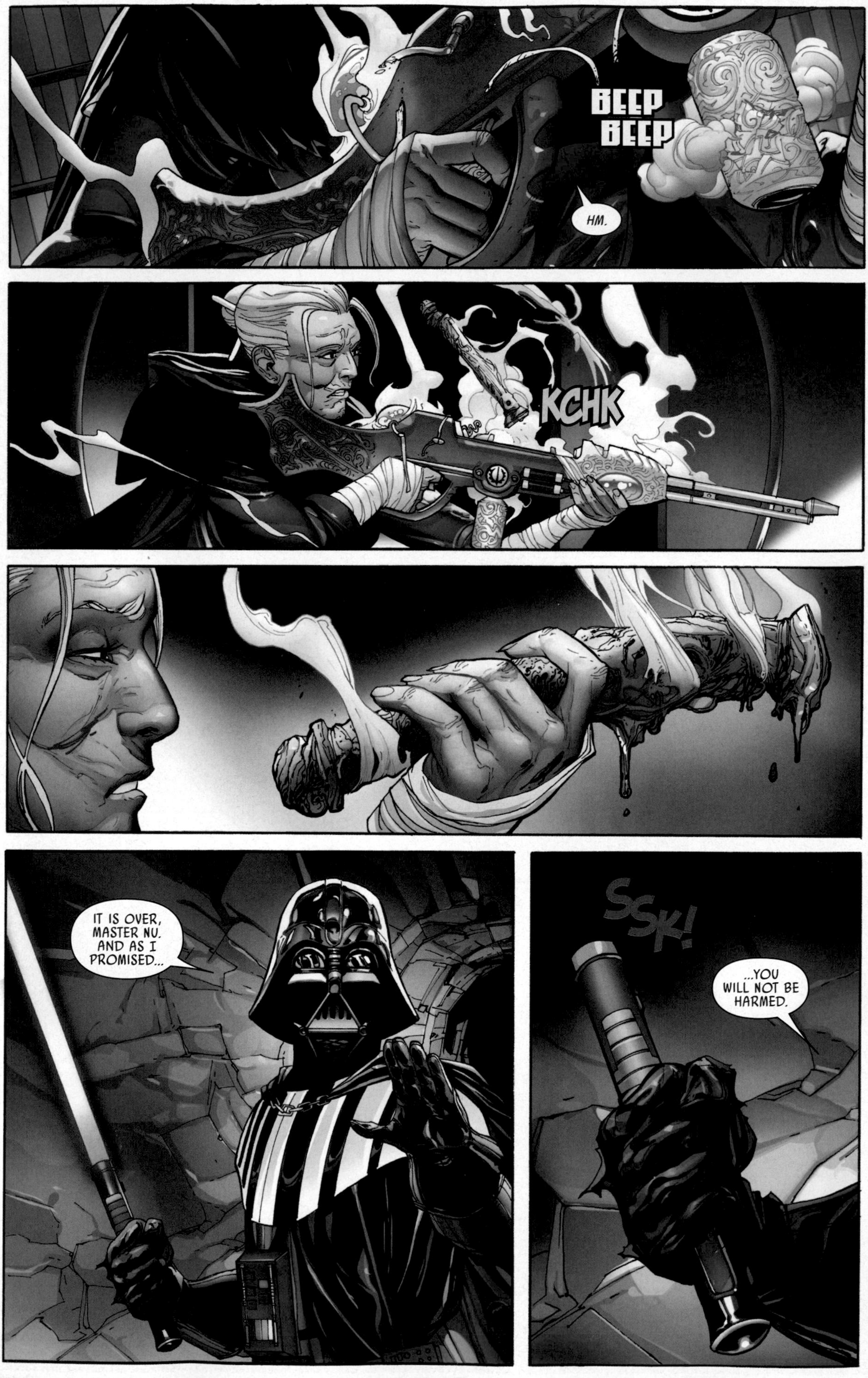
BEEP BEEP
HM.
KCHK
IT IS OVER, MASTER NU. AND AS I PROMISED...
SSK!
...YOU WILL NOT BE HARMED.

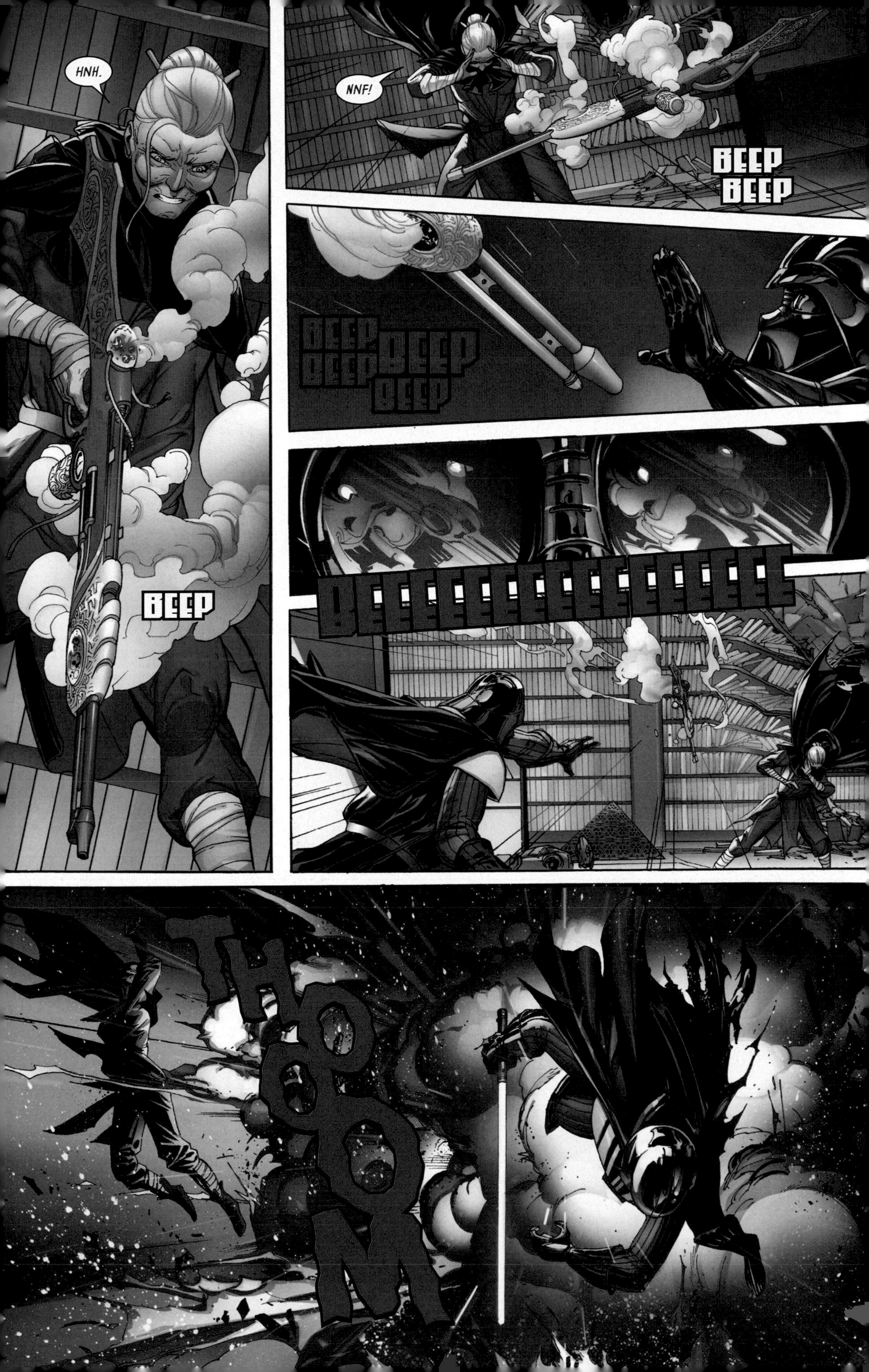
HNH.
BEEP
NNF!
BEEP
BEEP
BEEP
BEEP
BEEP
BEEP
BEEEEEEEEEEEEEEEEE
THOOOM

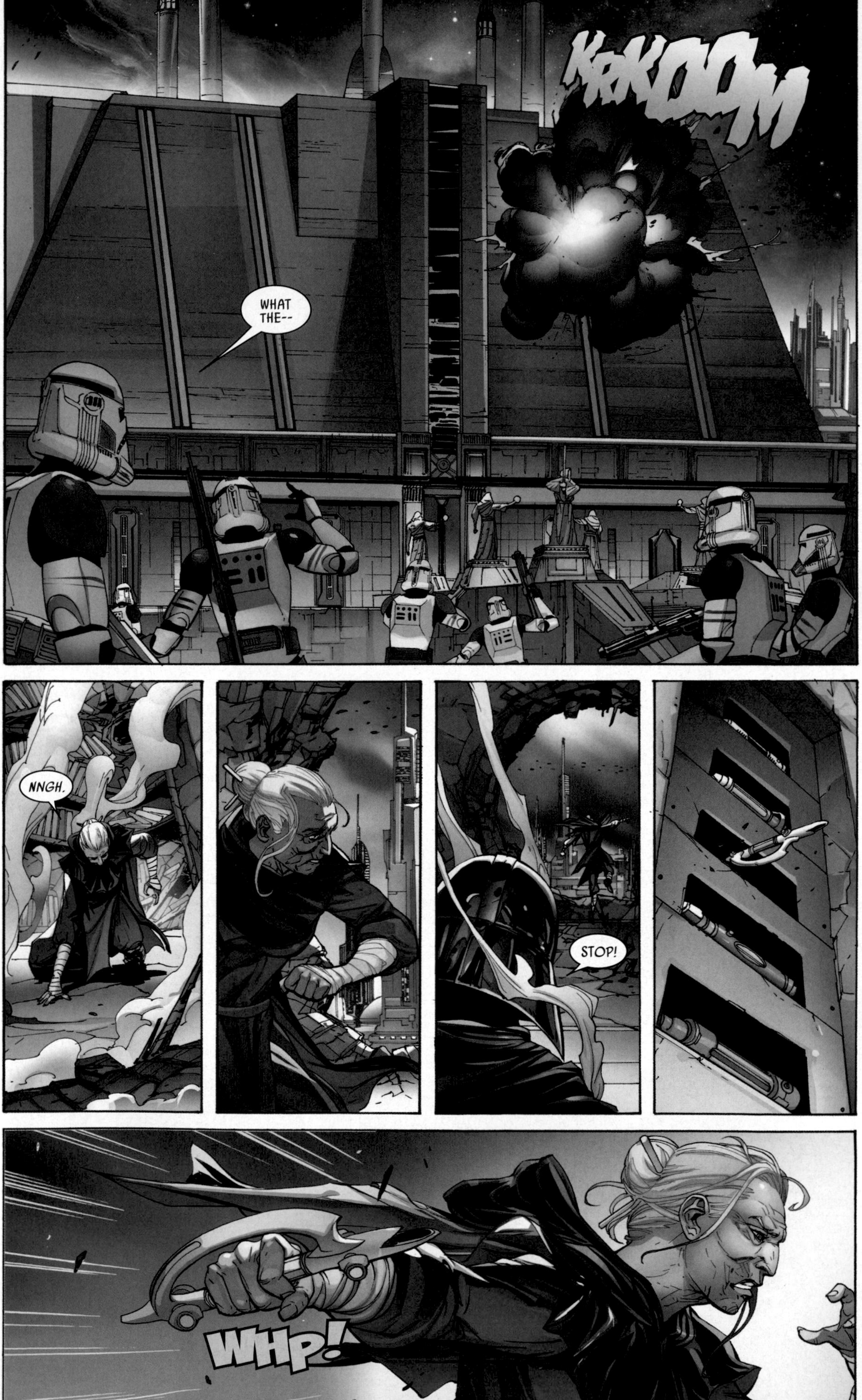
KRKOOM
WHAT THE--
NNGH.
STOP!
WHP!

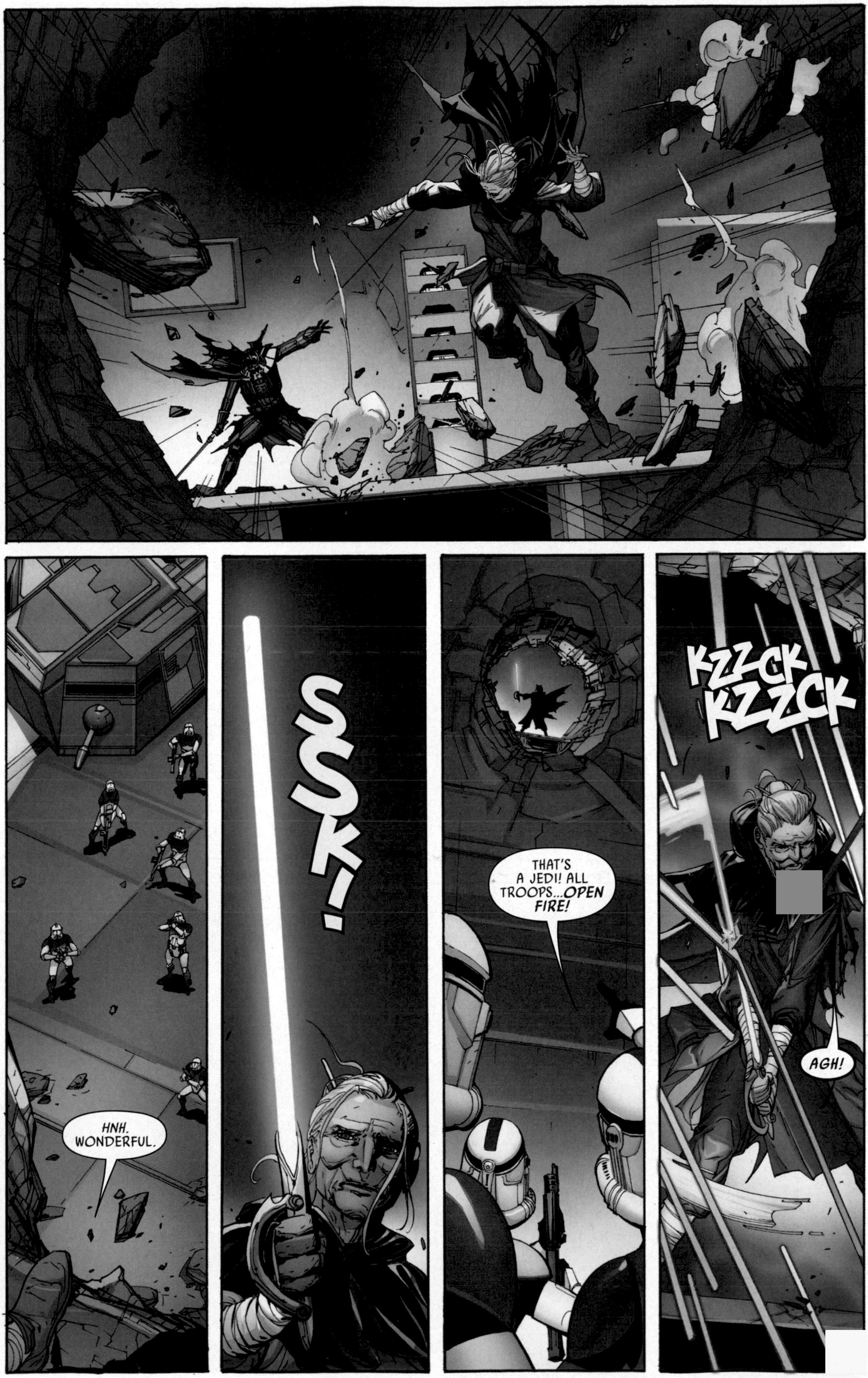
HNH. WONDERFUL.
SSSK!
THAT'S A JEDI! ALL TROOPS...OPEN FIRE!
KZZZCK KZZZCK
AGH!

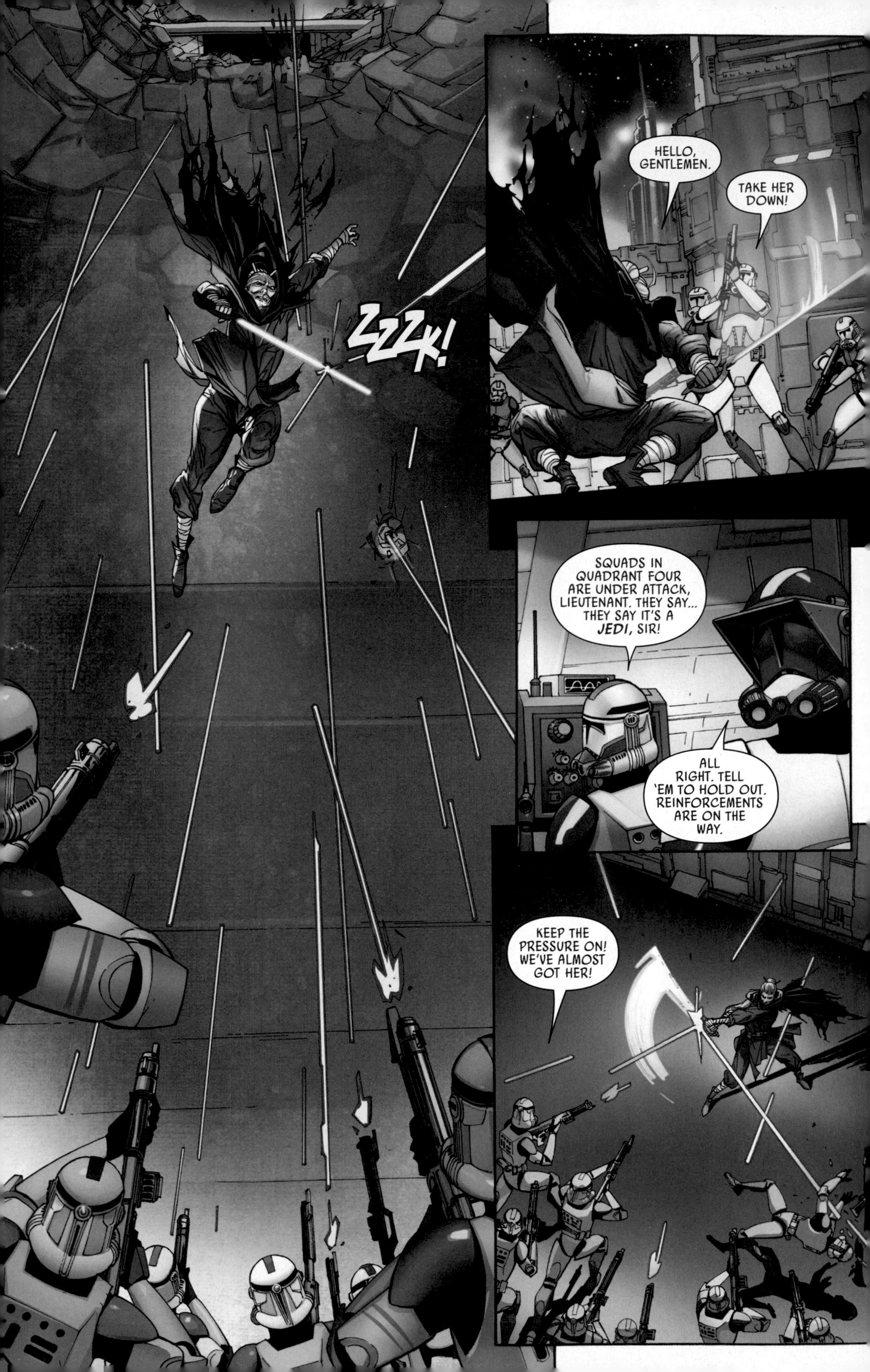
ZZZK!
HELLO, GENTLEMEN.
TAKE HER DOWN!
SQUADS IN QUADRANT FOUR ARE UNDER ATTACK, LIEUTENANT. THEY SAY... THEY SAY IT'S A JEDI, SIR!
ALL RIGHT. TELL 'EM TO HOLD OUT. REINFORCEMENTS ARE ON THE WAY.
KEEP THE PRESSURE ON! WE'VE ALMOST GOT HER!

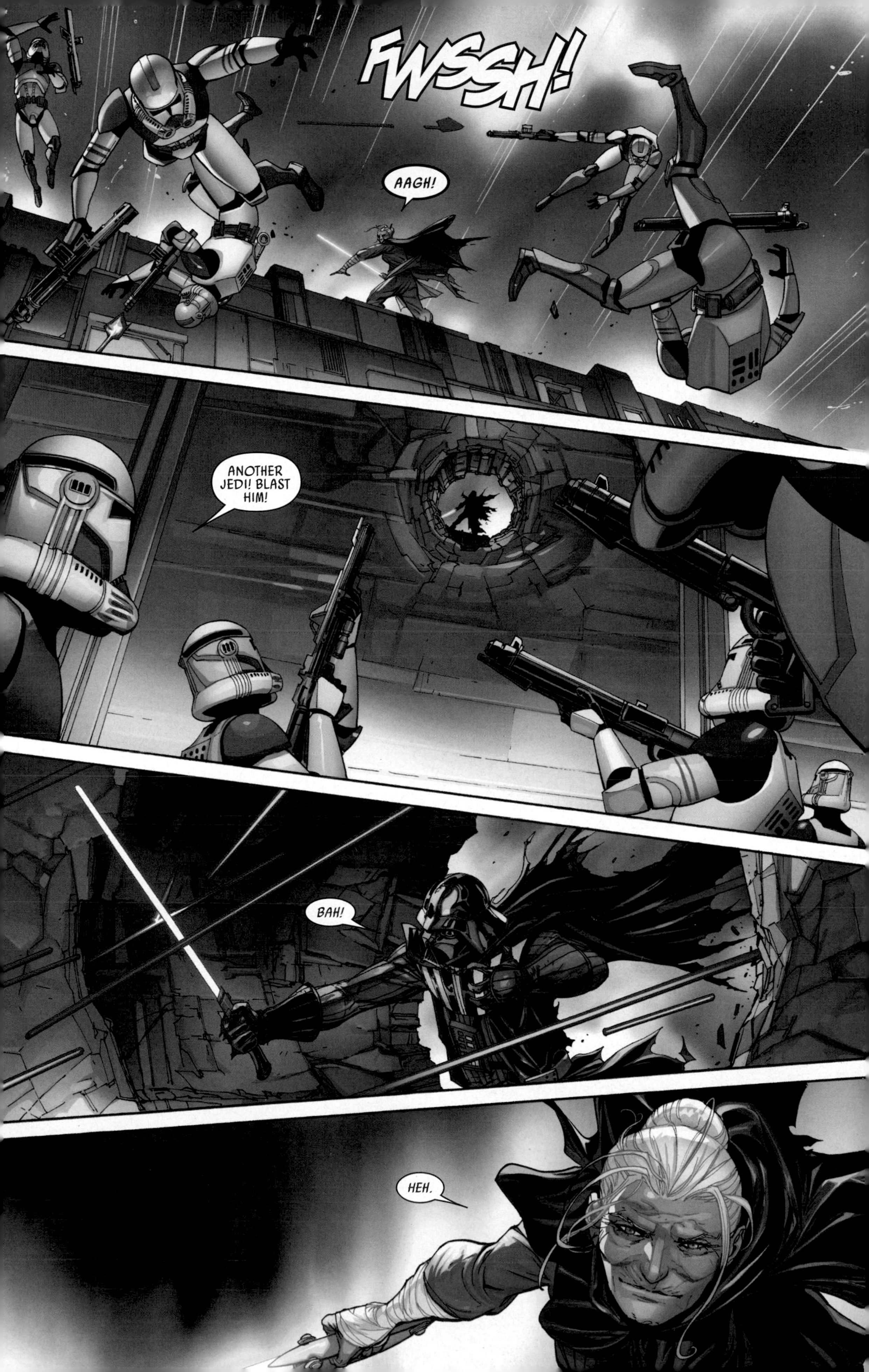
FWSSH!
AAGH!
ANOTHER JEDI! BLAST HIM!
BAH!
HEH.

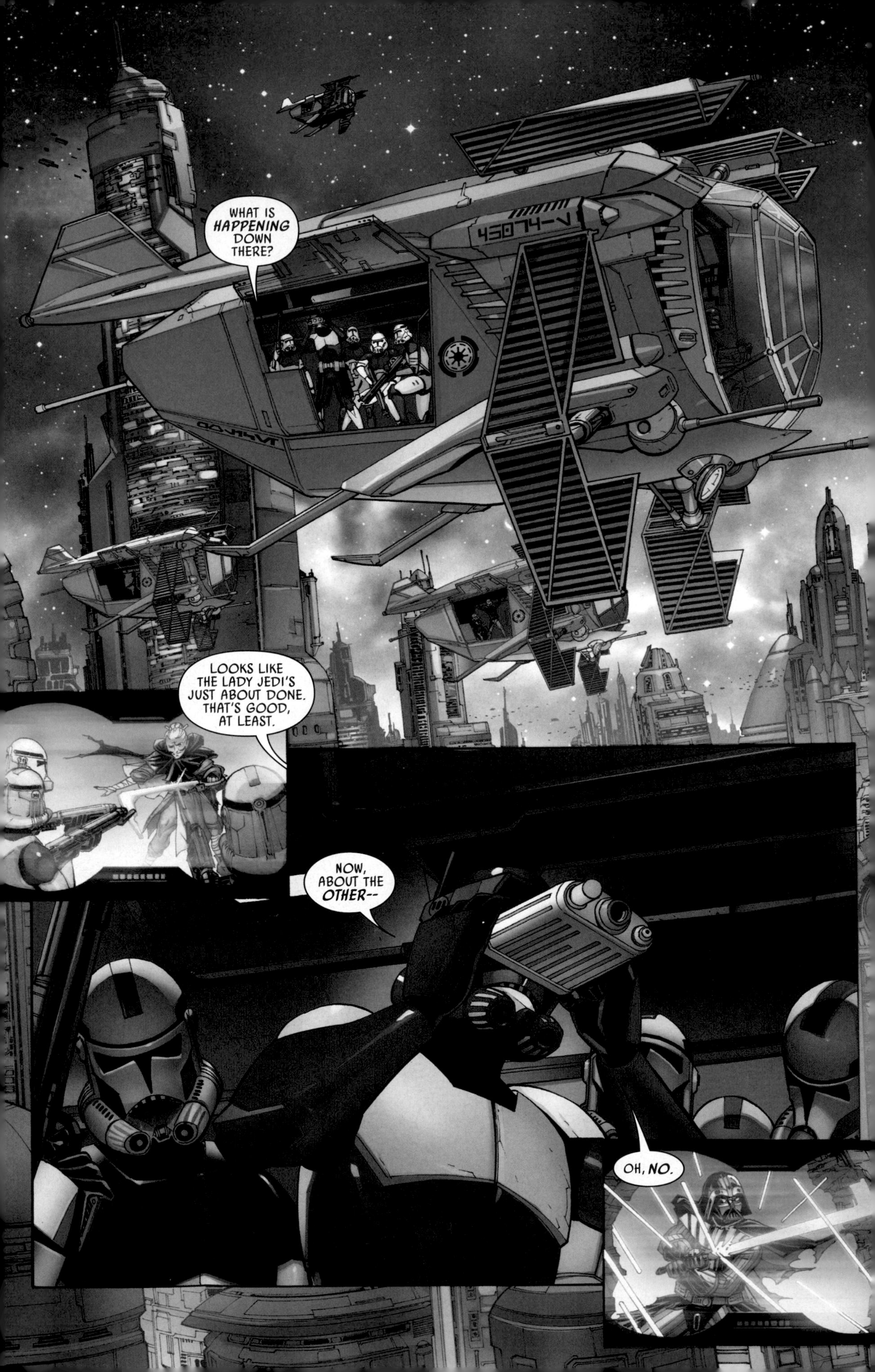

WHAT IS *HAPPENING* DOWN THERE?
45074-V
LOOKS LIKE THE LADY JEDI'S JUST ABOUT DONE. THAT'S GOOD, AT LEAST.
NOW, ABOUT THE *OTHER*--
OH, **NO.**

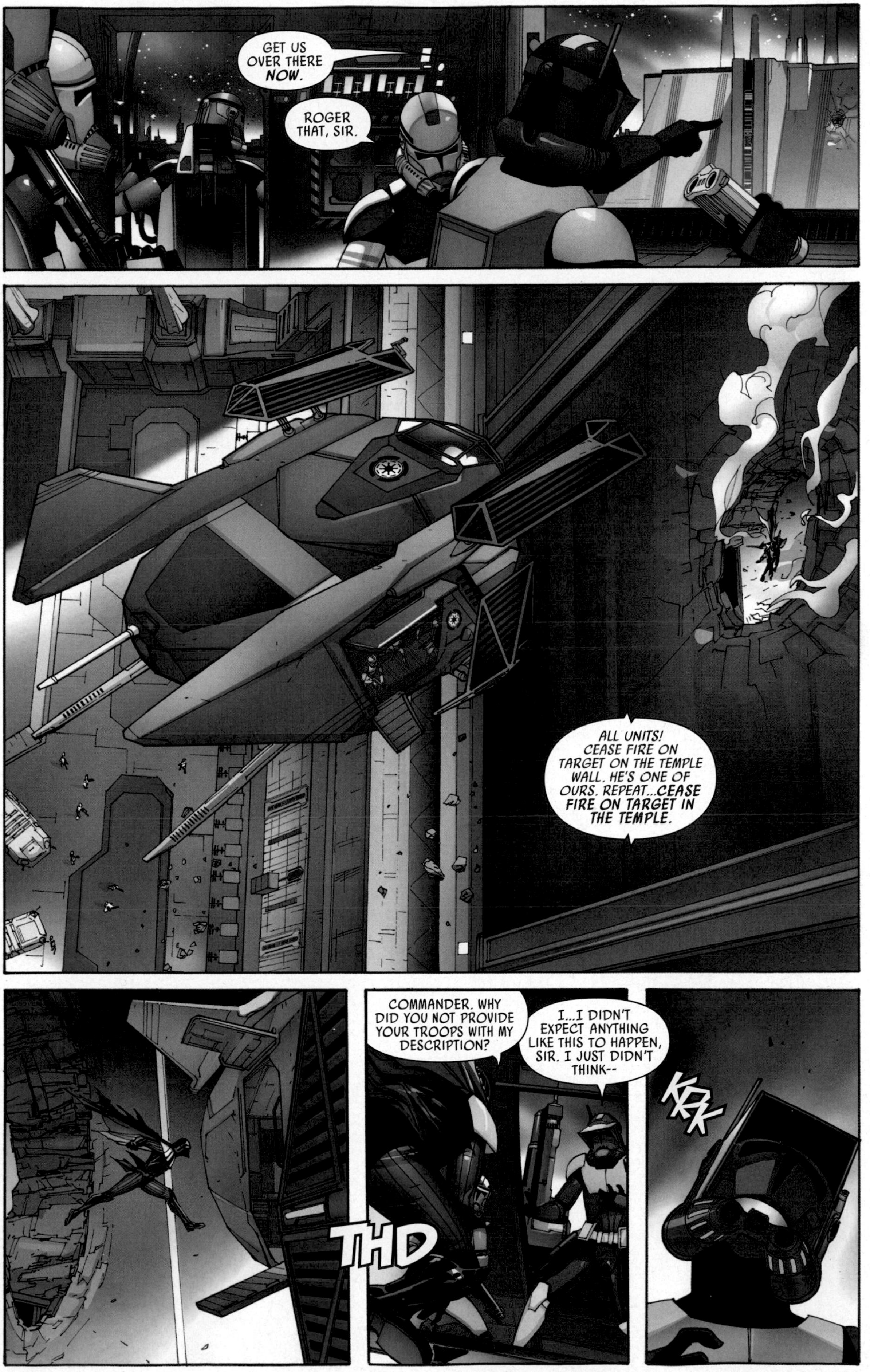
GET US OVER THERE NOW.
ROGER THAT, SIR.
ALL UNITS! CEASE FIRE ON TARGET ON THE TEMPLE WALL. HE'S ONE OF OURS. REPEAT...CEASE FIRE ON TARGET IN THE TEMPLE.
THD
COMMANDER. WHY DID YOU NOT PROVIDE YOUR TROOPS WITH MY DESCRIPTION?
I...I DIDN'T EXPECT ANYTHING LIKE THIS TO HAPPEN, SIR. I JUST DIDN'T THINK--
KRK

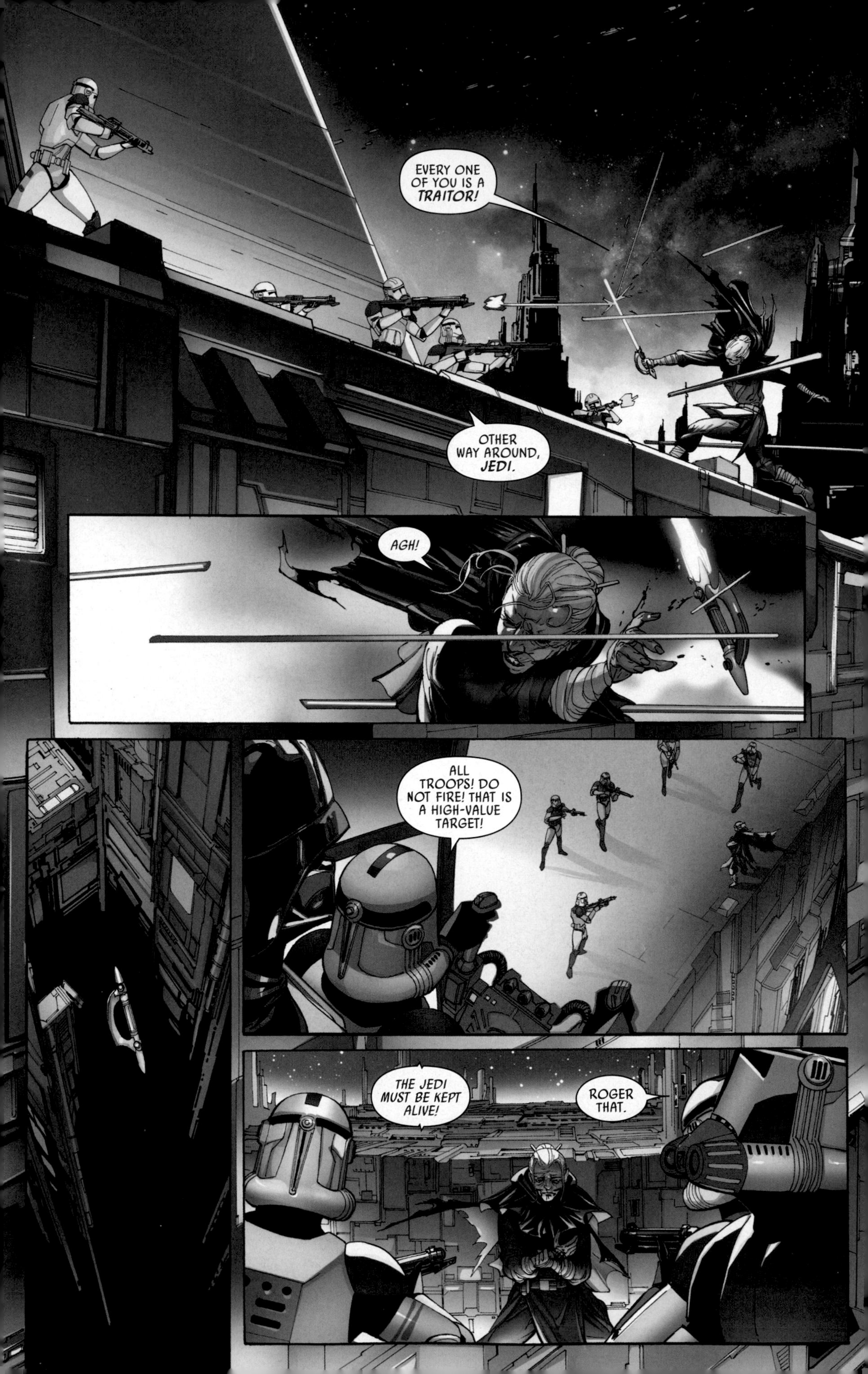
EVERY ONE OF YOU IS A TRAITOR!
OTHER WAY AROUND, JEDI.
AGH!
ALL TROOPS! DO NOT FIRE! THAT IS A HIGH-VALUE TARGET!
THE JEDI MUST BE KEPT ALIVE!
ROGER THAT.

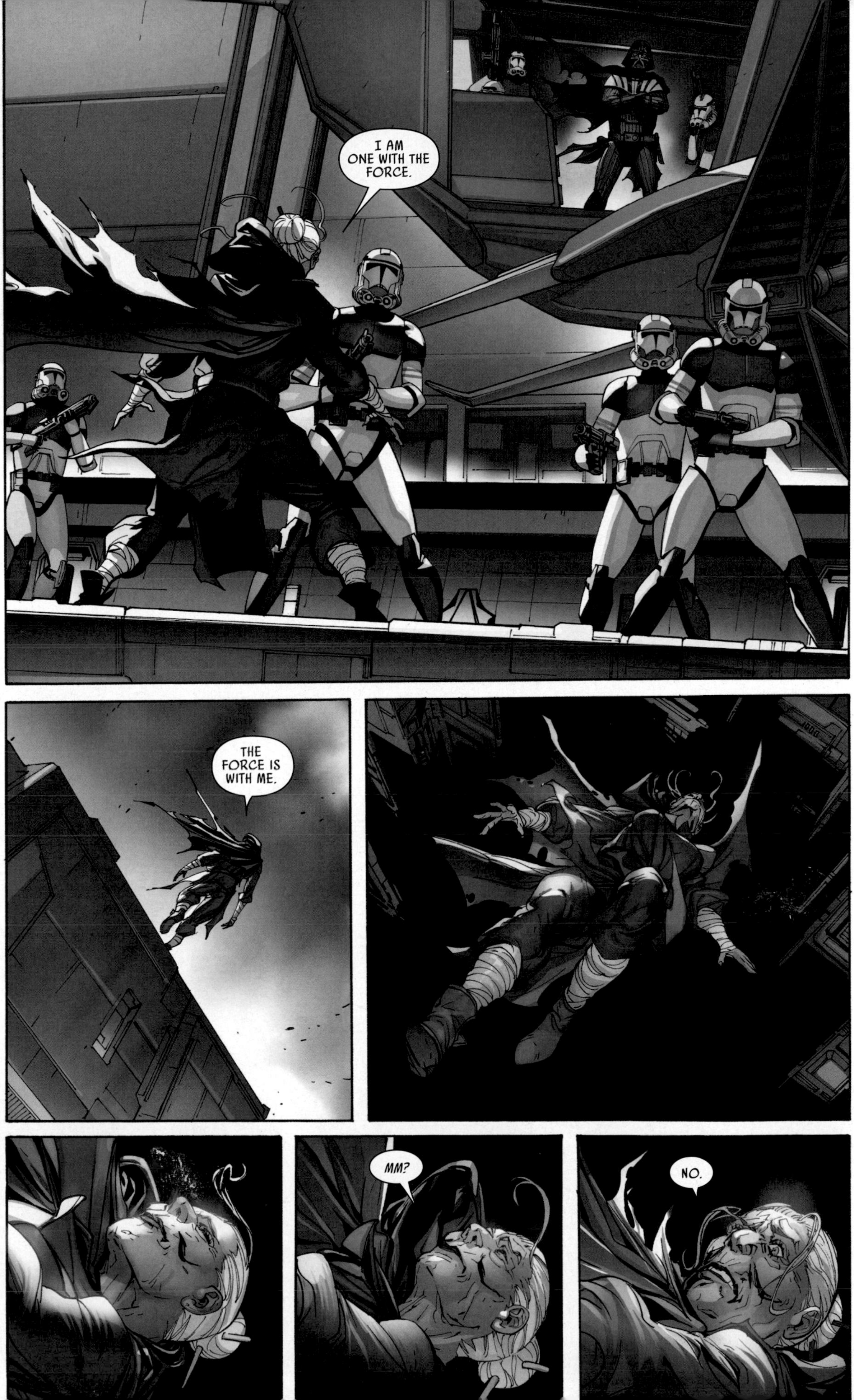
I AM ONE WITH THE FORCE.
THE FORCE IS WITH ME.
MM?
NO.

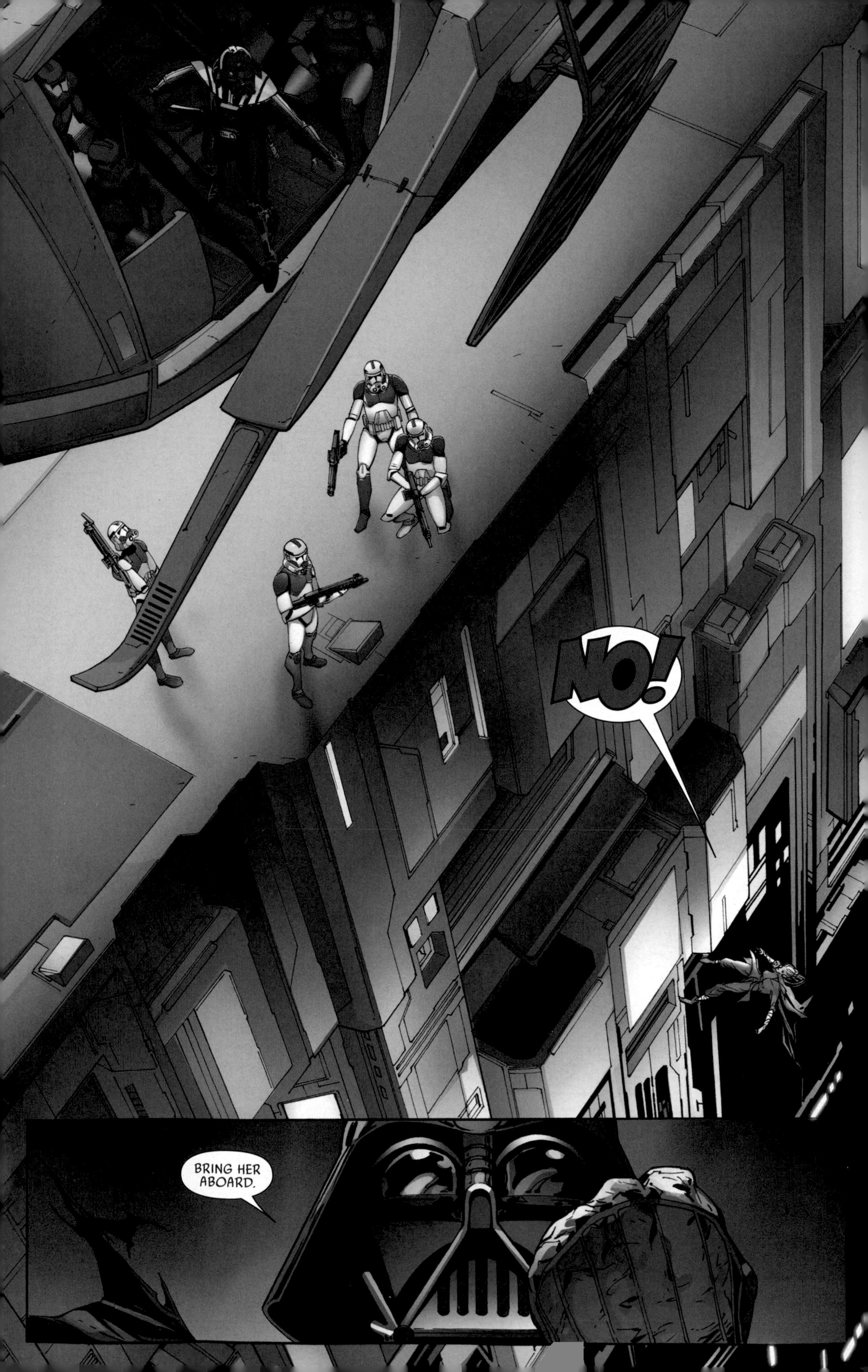
NO!
BRING HER ABOARD.

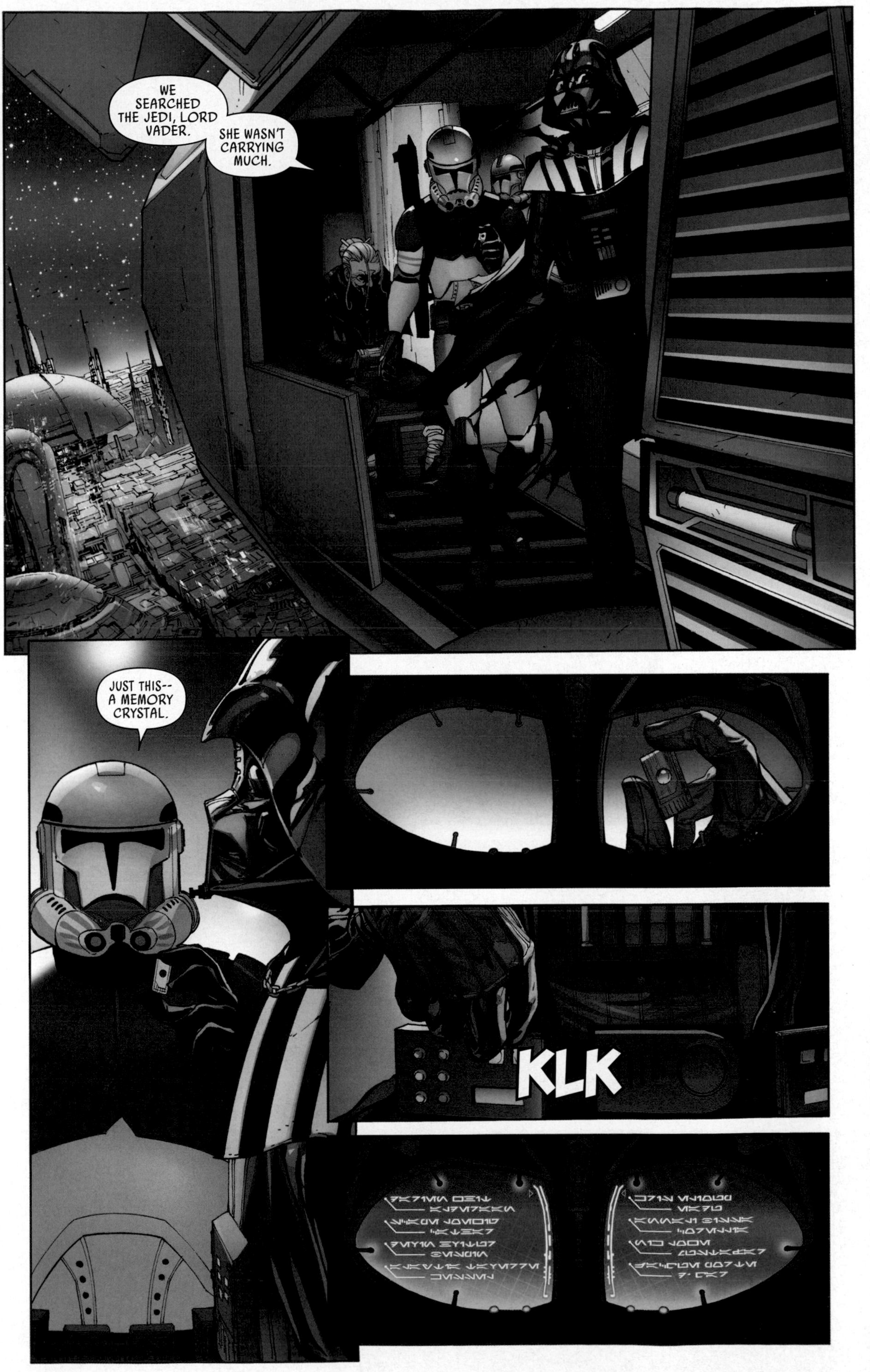

WE SEARCHED THE JEDI, LORD VADER.
SHE WASN'T CARRYING MUCH.
JUST THIS-- A MEMORY CRYSTAL.
KLK

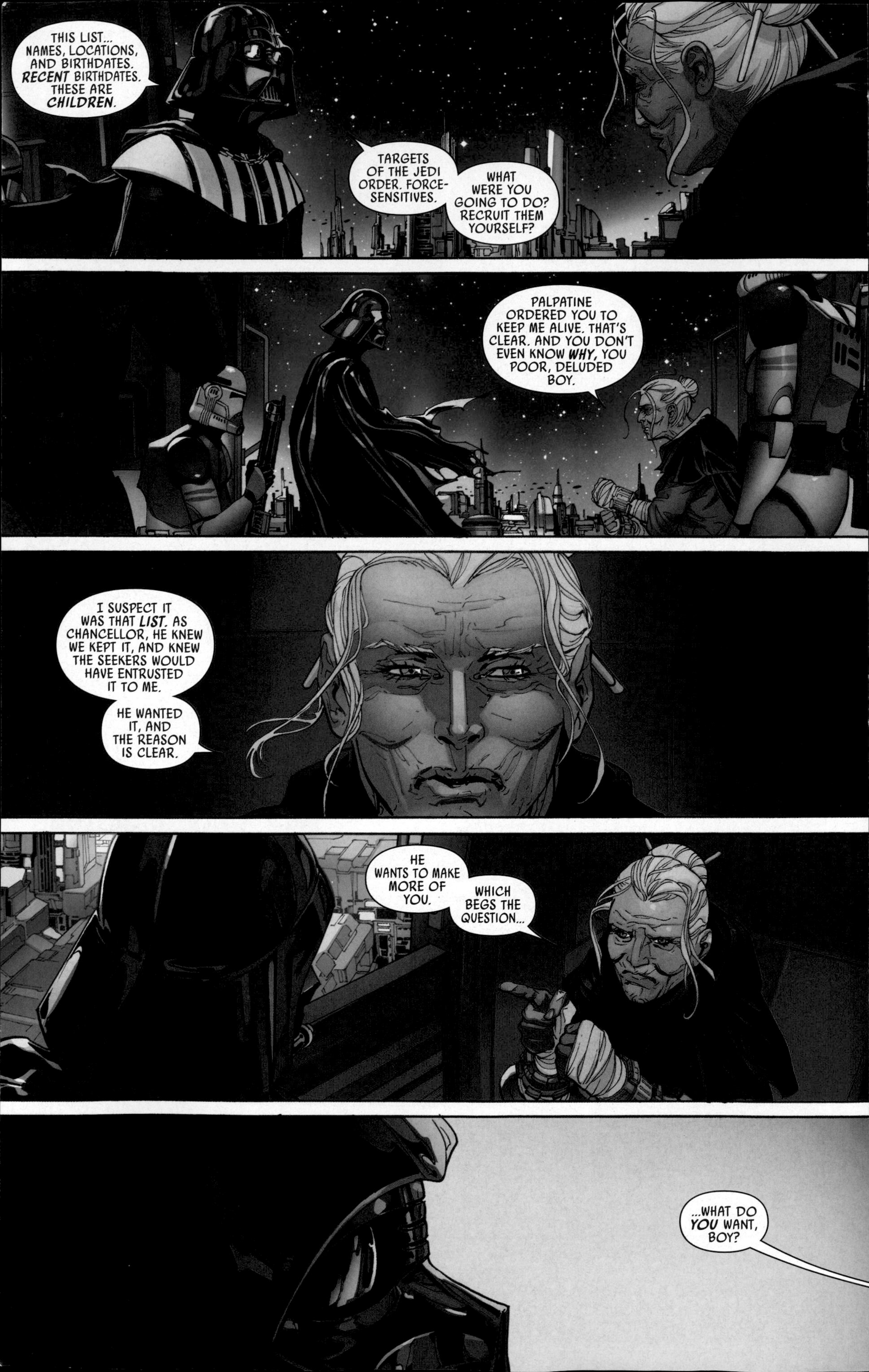

THIS LIST... NAMES, LOCATIONS, AND BIRTHDATES. RECENT BIRTHDATES. THESE ARE CHILDREN.
TARGETS OF THE JEDI ORDER. FORCE-SENSITIVES.
WHAT WERE YOU GOING TO DO? RECRUIT THEM YOURSELF?
PALPATINE ORDERED YOU TO KEEP ME ALIVE. THAT'S CLEAR. AND YOU DON'T EVEN KNOW WHY, YOU POOR, DELUDED BOY.
I SUSPECT IT WAS THAT LIST. AS CHANCELLOR, HE KNEW WE KEPT IT, AND KNEW THE SEEKERS WOULD HAVE ENTRUSTED IT TO ME.
HE WANTED IT, AND THE REASON IS CLEAR.
HE WANTS TO MAKE MORE OF YOU.
WHICH BEGS THE QUESTION...
...WHAT DO YOU WANT, BOY?

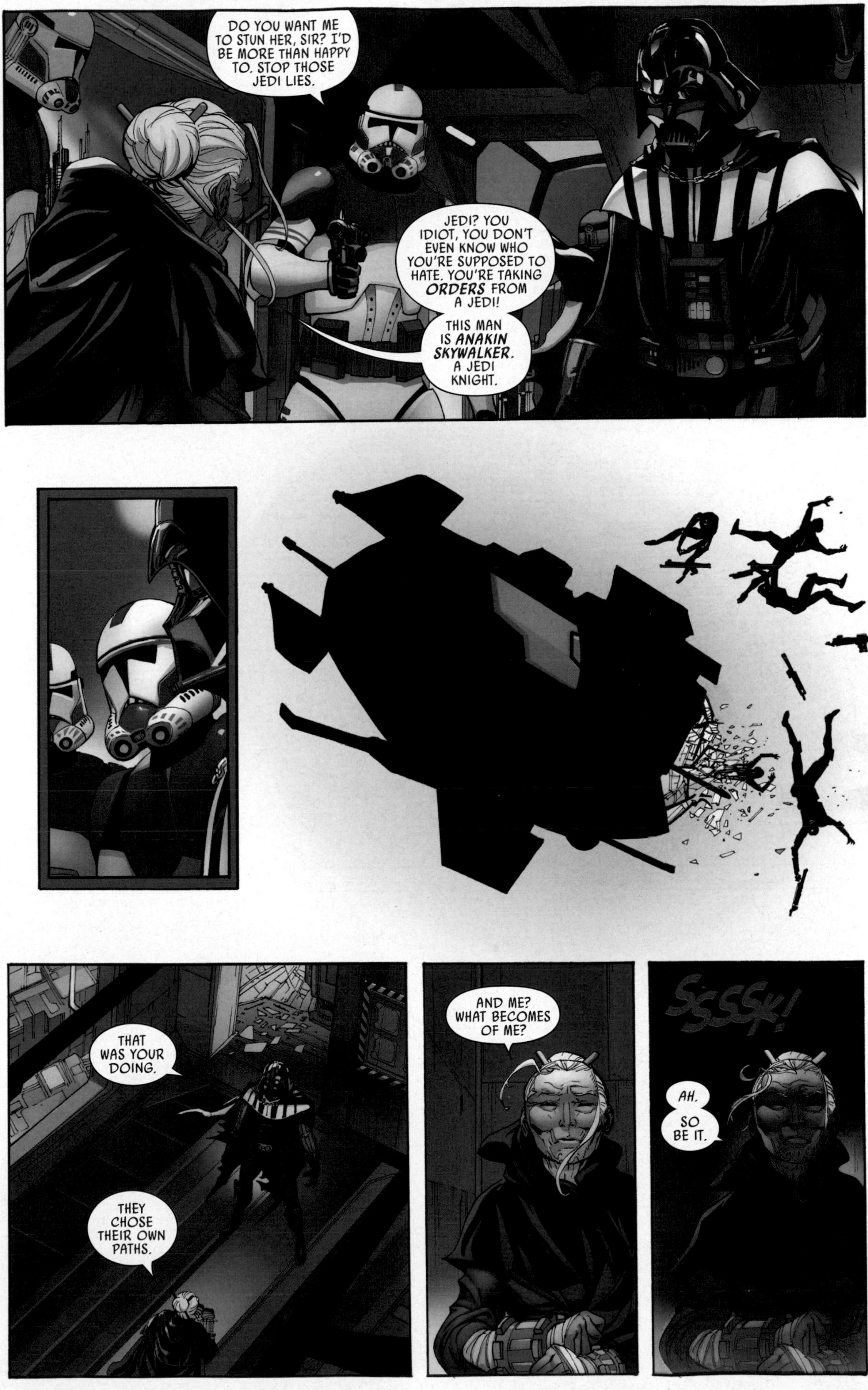

DO YOU WANT ME TO STUN HER, SIR? I'D BE MORE THAN HAPPY TO. STOP THOSE JEDI LIES.
JEDI? YOU IDIOT, YOU DON'T EVEN KNOW WHO YOU'RE SUPPOSED TO HATE. YOU'RE TAKING ORDERS FROM A JEDI!
THIS MAN IS ANAKIN SKYWALKER. A JEDI KNIGHT.
THAT WAS YOUR DOING.
THEY CHOSE THEIR OWN PATHS.
AND ME? WHAT BECOMES OF ME?
SSSSK!
AH.
SO BE IT.

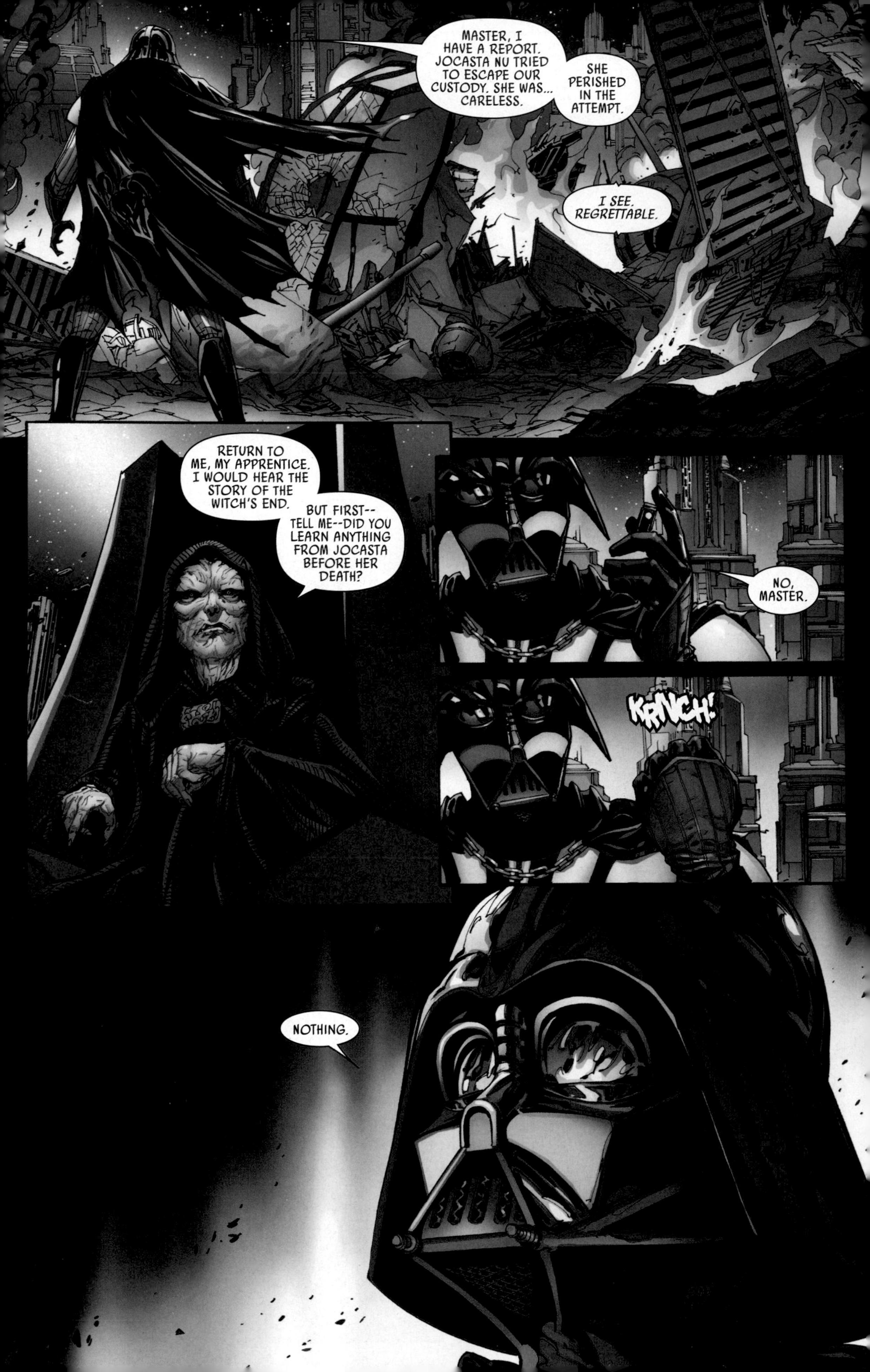
MASTER, I HAVE A REPORT. JOCASTA NU TRIED TO ESCAPE OUR CUSTODY. SHE WAS... CARELESS.
SHE PERISHED IN THE ATTEMPT.
I SEE. REGRETTABLE.
RETURN TO ME, MY APPRENTICE. I WOULD HEAR THE STORY OF THE WITCH'S END.
BUT FIRST-- TELL ME--DID YOU LEARN ANYTHING FROM JOCASTA BEFORE HER DEATH?
NO, MASTER.
KRNCH!
NOTHING.

Elsewhere.

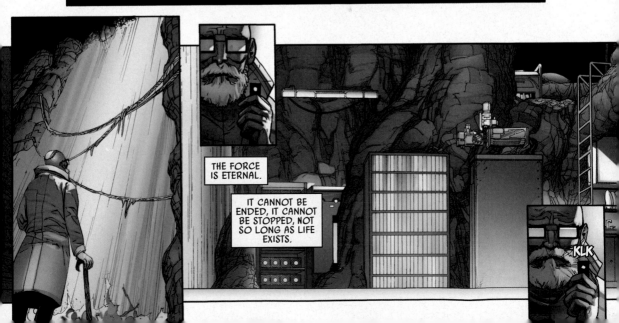

THE FORCE IS ETERNAL.

IT CANNOT BE ENDED, IT CANNOT BE STOPPED, NOT SO LONG AS LIFE EXISTS.

KLK

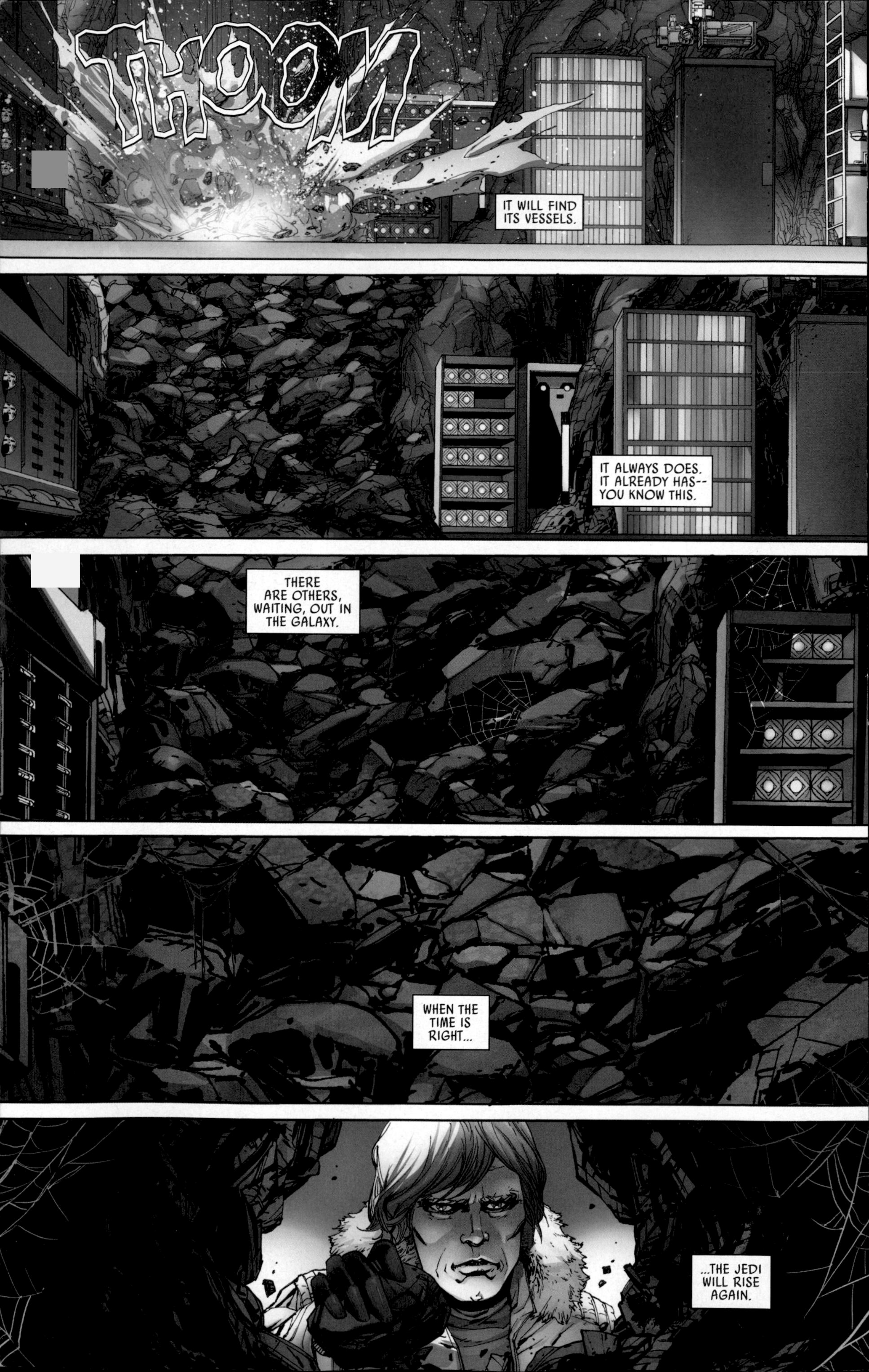
THOOM
IT WILL FIND ITS VESSELS.
IT ALWAYS DOES. IT ALREADY HAS-- YOU KNOW THIS.
THERE ARE OTHERS, WAITING, OUT IN THE GALAXY.
WHEN THE TIME IS RIGHT...
...THE JEDI WILL RISE AGAIN.

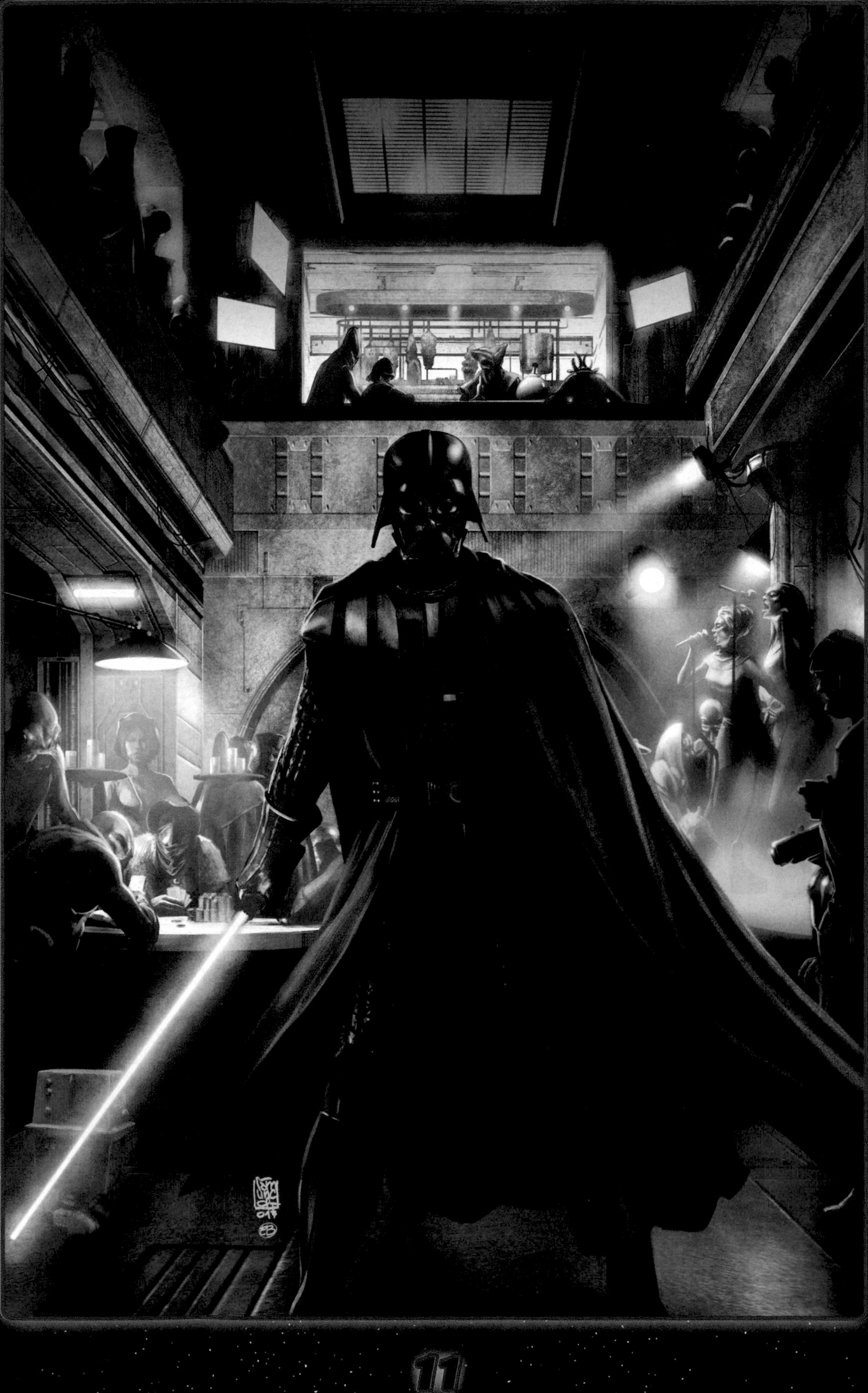
11

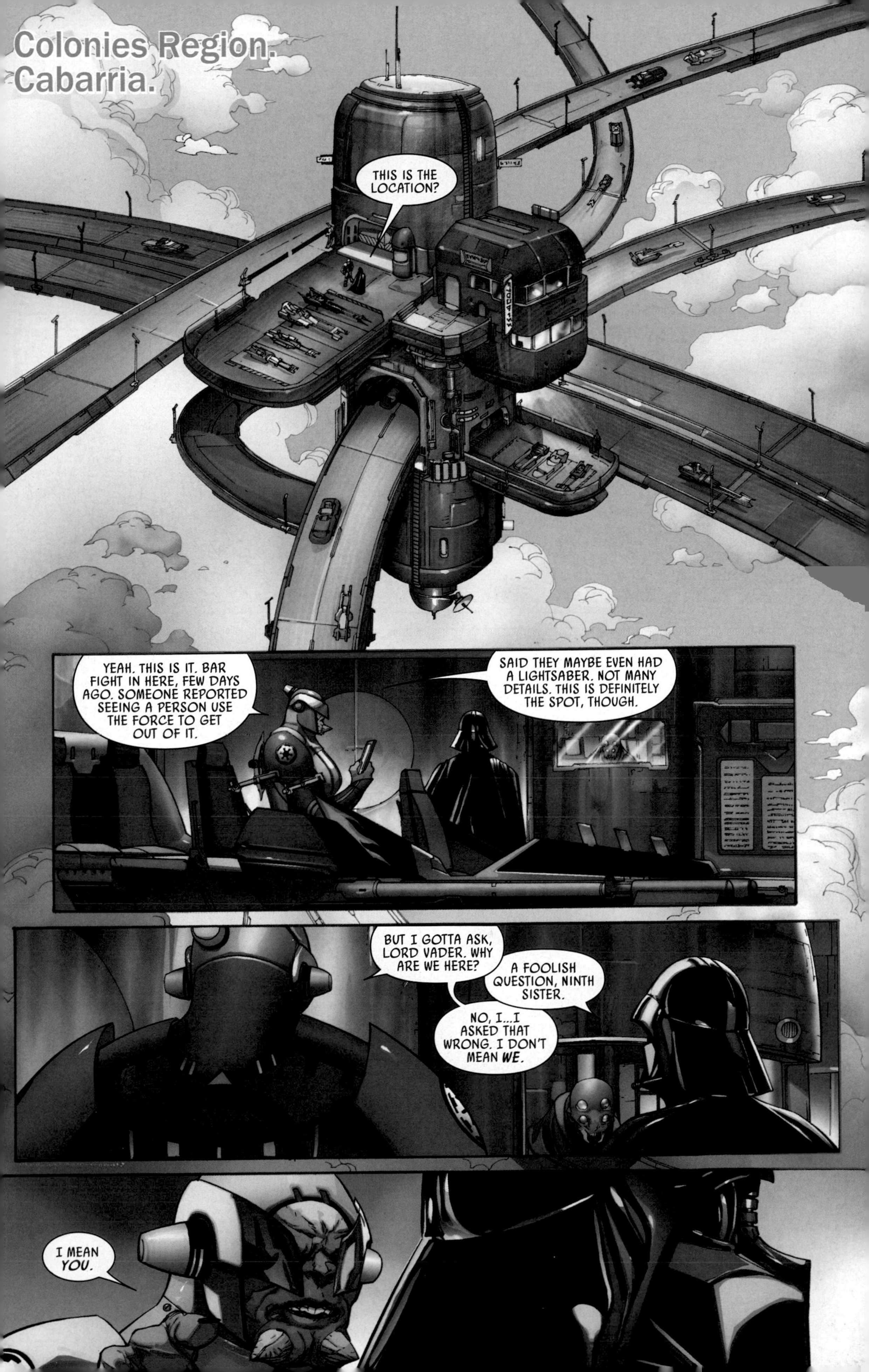
Colonies Region. Cabarria.
THIS IS THE LOCATION?
YEAH. THIS IS IT. BAR FIGHT IN HERE, FEW DAYS AGO. SOMEONE REPORTED SEEING A PERSON USE THE FORCE TO GET OUT OF IT.
SAID THEY MAYBE EVEN HAD A LIGHTSABER. NOT MANY DETAILS. THIS IS DEFINITELY THE SPOT, THOUGH.
BUT I GOTTA ASK, LORD VADER. WHY ARE WE HERE?
A FOOLISH QUESTION, NINTH SISTER.
NO, I...I ASKED THAT WRONG. I DON'T MEAN *WE*.
I MEAN *YOU*.

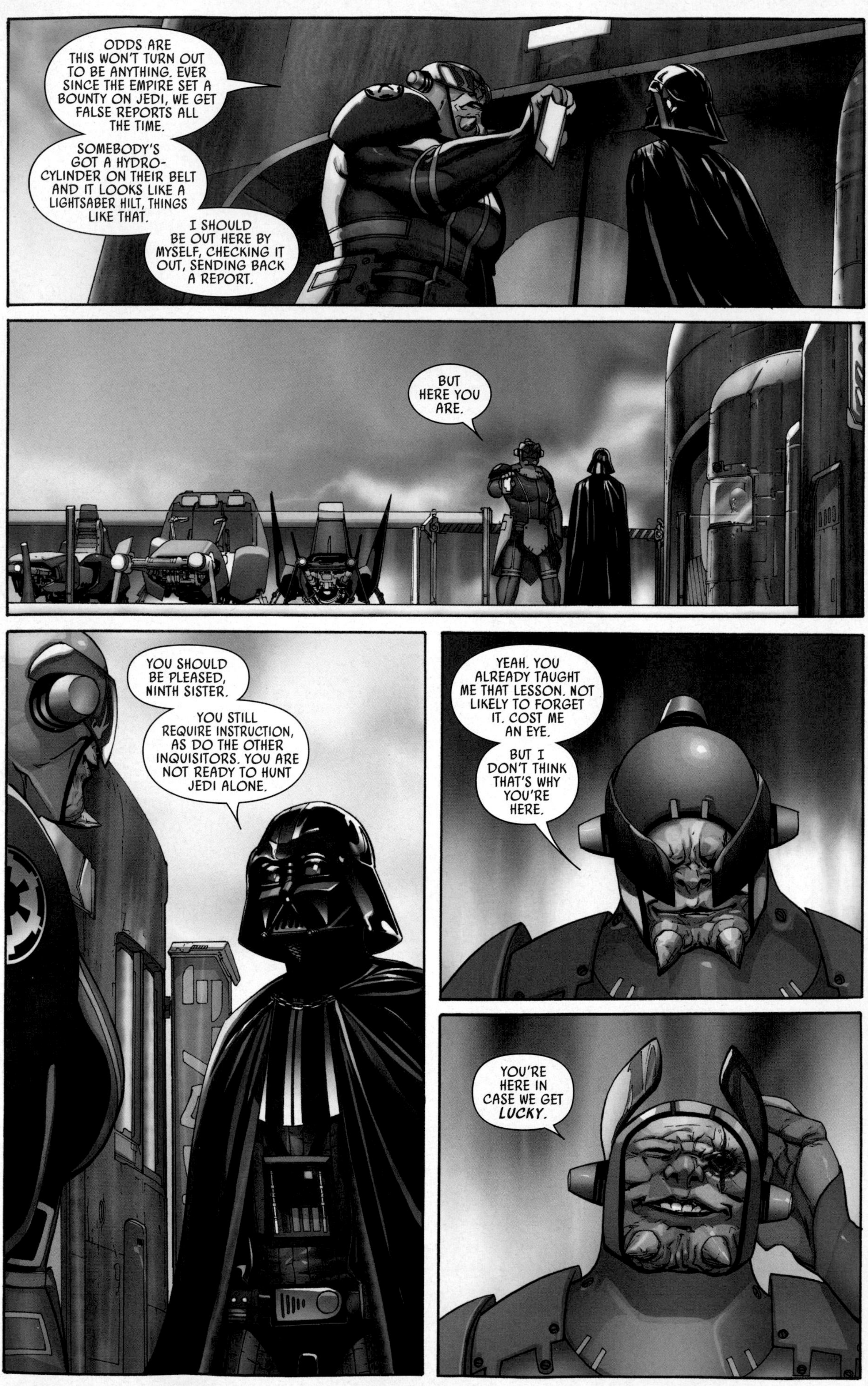
ODDS ARE THIS WON'T TURN OUT TO BE ANYTHING. EVER SINCE THE EMPIRE SET A BOUNTY ON JEDI, WE GET FALSE REPORTS ALL THE TIME.
SOMEBODY'S GOT A HYDRO-CYLINDER ON THEIR BELT AND IT LOOKS LIKE A LIGHTSABER HILT, THINGS LIKE THAT.
I SHOULD BE OUT HERE BY MYSELF, CHECKING IT OUT, SENDING BACK A REPORT.
BUT HERE YOU ARE.
YOU SHOULD BE PLEASED, NINTH SISTER.
YOU STILL REQUIRE INSTRUCTION, AS DO THE OTHER INQUISITORS. YOU ARE NOT READY TO HUNT JEDI ALONE.
YEAH. YOU ALREADY TAUGHT ME THAT LESSON. NOT LIKELY TO FORGET IT. COST ME AN EYE.
BUT I DON'T THINK THAT'S WHY YOU'RE HERE.
YOU'RE HERE IN CASE WE GET ***LUCKY***.

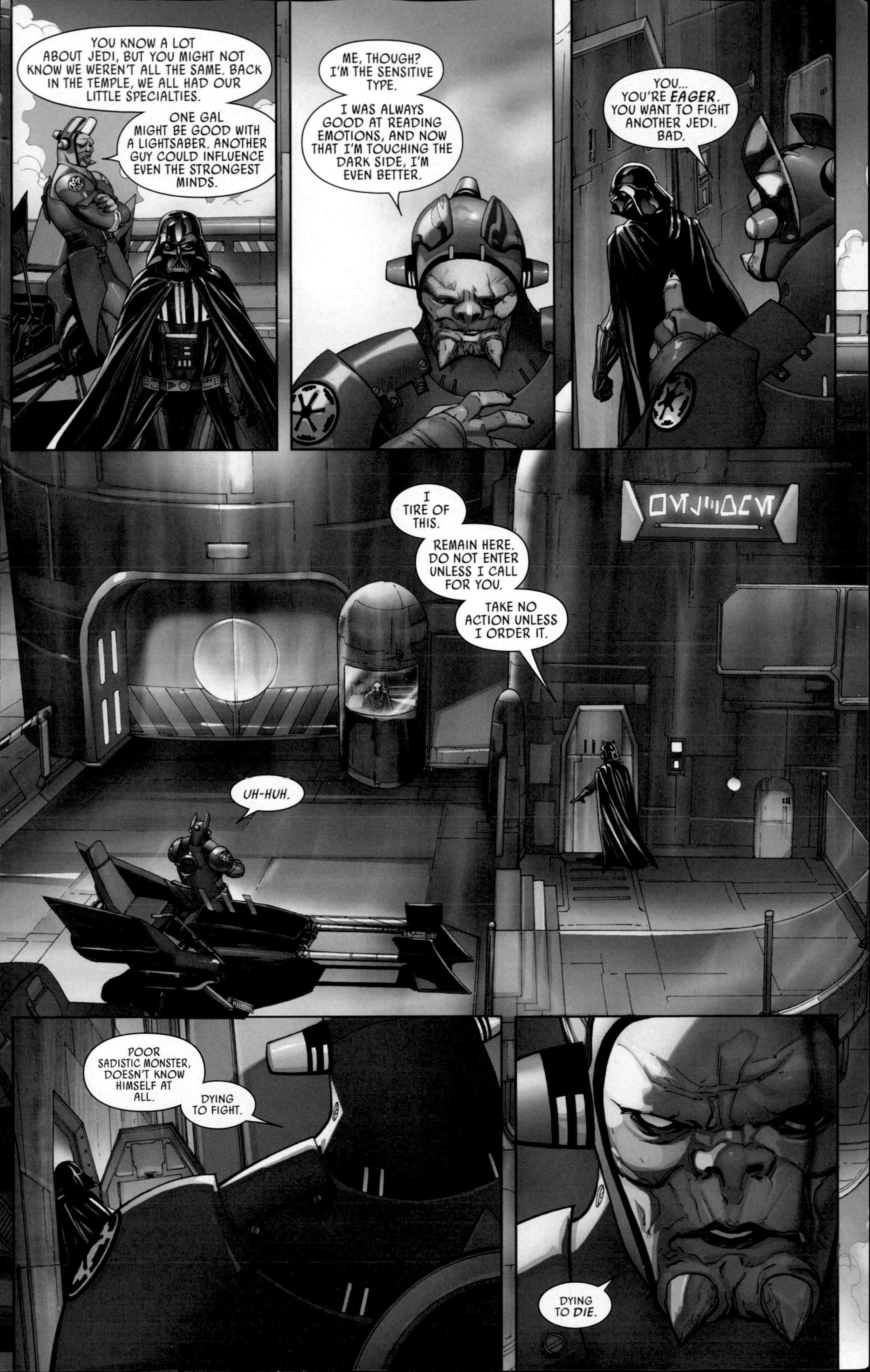
YOU KNOW A LOT ABOUT JEDI, BUT YOU MIGHT NOT KNOW WE WEREN'T ALL THE SAME. BACK IN THE TEMPLE, WE ALL HAD OUR LITTLE SPECIALTIES.
ONE GAL MIGHT BE GOOD WITH A LIGHTSABER. ANOTHER GUY COULD INFLUENCE EVEN THE STRONGEST MINDS.
ME, THOUGH? I'M THE SENSITIVE TYPE.
I WAS ALWAYS GOOD AT READING EMOTIONS, AND NOW THAT I'M TOUCHING THE DARK SIDE, I'M EVEN BETTER.
YOU... YOU'RE EAGER. YOU WANT TO FIGHT ANOTHER JEDI. BAD.
I TIRE OF THIS.
REMAIN HERE. DO NOT ENTER UNLESS I CALL FOR YOU.
TAKE NO ACTION UNLESS I ORDER IT.
UH-HUH.
POOR SADISTIC MONSTER, DOESN'T KNOW HIMSELF AT ALL.
DYING TO FIGHT.
DYING TO DIE.

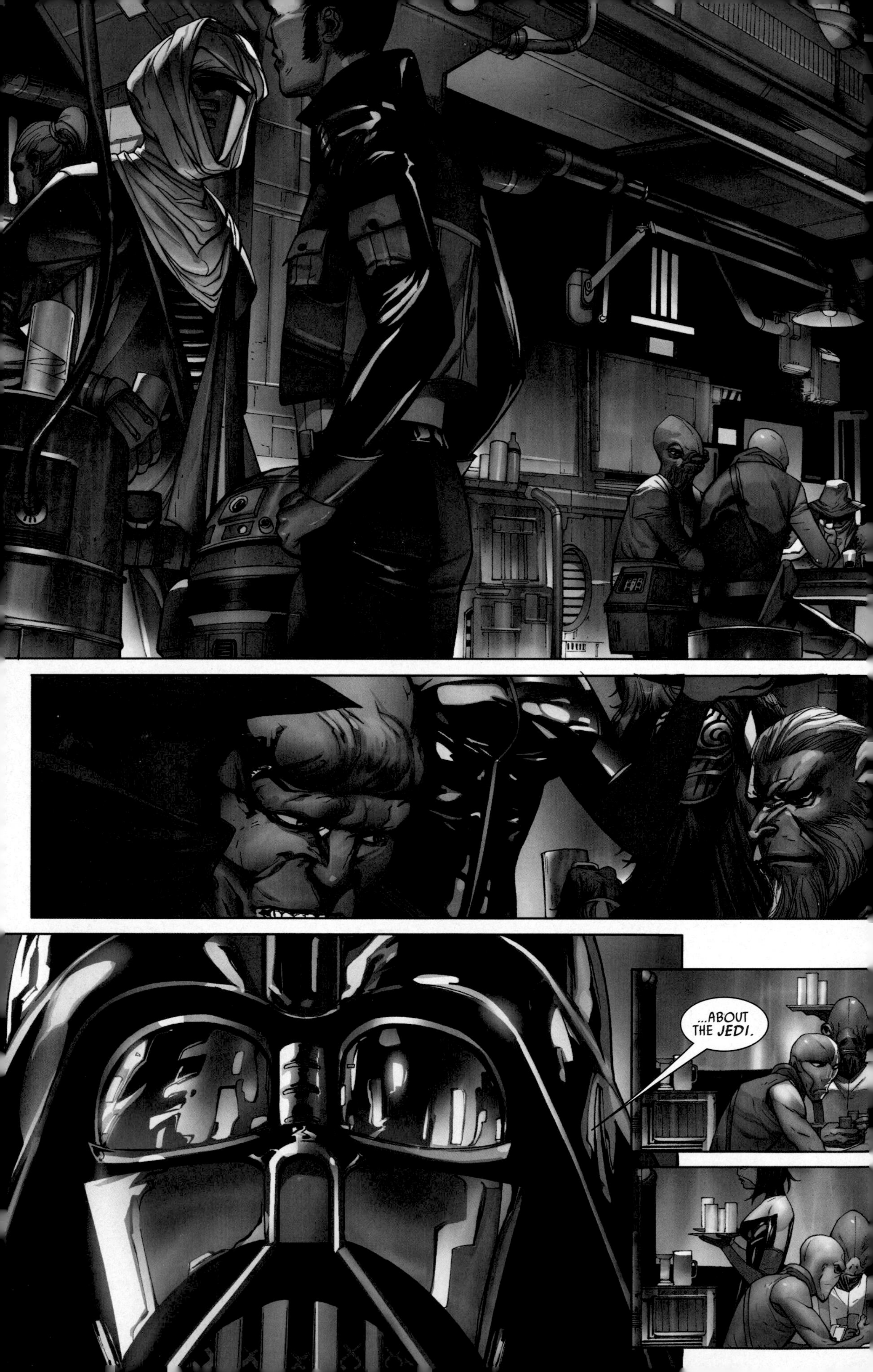
...ABOUT THE JEDI.

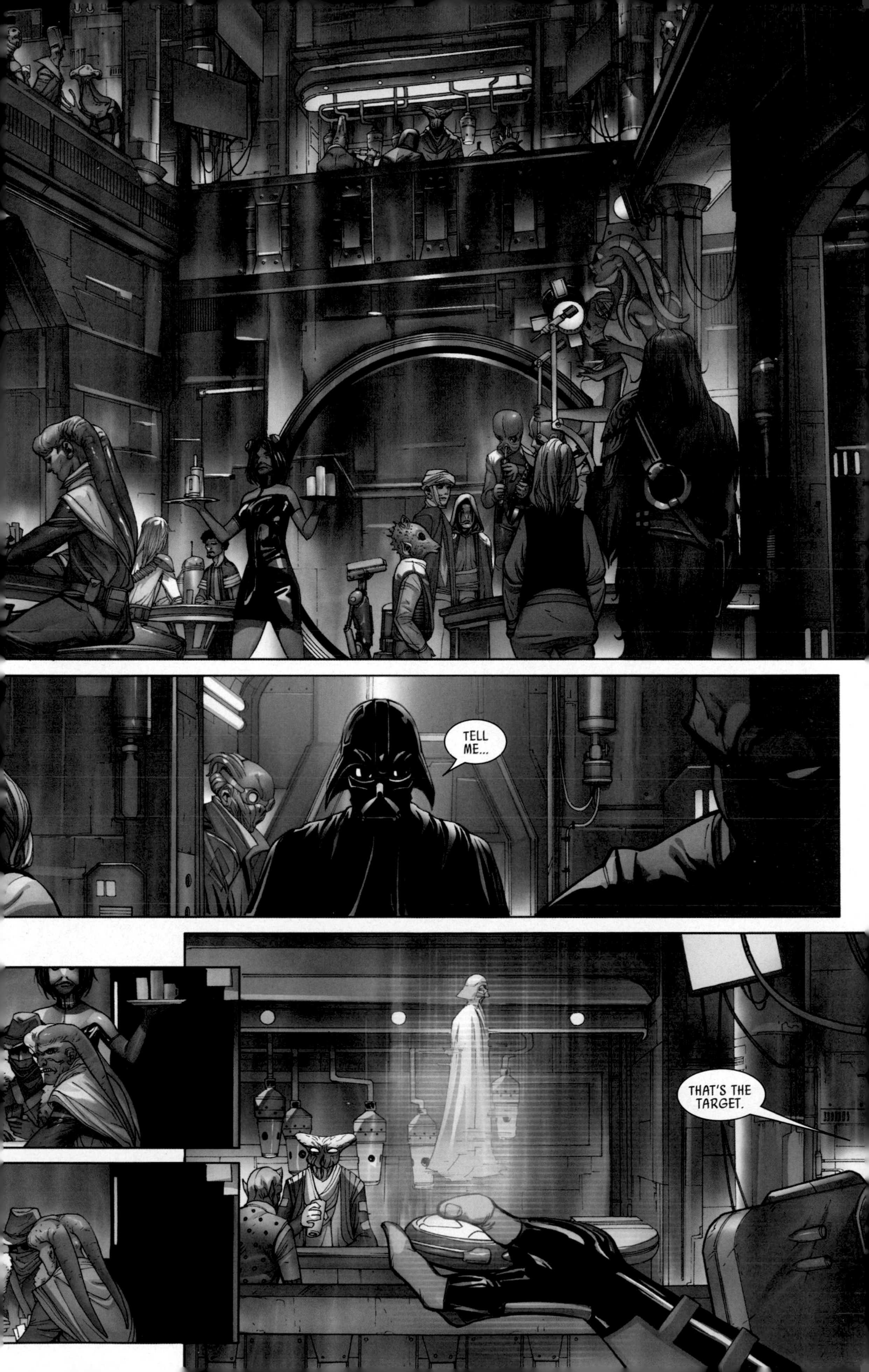
TELL ME...
THAT'S THE TARGET.

YOU ARE CERTAIN, FATHER?

YES, DAUGHTER.

DO YOUR PART, AND WE WILL DO OURS.

KSSHT

I HAVE IT. IT'S COMING.

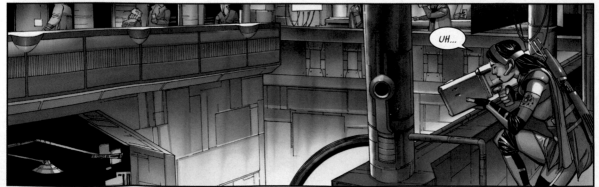

UH...

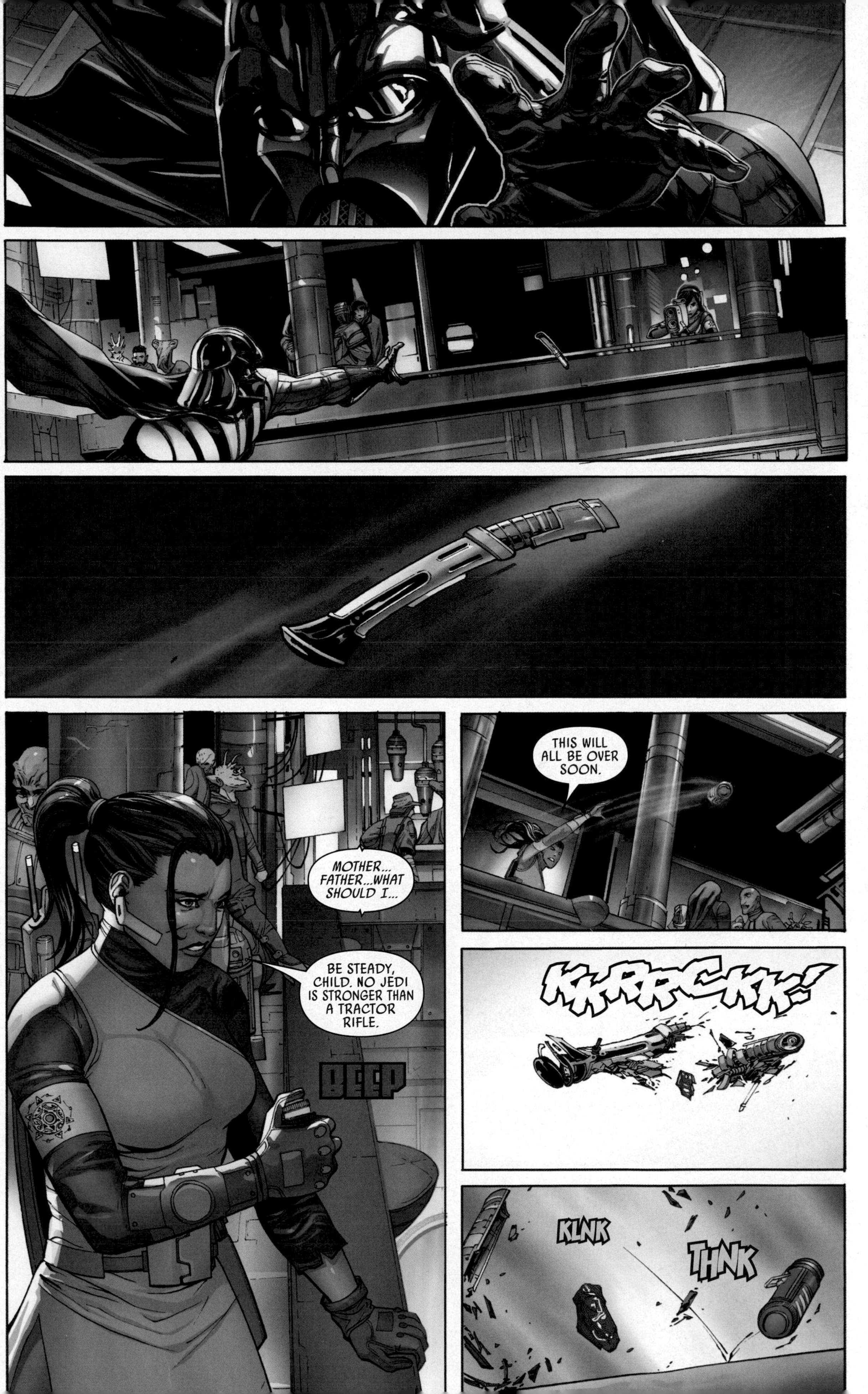
MOTHER... FATHER...WHAT SHOULD I...
BE STEADY, CHILD. NO JEDI IS STRONGER THAN A TRACTOR RIFLE.
BEEP
THIS WILL ALL BE OVER SOON.
KKRRCKK!
KLNK
THNK

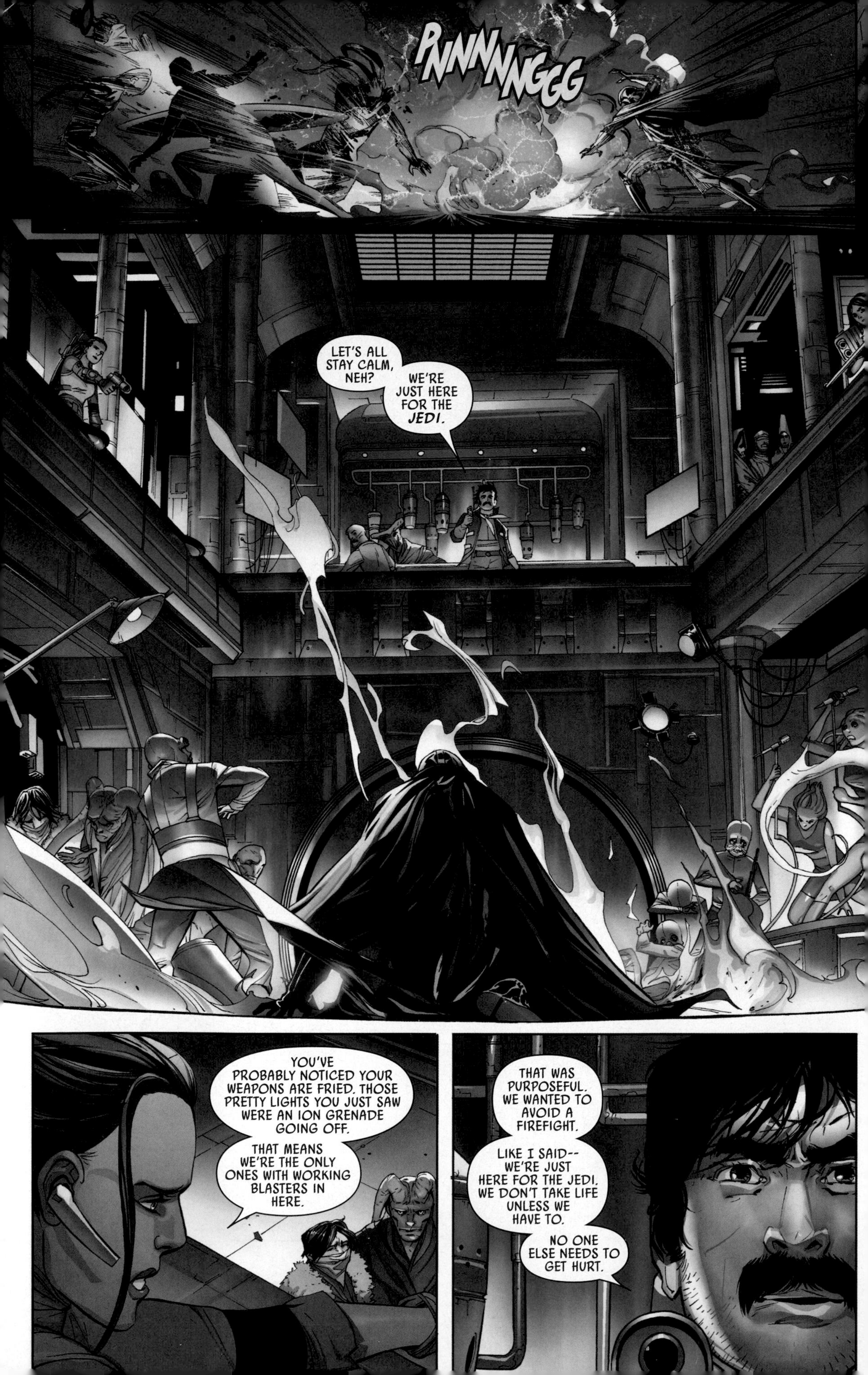
PNNNNNGGG
LET'S ALL STAY CALM, NEH?
WE'RE JUST HERE FOR THE JEDI.
YOU'VE PROBABLY NOTICED YOUR WEAPONS ARE FRIED. THOSE PRETTY LIGHTS YOU JUST SAW WERE AN ION GRENADE GOING OFF.
THAT MEANS WE'RE THE ONLY ONES WITH WORKING BLASTERS IN HERE.
THAT WAS PURPOSEFUL. WE WANTED TO AVOID A FIREFIGHT.
LIKE I SAID-- WE'RE JUST HERE FOR THE JEDI. WE DON'T TAKE LIFE UNLESS WE HAVE TO.
NO ONE ELSE NEEDS TO GET HURT.

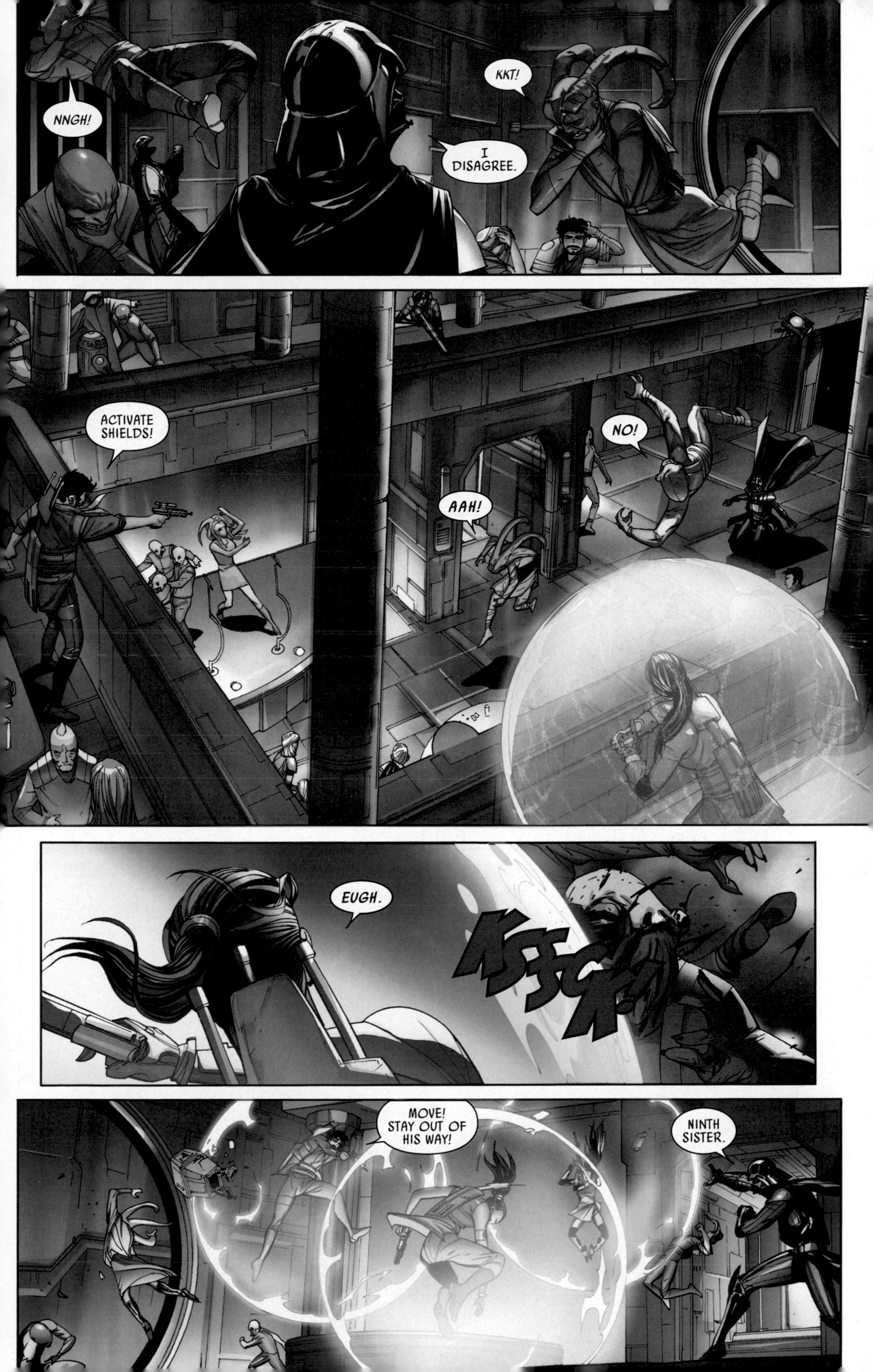
NNGH!
KKT!
I DISAGREE.
ACTIVATE SHIELDS!
NO!
AAH!
EUGH.
KSSCH!
MOVE! STAY OUT OF HIS WAY!
NINTH SISTER.

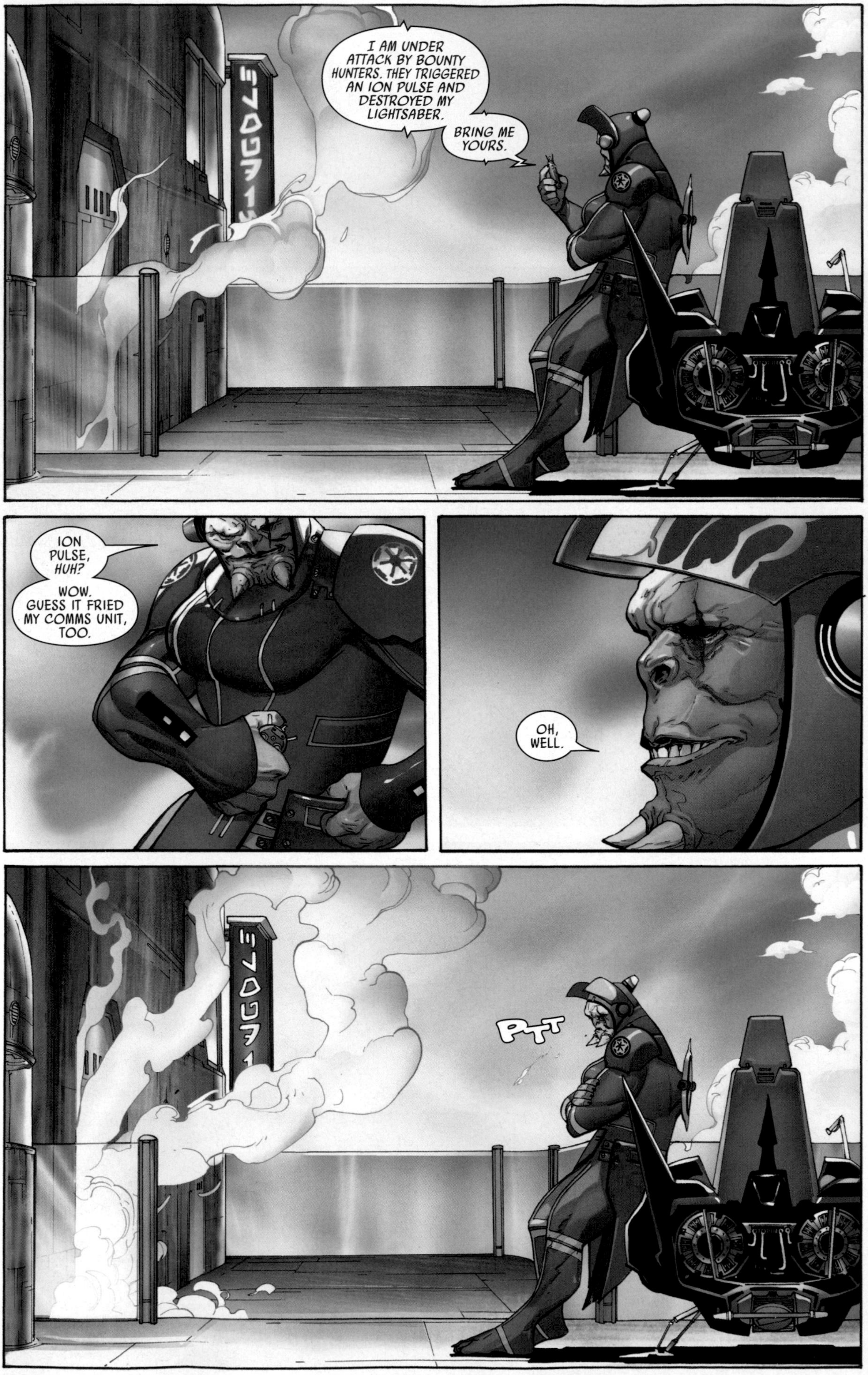
I AM UNDER ATTACK BY BOUNTY HUNTERS. THEY TRIGGERED AN ION PULSE AND DESTROYED MY LIGHTSABER.
BRING ME YOURS.
ION PULSE, HUH?
WOW. GUESS IT FRIED MY COMMS UNIT, TOO.
OH, WELL.
PTT

BHADA, THIS IS TOO MUCH! HE'LL KILL EVERYONE IN HERE--AND OUR SHIELD BATTERIES WON'T LAST FOREVER.

AGREED. WE NEED TO GO.

CHANATH! WE'RE DONE HERE. PULL BACK! NOW!

SMSH

YES, FATHER.

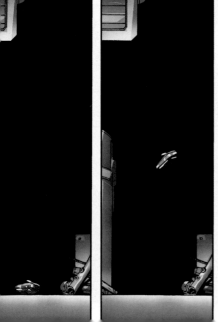

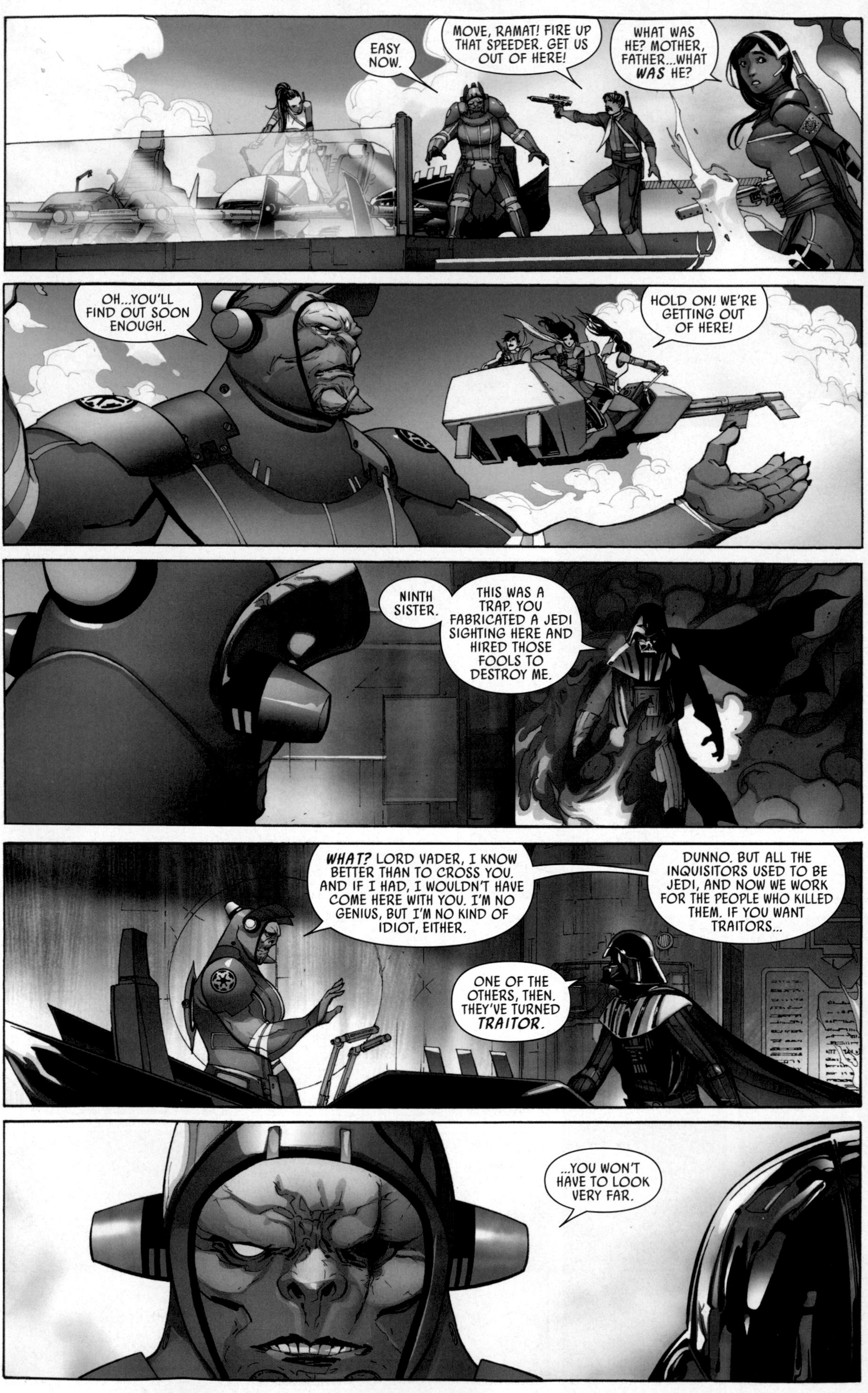
EASY NOW.
MOVE, RAMAT! FIRE UP THAT SPEEDER. GET US OUT OF HERE!
WHAT WAS HE? MOTHER, FATHER...WHAT WAS HE?
OH...YOU'LL FIND OUT SOON ENOUGH.
HOLD ON! WE'RE GETTING OUT OF HERE!
NINTH SISTER.
THIS WAS A TRAP. YOU FABRICATED A JEDI SIGHTING HERE AND HIRED THOSE FOOLS TO DESTROY ME.
WHAT? LORD VADER, I KNOW BETTER THAN TO CROSS YOU. AND IF I HAD, I WOULDN'T HAVE COME HERE WITH YOU. I'M NO GENIUS, BUT I'M NO KIND OF IDIOT, EITHER.
ONE OF THE OTHERS, THEN. THEY'VE TURNED TRAITOR.
DUNNO. BUT ALL THE INQUISITORS USED TO BE JEDI, AND NOW WE WORK FOR THE PEOPLE WHO KILLED THEM. IF YOU WANT TRAITORS...
...YOU WON'T HAVE TO LOOK VERY FAR.

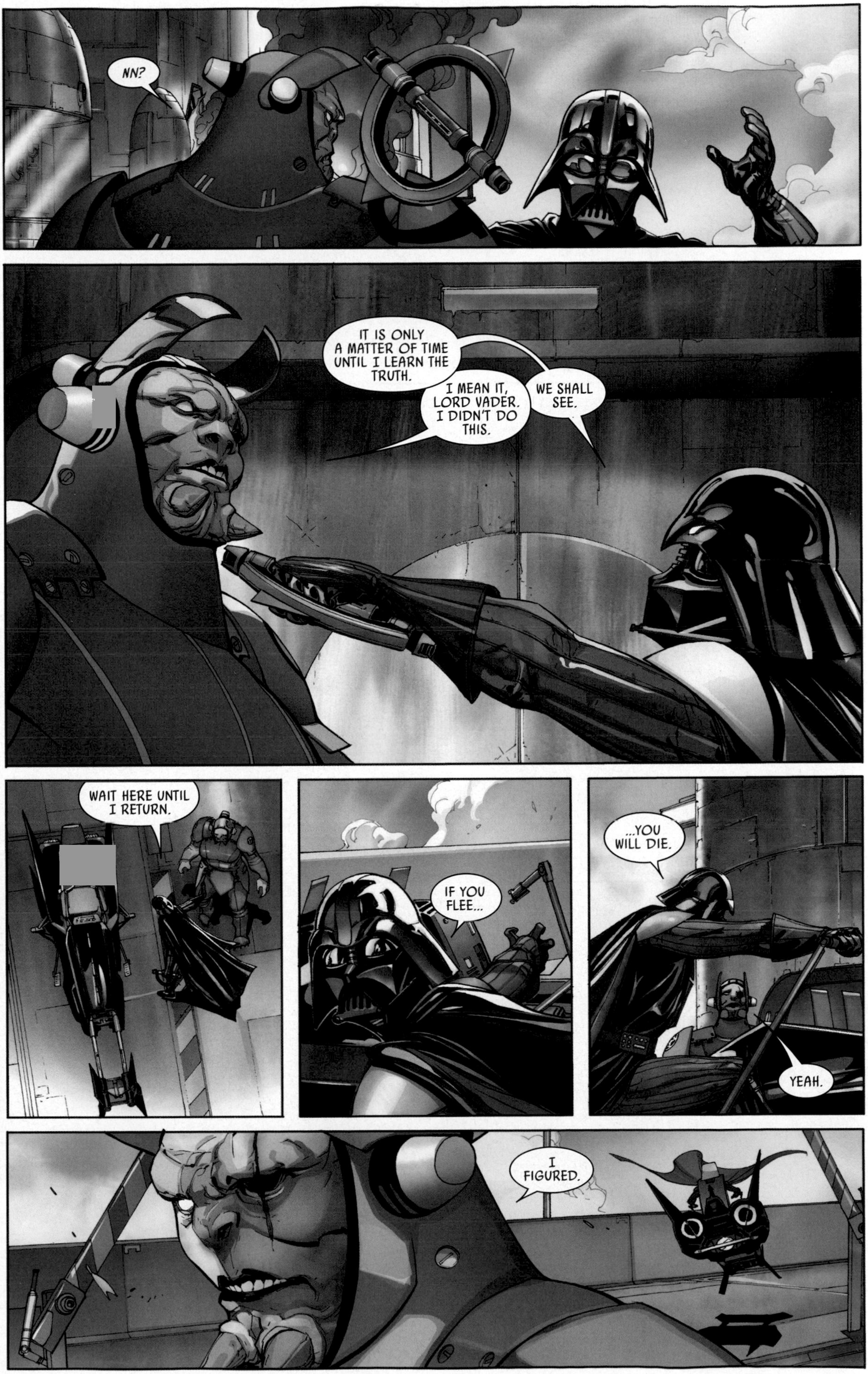
NN?
IT IS ONLY A MATTER OF TIME UNTIL I LEARN THE TRUTH.
I MEAN IT, LORD VADER. I DIDN'T DO THIS.
WE SHALL SEE.
WAIT HERE UNTIL I RETURN.
IF YOU FLEE...
...YOU WILL DIE.
YEAH.
I FIGURED.

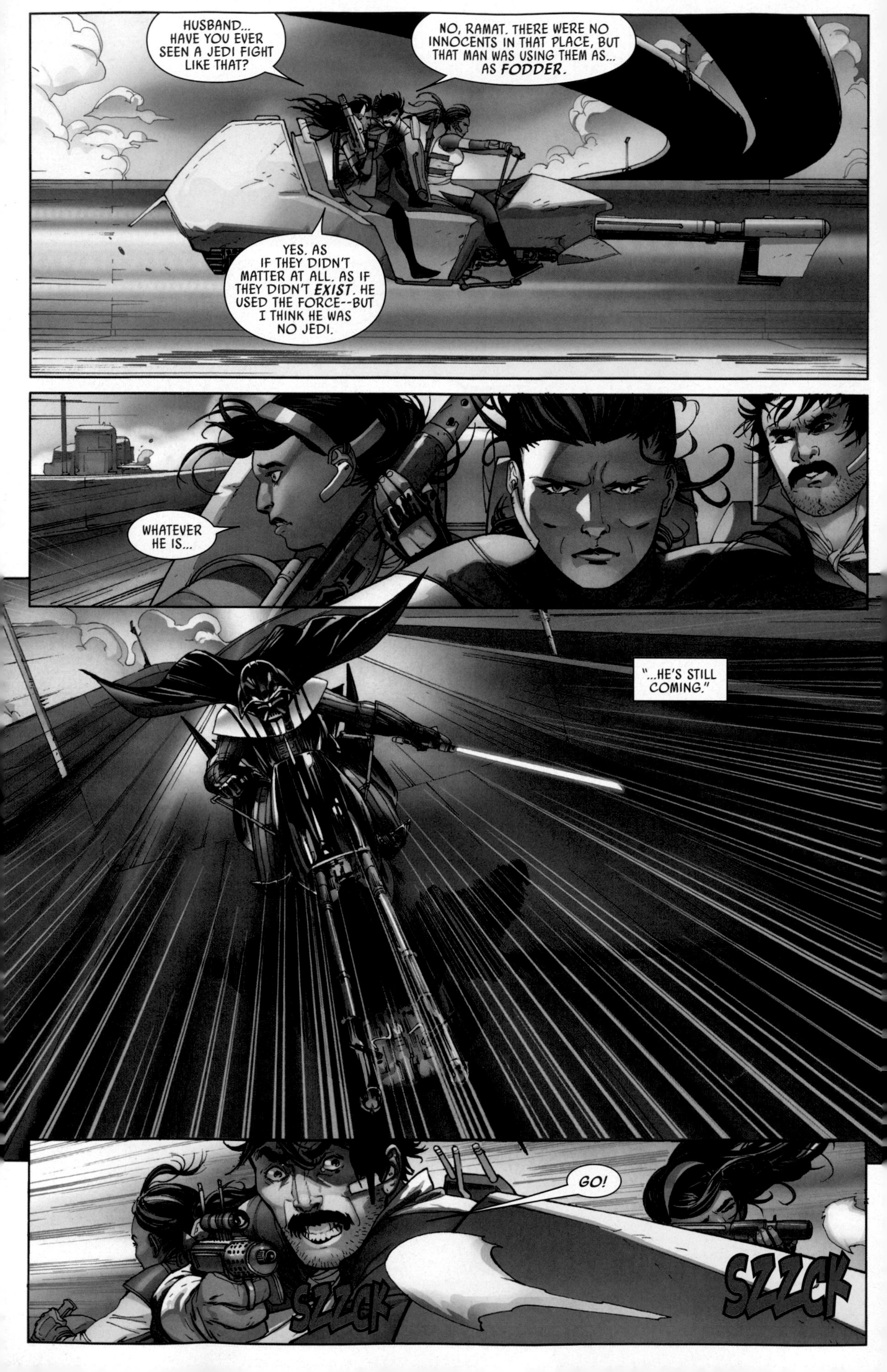
HUSBAND... HAVE YOU EVER SEEN A JEDI FIGHT LIKE THAT?
NO, RAMAT. THERE WERE NO INNOCENTS IN THAT PLACE, BUT THAT MAN WAS USING THEM AS... AS *FODDER*.
YES. AS IF THEY DIDN'T MATTER AT ALL. AS IF THEY DIDN'T *EXIST*. HE USED THE FORCE--BUT I THINK HE WAS NO JEDI.
WHATEVER HE IS...
"...HE'S STILL COMING."
GO!
SZZCK
SZZCK

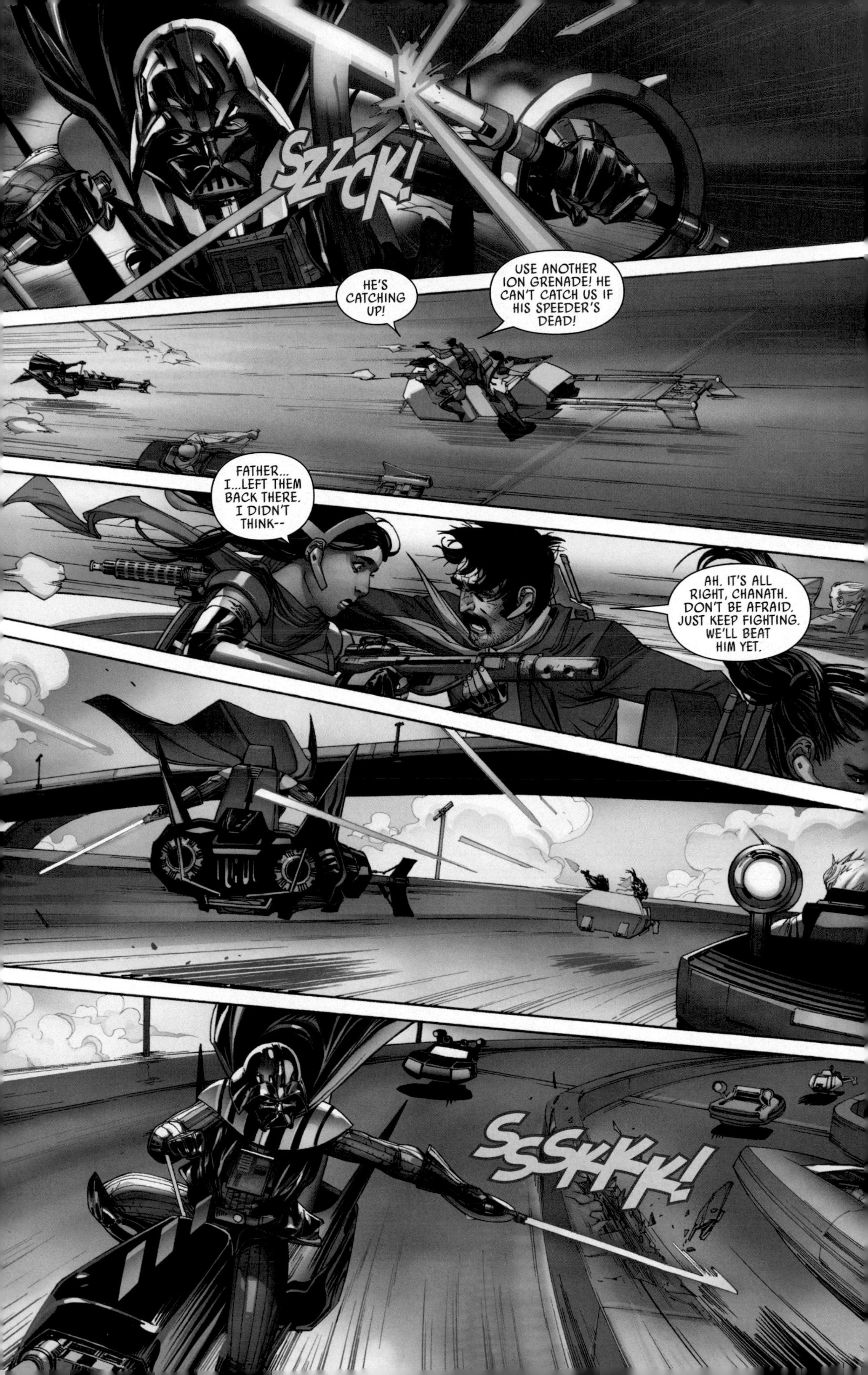
SZZCK!
HE'S CATCHING UP!
USE ANOTHER ION GRENADE! HE CAN'T CATCH US IF HIS SPEEDER'S DEAD!
FATHER... I...LEFT THEM BACK THERE. I DIDN'T THINK--
AH. IT'S ALL RIGHT, CHANATH. DON'T BE AFRAID. JUST KEEP FIGHTING. WE'LL BEAT HIM YET.
SSSKKK!

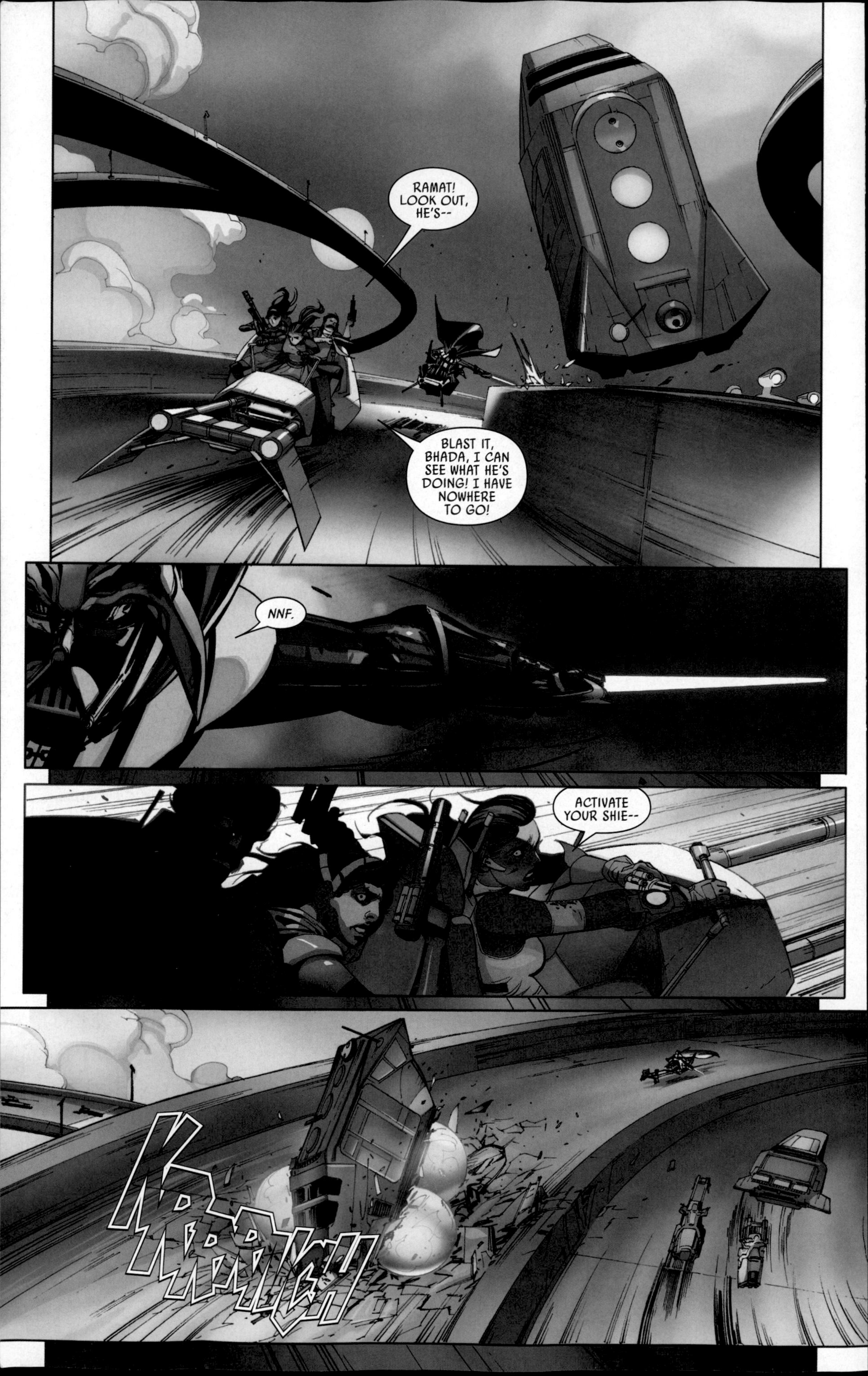
RAMAT! LOOK OUT, HE'S--
BLAST IT, BHADA, I CAN SEE WHAT HE'S DOING! I HAVE NOWHERE TO GO!
NNF.
ACTIVATE YOUR SHIE--
KRRRUNCH

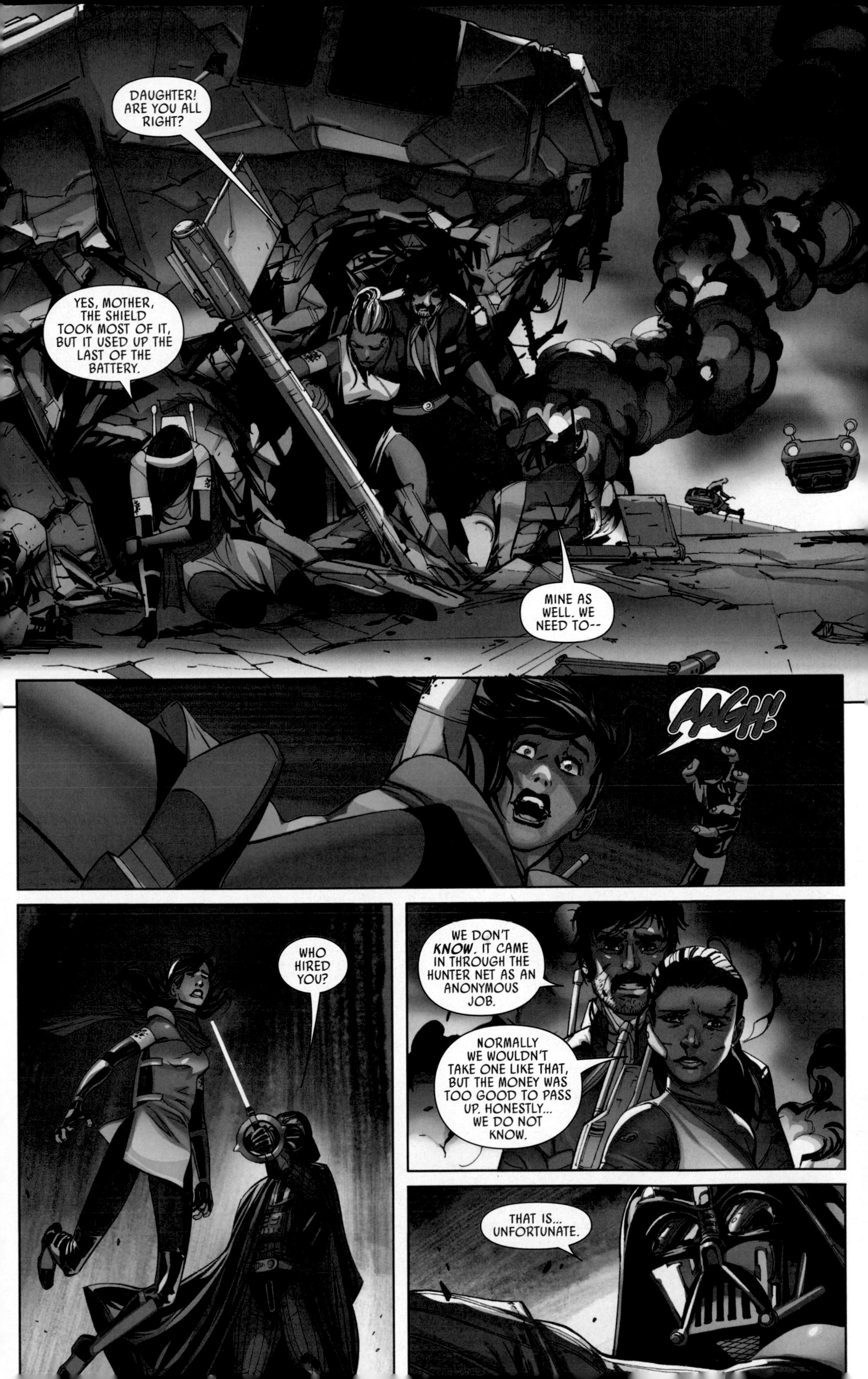
DAUGHTER! ARE YOU ALL RIGHT?
YES, MOTHER, THE SHIELD TOOK MOST OF IT, BUT IT USED UP THE LAST OF THE BATTERY.
MINE AS WELL. WE NEED TO--
AAGH!
WHO HIRED YOU?
WE DON'T KNOW. IT CAME IN THROUGH THE HUNTER NET AS AN ANONYMOUS JOB.
NORMALLY WE WOULDN'T TAKE ONE LIKE THAT, BUT THE MONEY WAS TOO GOOD TO PASS UP. HONESTLY... WE DO NOT KNOW.
THAT IS... UNFORTUNATE.

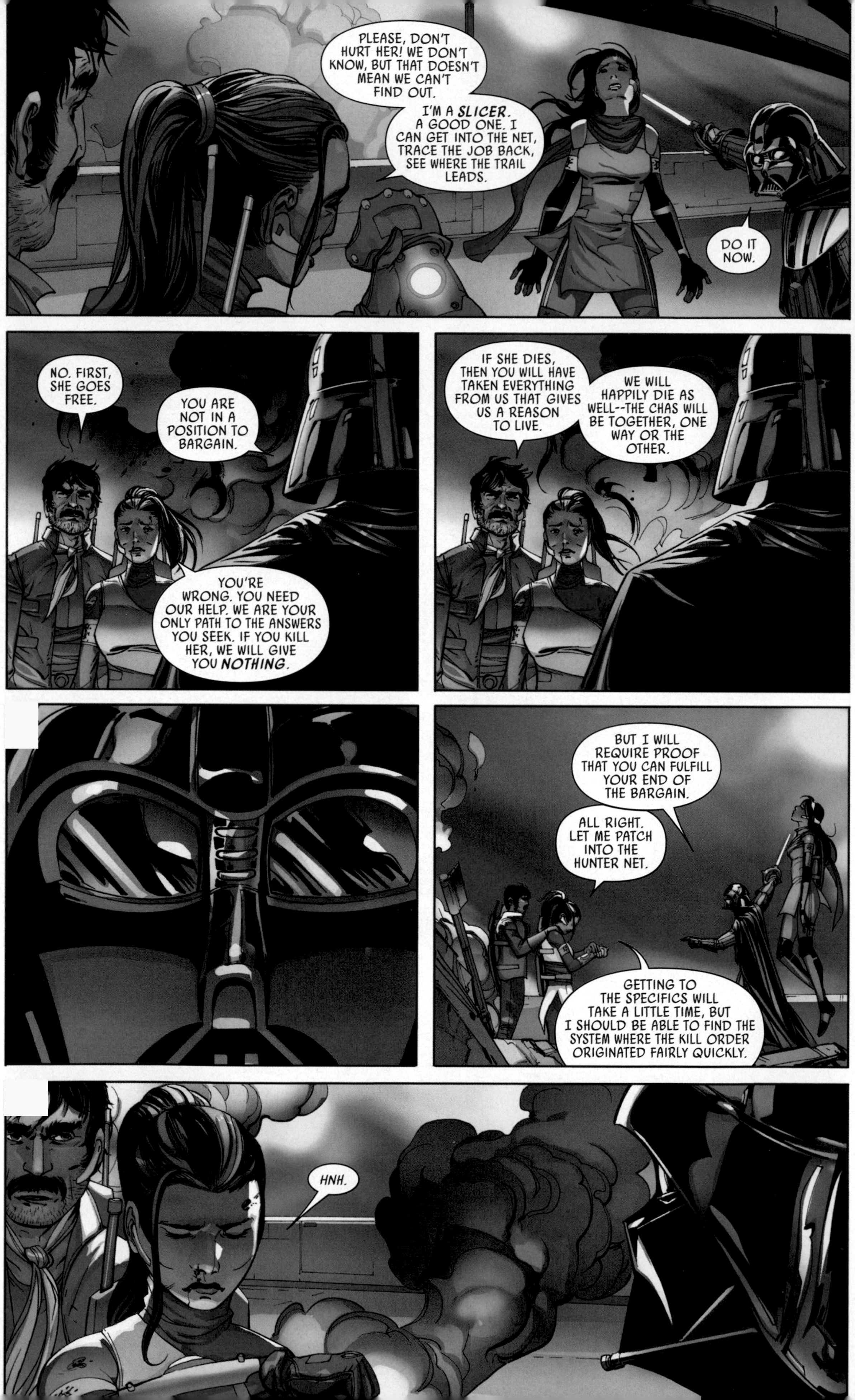
PLEASE, DON'T HURT HER! WE DON'T KNOW, BUT THAT DOESN'T MEAN WE CAN'T FIND OUT.
I'M A SLICER. A GOOD ONE. I CAN GET INTO THE NET, TRACE THE JOB BACK, SEE WHERE THE TRAIL LEADS.
DO IT NOW.
NO. FIRST, SHE GOES FREE.
YOU ARE NOT IN A POSITION TO BARGAIN.
YOU'RE WRONG. YOU NEED OUR HELP. WE ARE YOUR ONLY PATH TO THE ANSWERS YOU SEEK. IF YOU KILL HER, WE WILL GIVE YOU NOTHING.
IF SHE DIES, THEN YOU WILL HAVE TAKEN EVERYTHING FROM US THAT GIVES US A REASON TO LIVE.
WE WILL HAPPILY DIE AS WELL--THE CHAS WILL BE TOGETHER, ONE WAY OR THE OTHER.
BUT I WILL REQUIRE PROOF THAT YOU CAN FULFILL YOUR END OF THE BARGAIN.
ALL RIGHT. LET ME PATCH INTO THE HUNTER NET.
GETTING TO THE SPECIFICS WILL TAKE A LITTLE TIME, BUT I SHOULD BE ABLE TO FIND THE SYSTEM WHERE THE KILL ORDER ORIGINATED FAIRLY QUICKLY.
HNH.

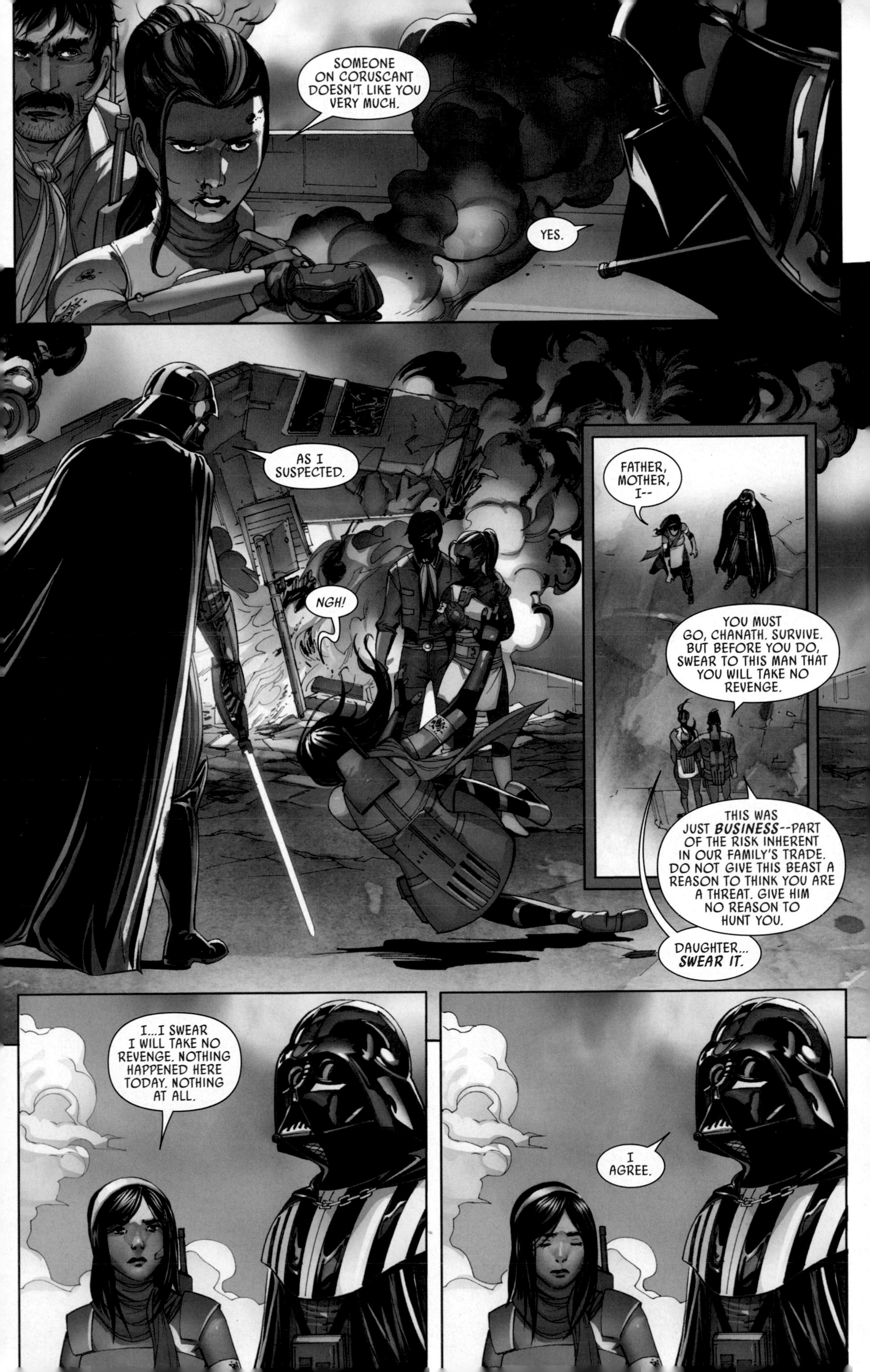
SOMEONE ON CORUSCANT DOESN'T LIKE YOU VERY MUCH.
YES.
AS I SUSPECTED.
NGH!
FATHER, MOTHER, I--
YOU MUST GO, CHANATH. SURVIVE. BUT BEFORE YOU DO, SWEAR TO THIS MAN THAT YOU WILL TAKE NO REVENGE.
THIS WAS JUST BUSINESS--PART OF THE RISK INHERENT IN OUR FAMILY'S TRADE. DO NOT GIVE THIS BEAST A REASON TO THINK YOU ARE A THREAT. GIVE HIM NO REASON TO HUNT YOU.
DAUGHTER... SWEAR IT.
I...I SWEAR I WILL TAKE NO REVENGE. NOTHING HAPPENED HERE TODAY. NOTHING AT ALL.
I AGREE.

CONTINUE.

I *AM*. THIS... THIS ACTUALLY ISN'T AS HARD AS I THOUGHT. I'M SLICING RIGHT THROUGH THE ENCRYPTION.

LOOKS LIKE...THE SENATE DISTRICT.

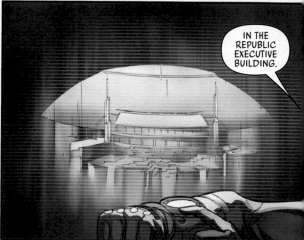

IN THE REPUBLIC EXECUTIVE BUILDING.

WHERE?

I THINK...

"...ALL THE WAY AT THE TOP."

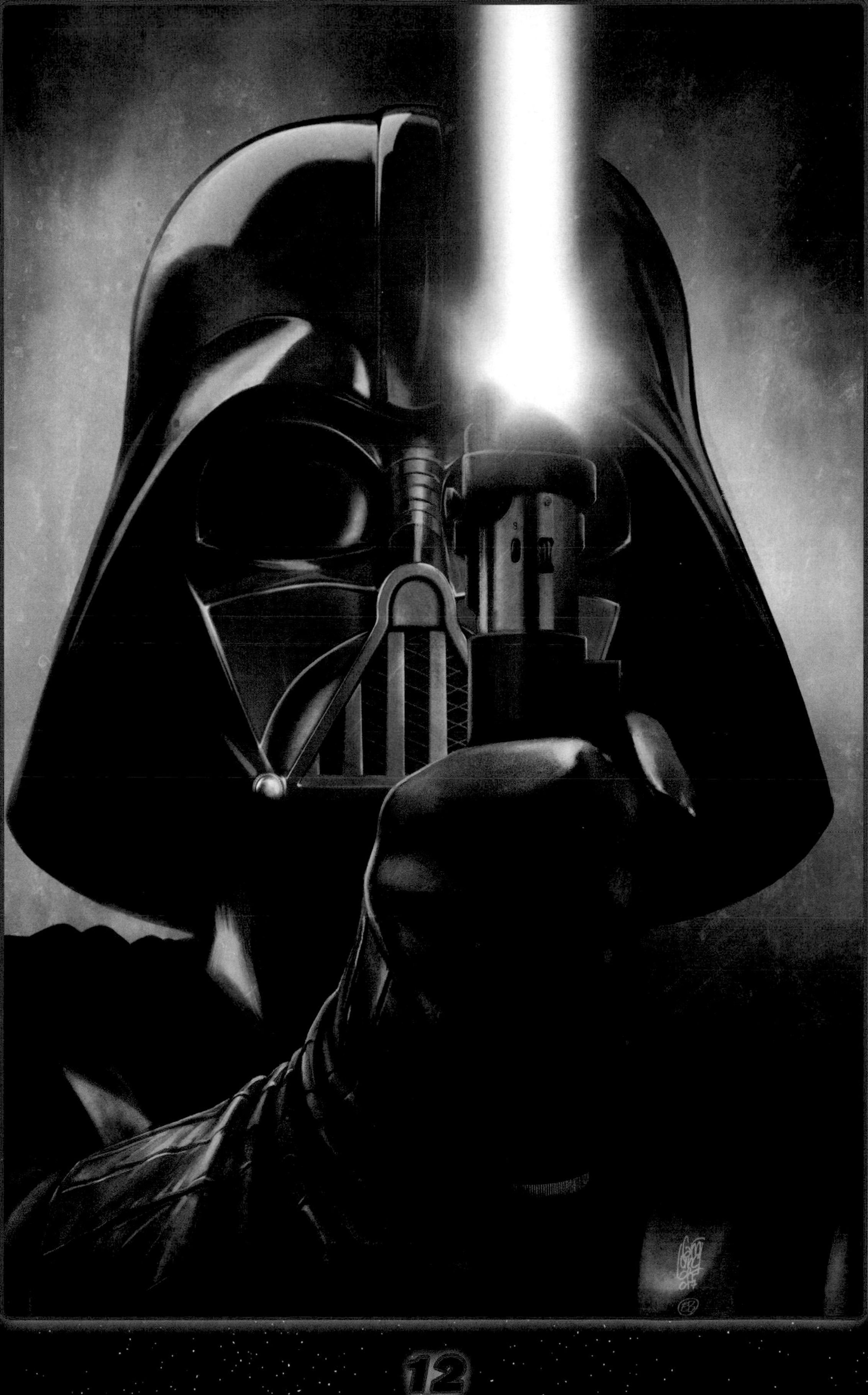
12

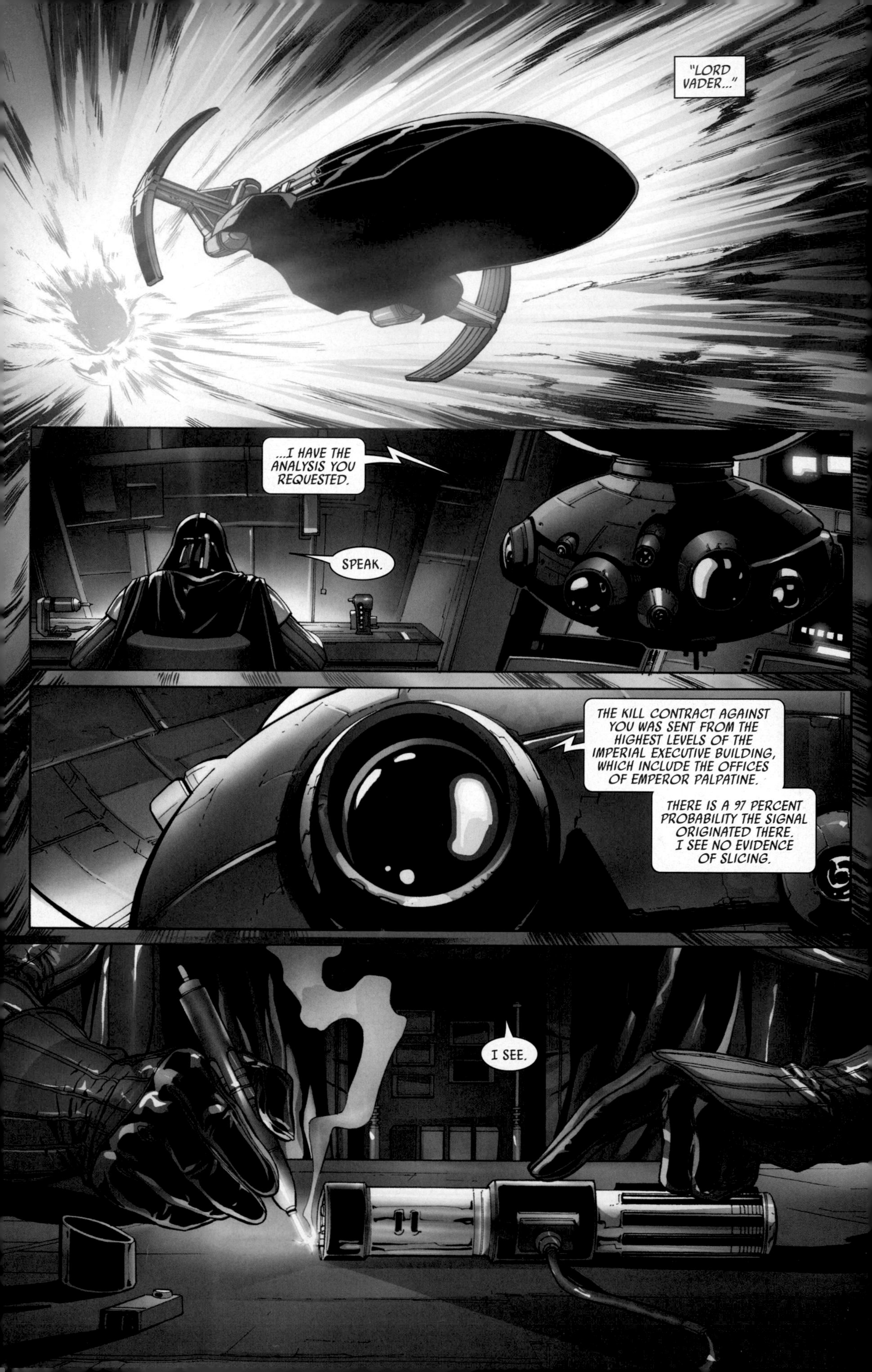
"LORD VADER..."
...I HAVE THE ANALYSIS YOU REQUESTED.
SPEAK.
THE KILL CONTRACT AGAINST YOU WAS SENT FROM THE HIGHEST LEVELS OF THE IMPERIAL EXECUTIVE BUILDING, WHICH INCLUDE THE OFFICES OF EMPEROR PALPATINE.
THERE IS A 97 PERCENT PROBABILITY THE SIGNAL ORIGINATED THERE. I SEE NO EVIDENCE OF SLICING.
I SEE.

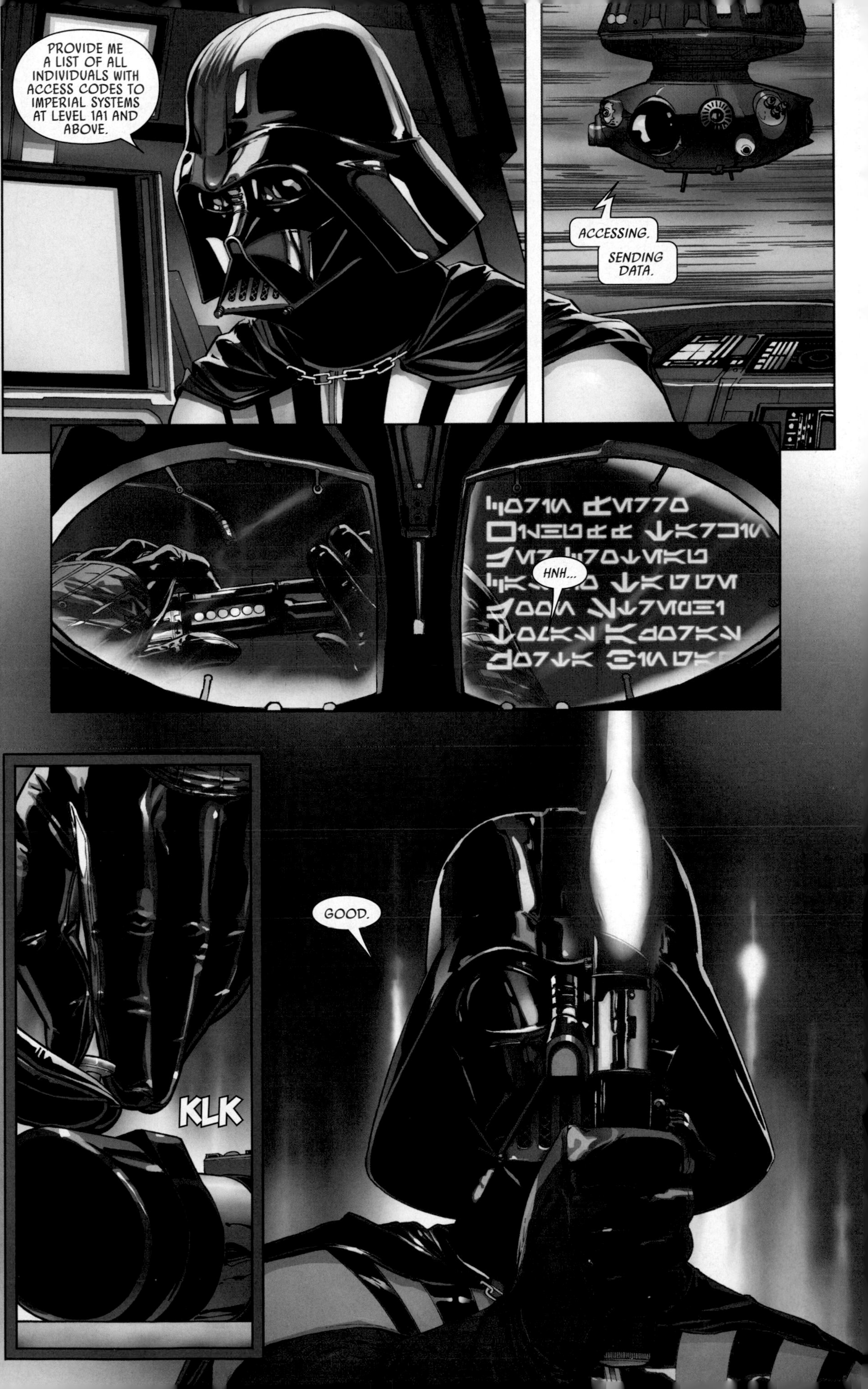

PROVIDE ME A LIST OF ALL INDIVIDUALS WITH ACCESS CODES TO IMPERIAL SYSTEMS AT LEVEL 1A1 AND ABOVE.
ACCESSING.
SENDING DATA.
HNH...
GOOD.
KLK

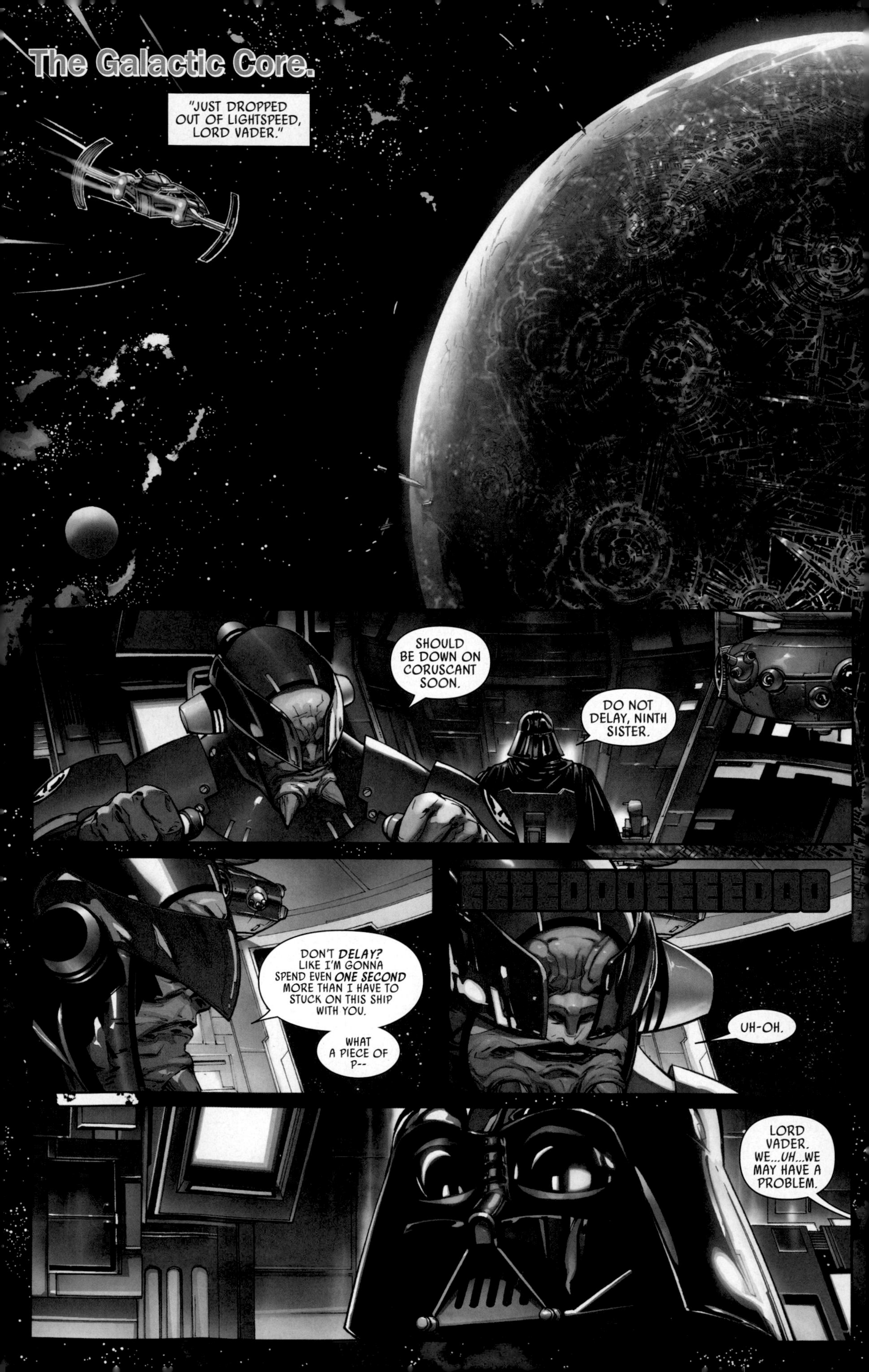
The Galactic Core.
"JUST DROPPED OUT OF LIGHTSPEED, LORD VADER."
SHOULD BE DOWN ON CORUSCANT SOON.
DO NOT DELAY, NINTH SISTER.
DON'T *DELAY?* LIKE I'M GONNA SPEND EVEN *ONE SECOND* MORE THAN I HAVE TO STUCK ON THIS SHIP WITH YOU.
WHAT A PIECE OF P--
EEEEDOOEEEEDOO
UH-OH.
LORD VADER. WE...*UH*...WE MAY HAVE A PROBLEM.

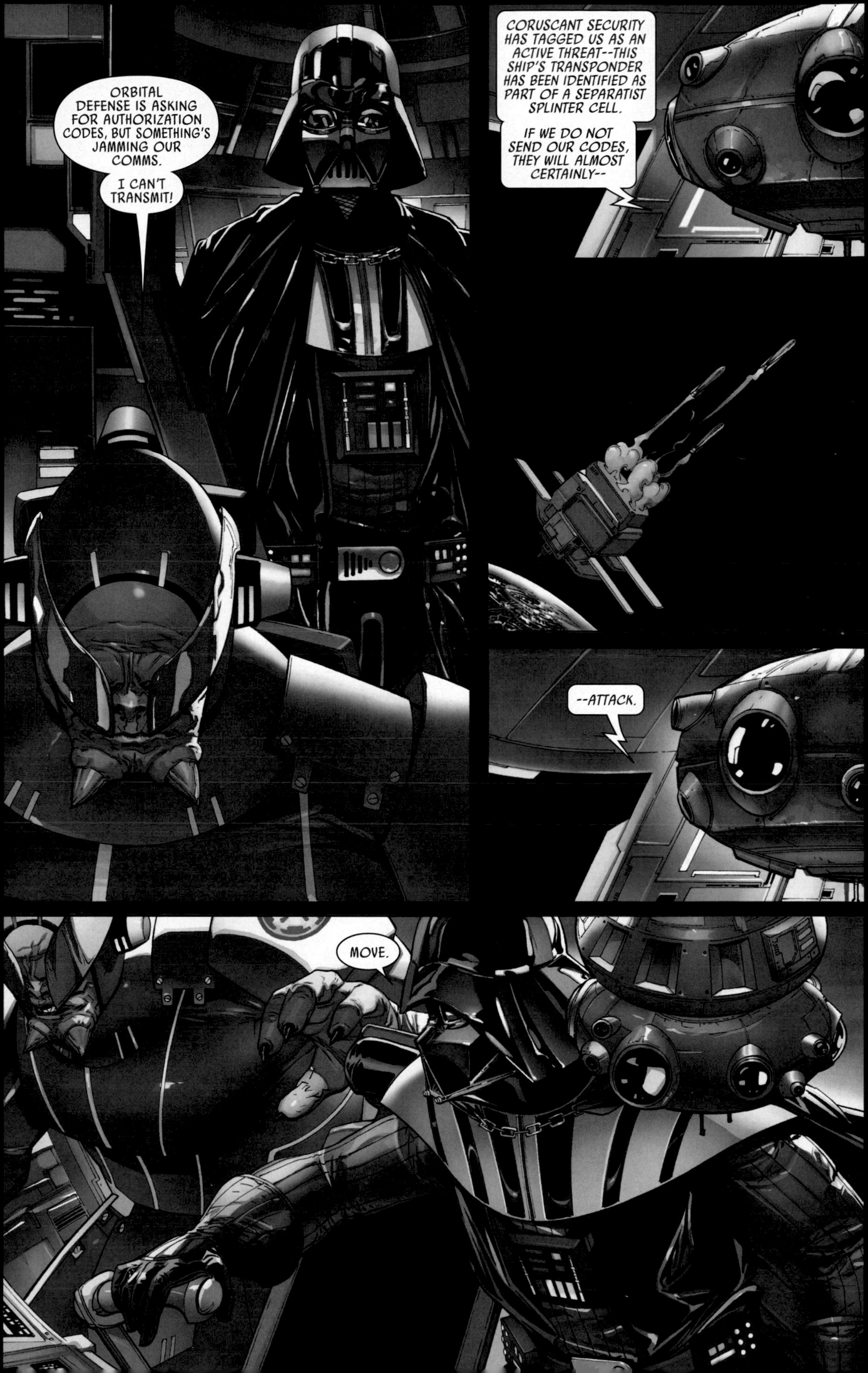
ORBITAL DEFENSE IS ASKING FOR AUTHORIZATION CODES, BUT SOMETHING'S JAMMING OUR COMMS.
I CAN'T TRANSMIT!
CORUSCANT SECURITY HAS TAGGED US AS AN ACTIVE THREAT--THIS SHIP'S TRANSPONDER HAS BEEN IDENTIFIED AS PART OF A SEPARATIST SPLINTER CELL.
IF WE DO NOT SEND OUR CODES, THEY WILL ALMOST CERTAINLY--
--ATTACK.
MOVE.

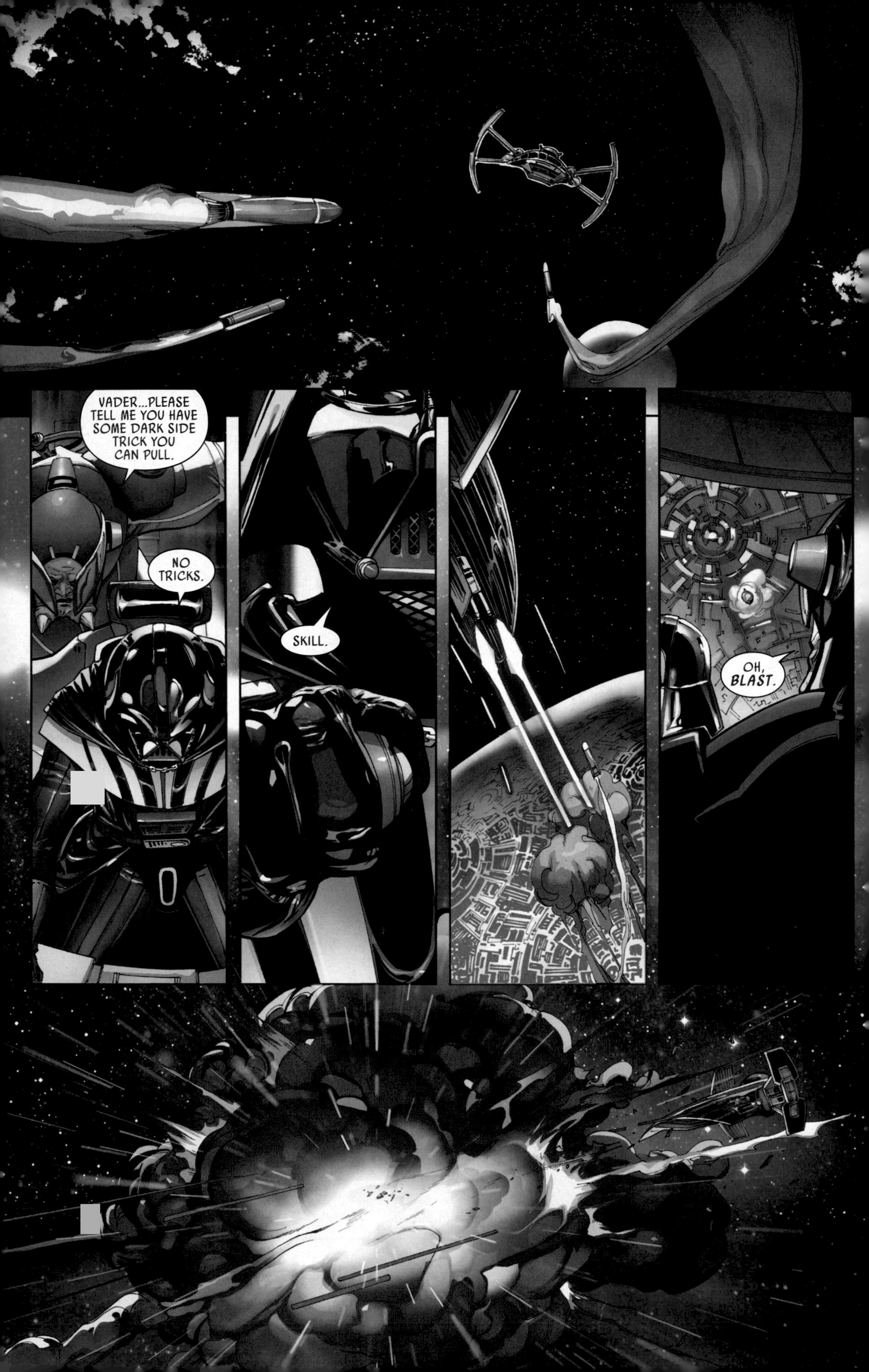
VADER...PLEASE TELL ME YOU HAVE SOME DARK SIDE TRICK YOU CAN PULL.
NO TRICKS.
SKILL.
OH, BLAST.

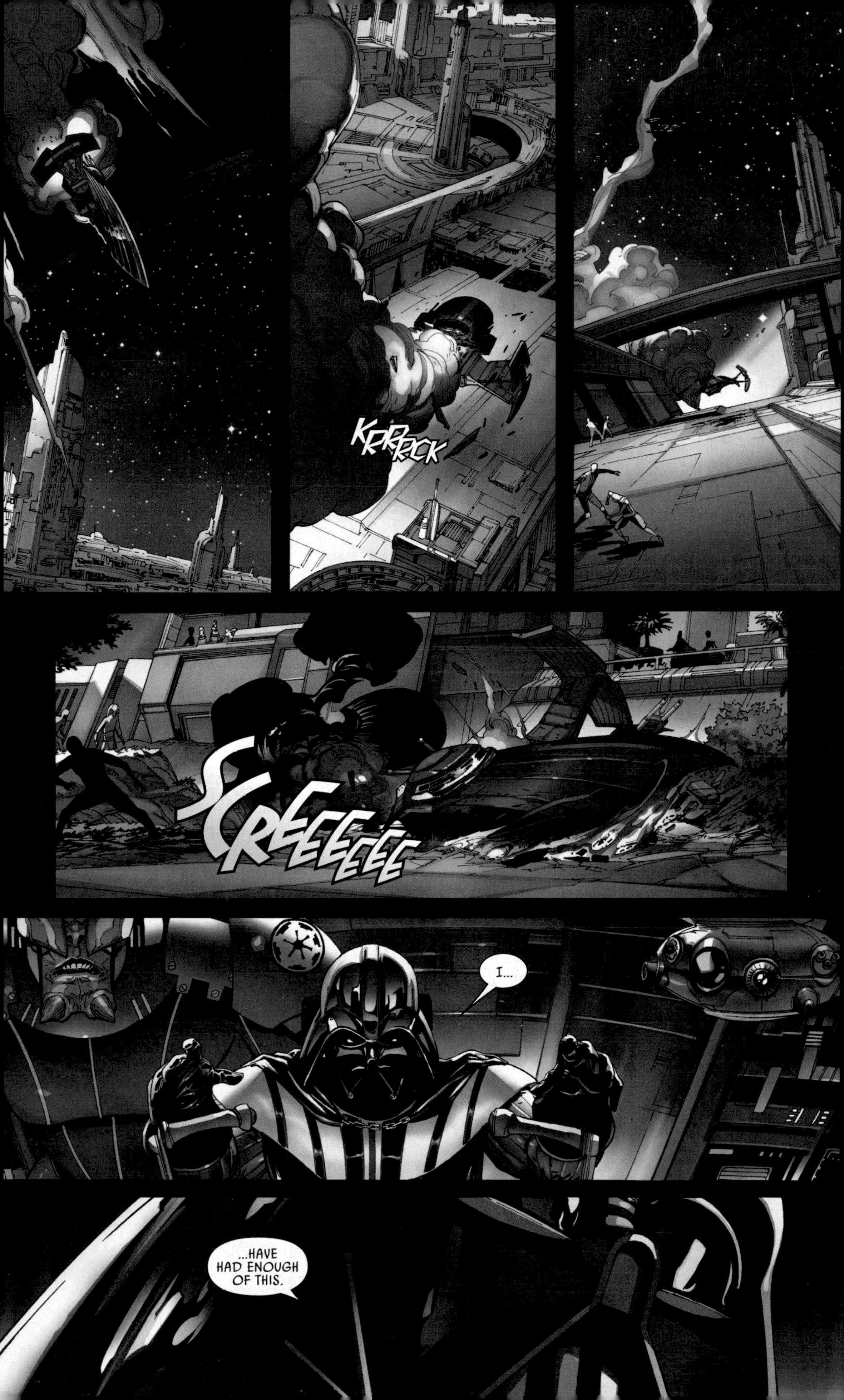
KRRRRACK
SCREEEEEEE
I...
...HAVE HAD ENOUGH OF THIS.

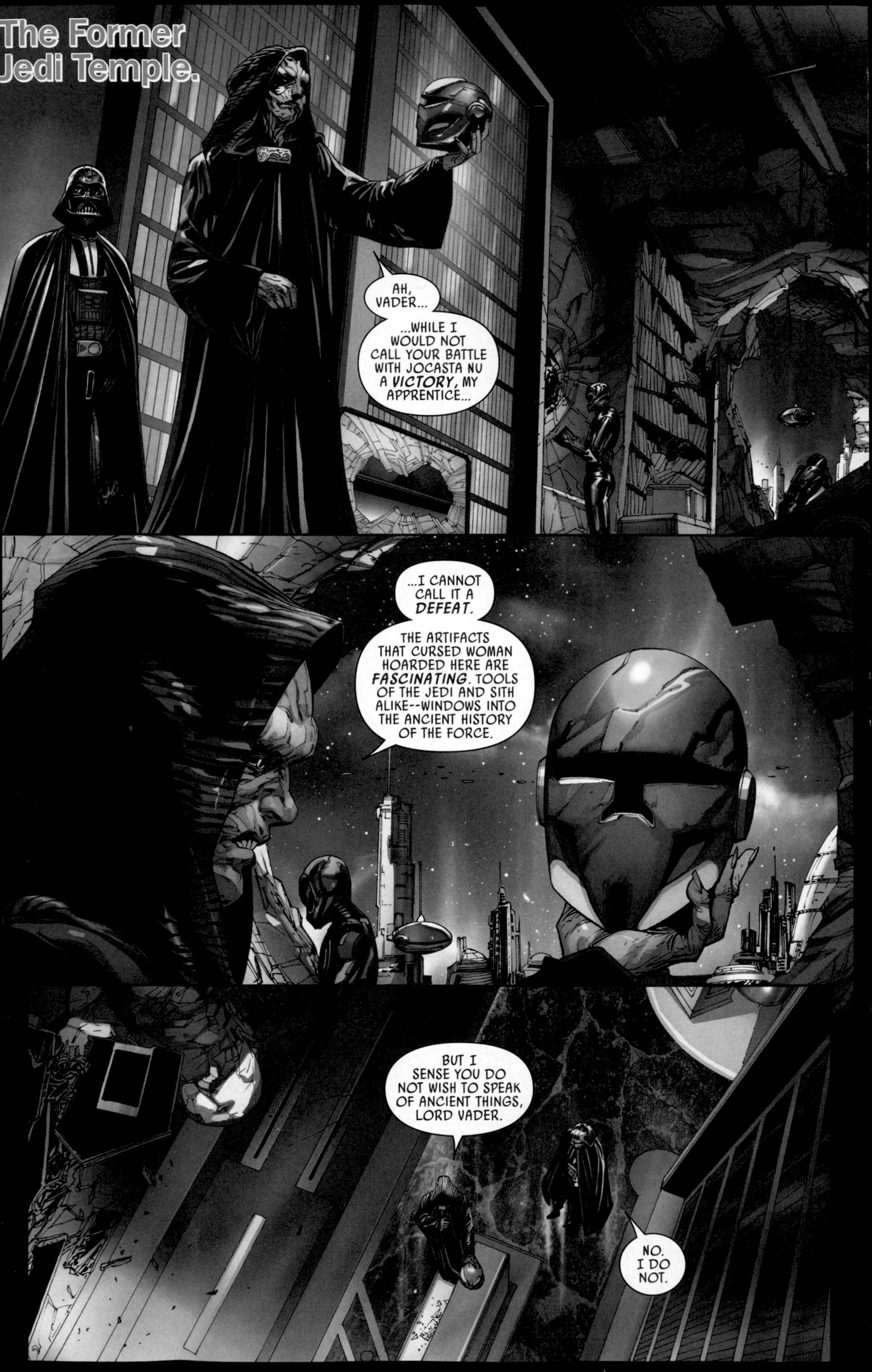
The Former Jedi Temple.
AH, VADER...
...WHILE I WOULD NOT CALL YOUR BATTLE WITH JOCASTA NU A VICTORY, MY APPRENTICE...
...I CANNOT CALL IT A DEFEAT.
THE ARTIFACTS THAT CURSED WOMAN HOARDED HERE ARE FASCINATING. TOOLS OF THE JEDI AND SITH ALIKE--WINDOWS INTO THE ANCIENT HISTORY OF THE FORCE.
BUT I SENSE YOU DO NOT WISH TO SPEAK OF ANCIENT THINGS, LORD VADER.
NO. I DO NOT.

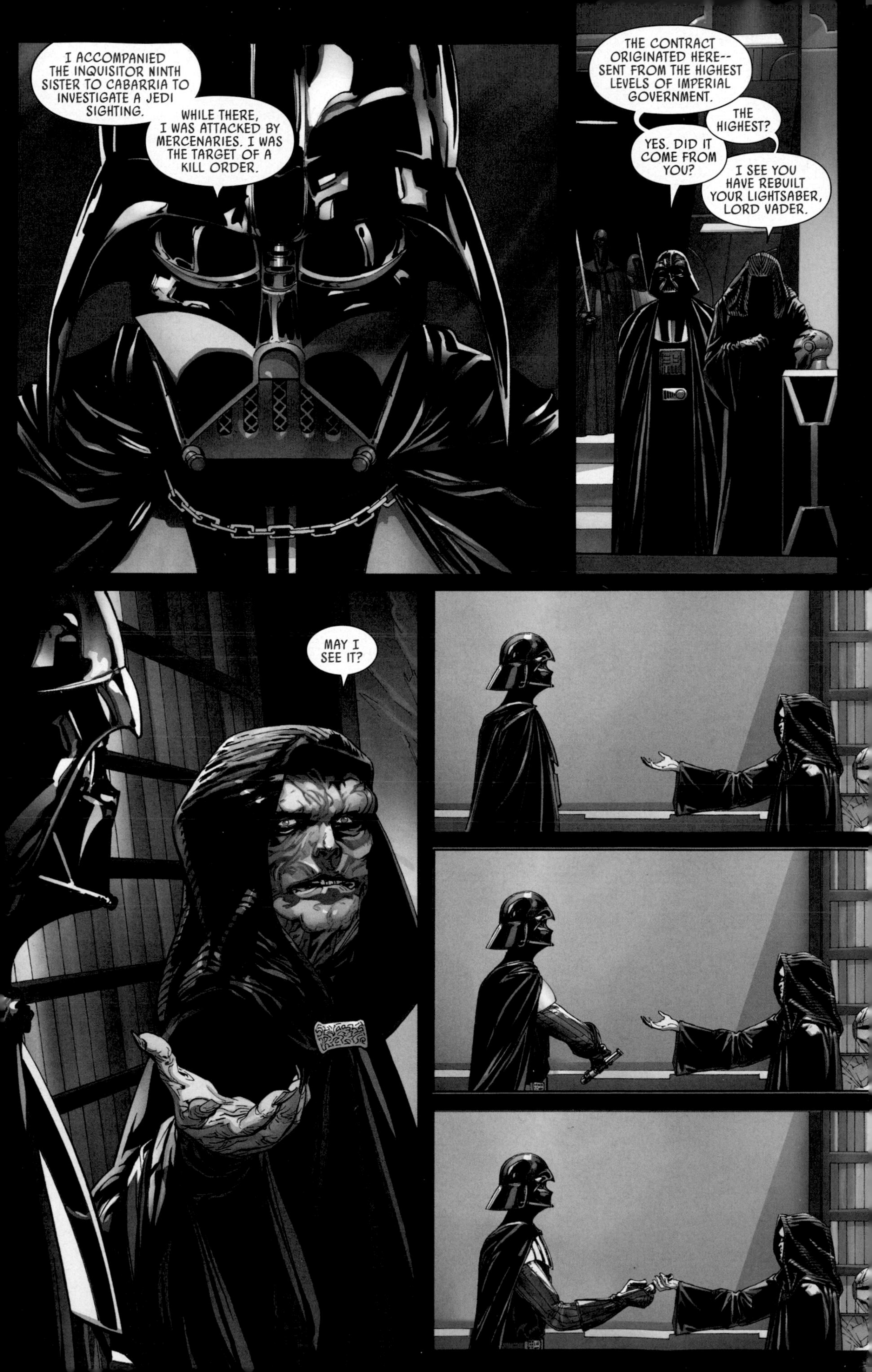
I ACCOMPANIED THE INQUISITOR NINTH SISTER TO CABARRIA TO INVESTIGATE A JEDI SIGHTING.
WHILE THERE, I WAS ATTACKED BY MERCENARIES. I WAS THE TARGET OF A KILL ORDER.
THE CONTRACT ORIGINATED HERE-- SENT FROM THE HIGHEST LEVELS OF IMPERIAL GOVERNMENT.
THE HIGHEST?
YES. DID IT COME FROM YOU?
I SEE YOU HAVE REBUILT YOUR LIGHTSABER, LORD VADER.
MAY I SEE IT?

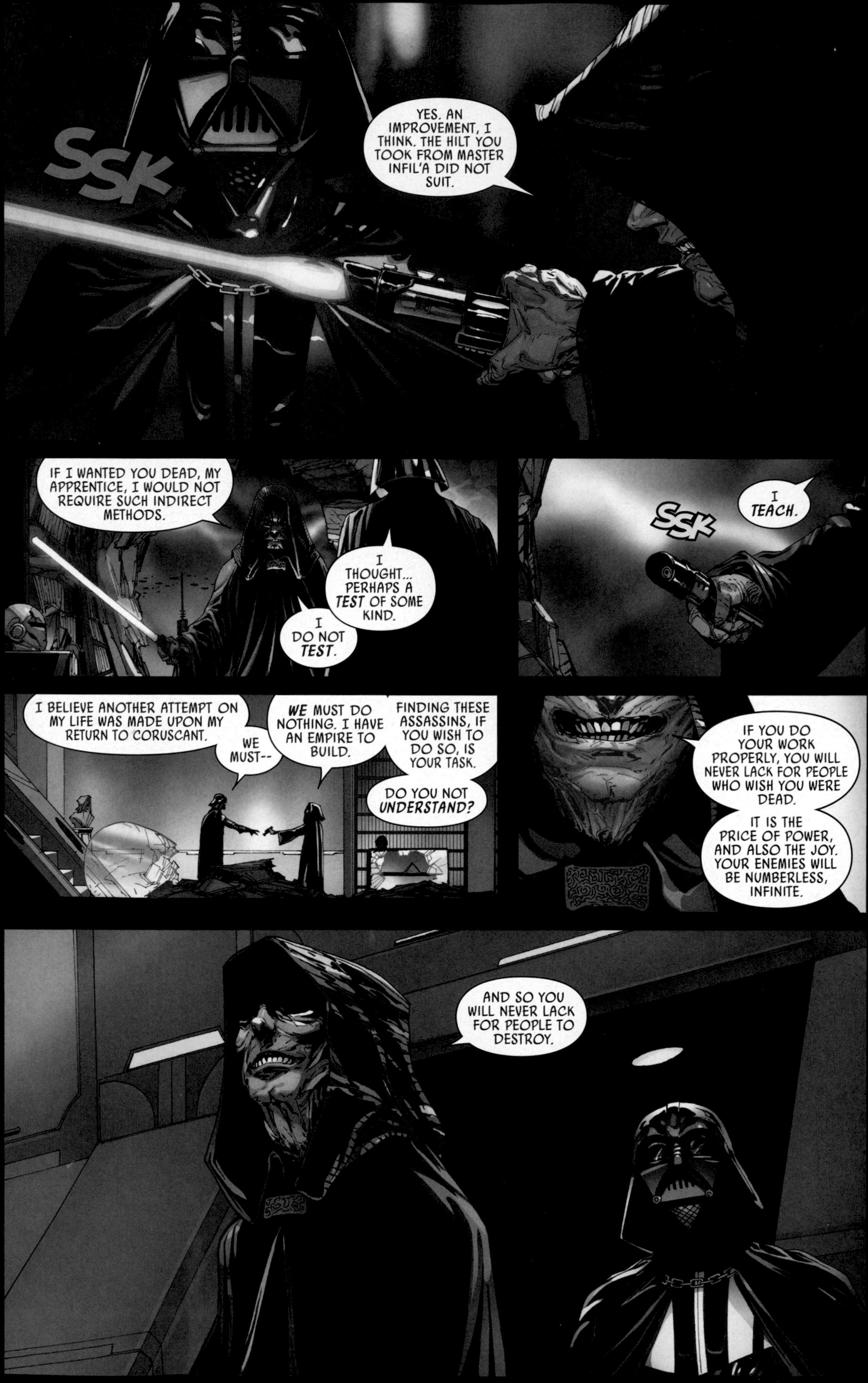
SSK
YES. AN IMPROVEMENT, I THINK. THE HILT YOU TOOK FROM MASTER INFIL'A DID NOT SUIT.
IF I WANTED YOU DEAD, MY APPRENTICE, I WOULD NOT REQUIRE SUCH INDIRECT METHODS.
I THOUGHT... PERHAPS A TEST OF SOME KIND.
I DO NOT TEST.
SSK
I TEACH.
I BELIEVE ANOTHER ATTEMPT ON MY LIFE WAS MADE UPON MY RETURN TO CORUSCANT.
WE MUST--
WE MUST DO NOTHING. I HAVE AN EMPIRE TO BUILD.
FINDING THESE ASSASSINS, IF YOU WISH TO DO SO, IS YOUR TASK.
DO YOU NOT UNDERSTAND?
IF YOU DO YOUR WORK PROPERLY, YOU WILL NEVER LACK FOR PEOPLE WHO WISH YOU WERE DEAD.
IT IS THE PRICE OF POWER, AND ALSO THE JOY. YOUR ENEMIES WILL BE NUMBERLESS, INFINITE.
AND SO YOU WILL NEVER LACK FOR PEOPLE TO DESTROY.

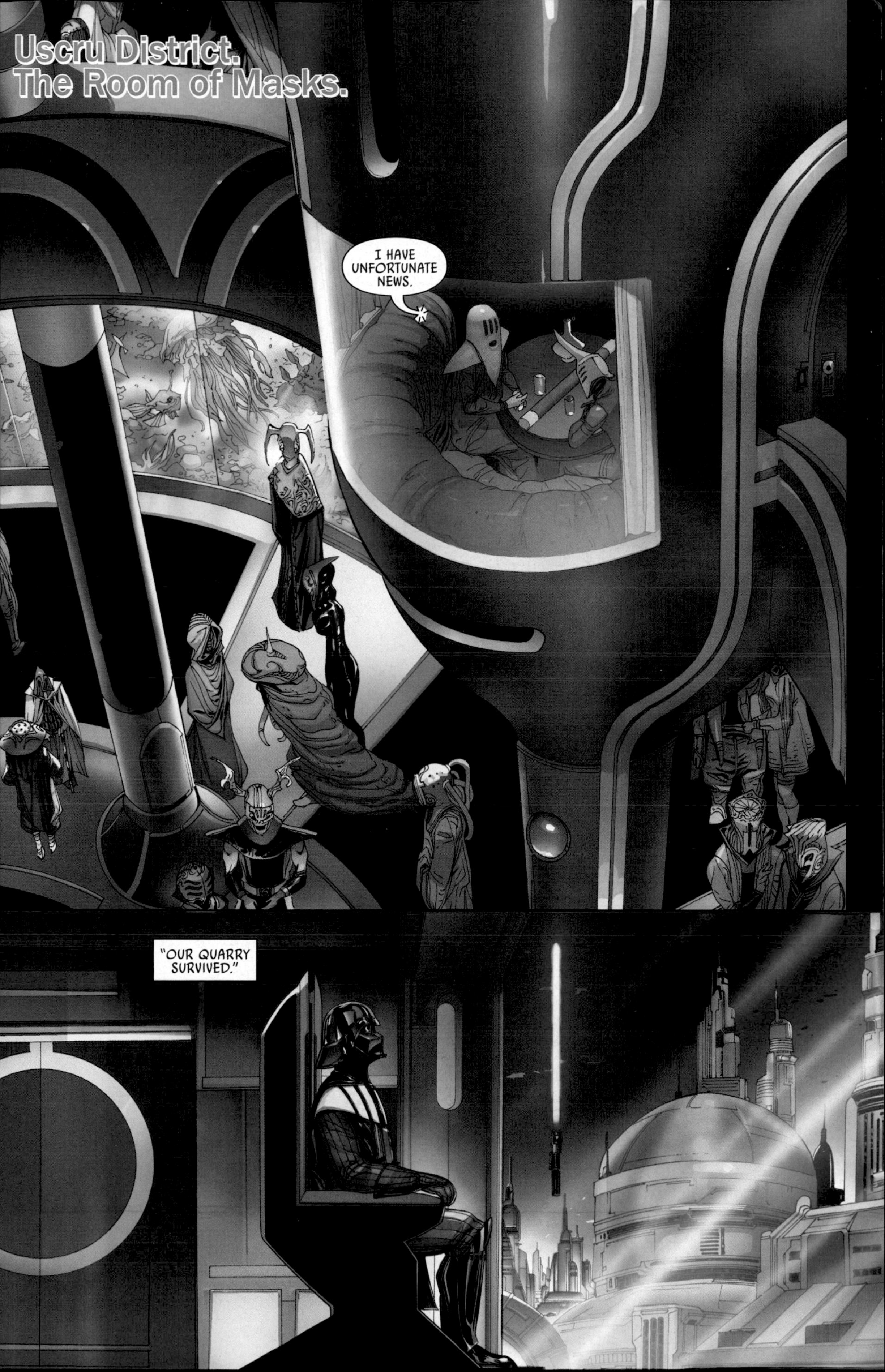
Uscru District.
The Room of Masks.
I HAVE UNFORTUNATE NEWS.
"OUR QUARRY SURVIVED."

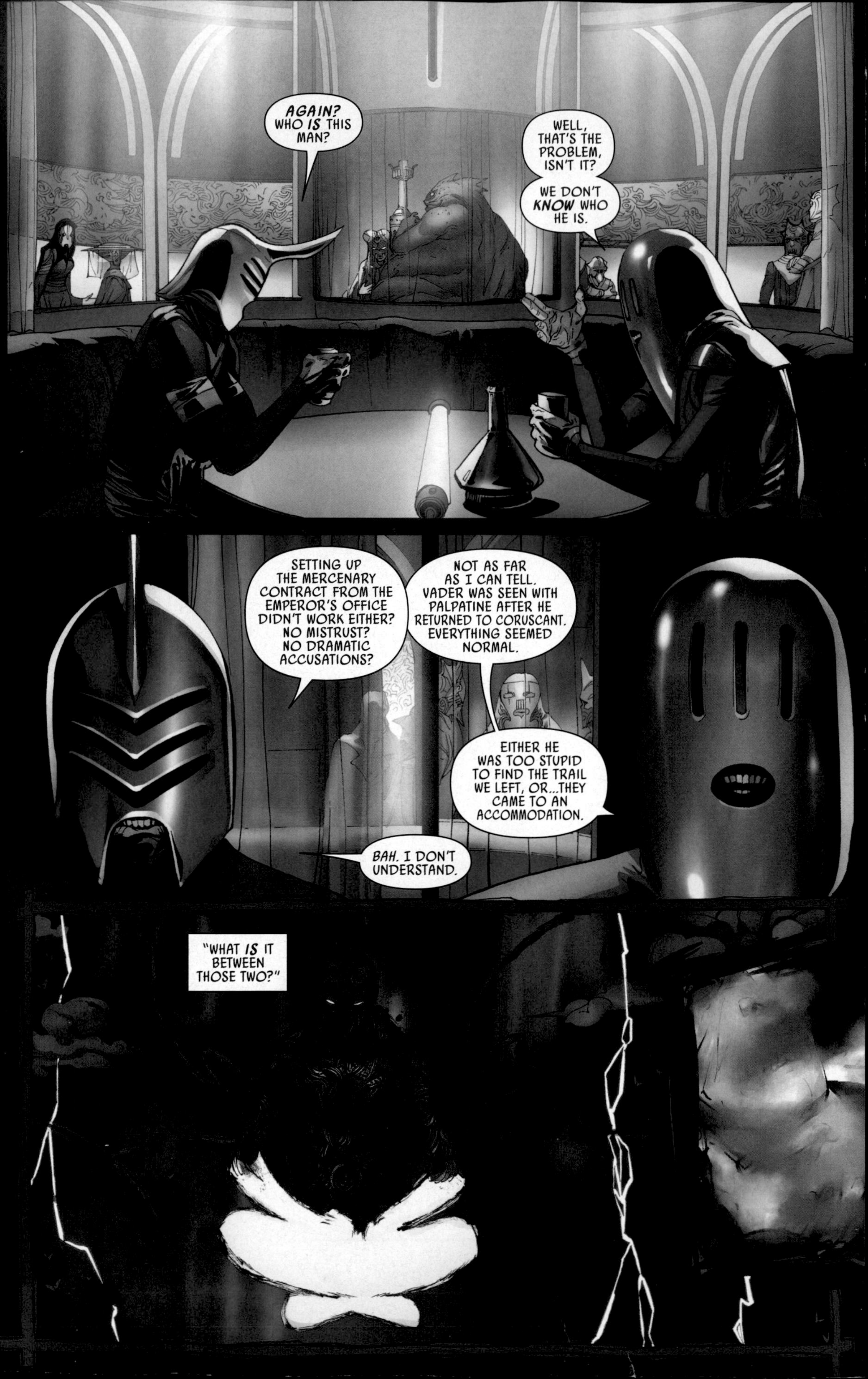
AGAIN? WHO IS THIS MAN?
WELL, THAT'S THE PROBLEM, ISN'T IT?
WE DON'T KNOW WHO HE IS.
SETTING UP THE MERCENARY CONTRACT FROM THE EMPEROR'S OFFICE DIDN'T WORK EITHER? NO MISTRUST? NO DRAMATIC ACCUSATIONS?
NOT AS FAR AS I CAN TELL. VADER WAS SEEN WITH PALPATINE AFTER HE RETURNED TO CORUSCANT. EVERYTHING SEEMED NORMAL.
EITHER HE WAS TOO STUPID TO FIND THE TRAIL WE LEFT, OR...THEY CAME TO AN ACCOMMODATION.
BAH. I DON'T UNDERSTAND.
"WHAT IS IT BETWEEN THOSE TWO?"

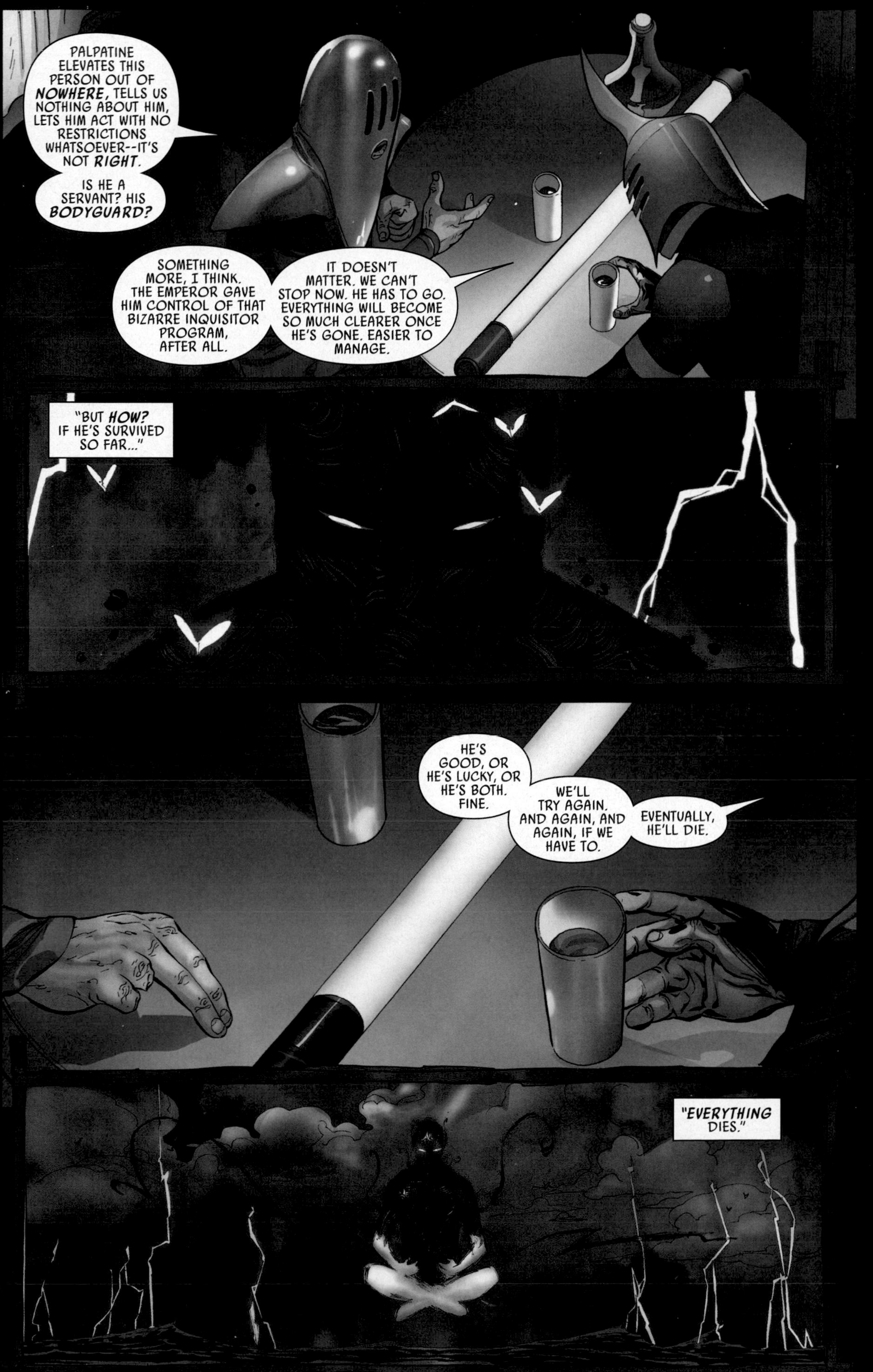
PALPATINE ELEVATES THIS PERSON OUT OF NOWHERE, TELLS US NOTHING ABOUT HIM, LETS HIM ACT WITH NO RESTRICTIONS WHATSOEVER--IT'S NOT RIGHT.
IS HE A SERVANT? HIS BODYGUARD?
SOMETHING MORE, I THINK. THE EMPEROR GAVE HIM CONTROL OF THAT BIZARRE INQUISITOR PROGRAM, AFTER ALL.
IT DOESN'T MATTER. WE CAN'T STOP NOW. HE HAS TO GO. EVERYTHING WILL BECOME SO MUCH CLEARER ONCE HE'S GONE. EASIER TO MANAGE.
"BUT HOW? IF HE'S SURVIVED SO FAR..."
HE'S GOOD, OR HE'S LUCKY, OR HE'S BOTH. FINE.
WE'LL TRY AGAIN. AND AGAIN, AND AGAIN, IF WE HAVE TO.
EVENTUALLY, HE'LL DIE.
"EVERYTHING DIES."

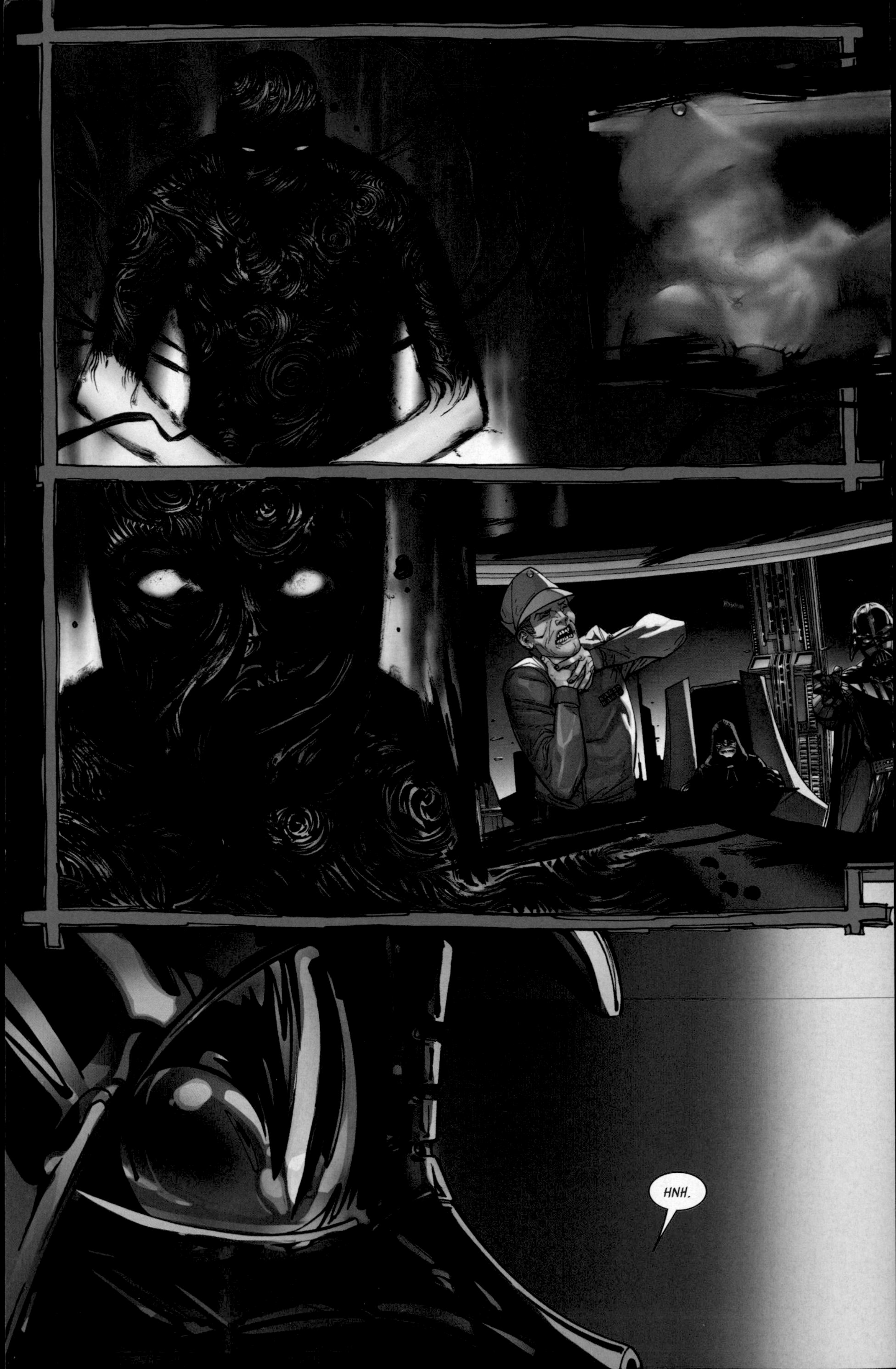
HNH.

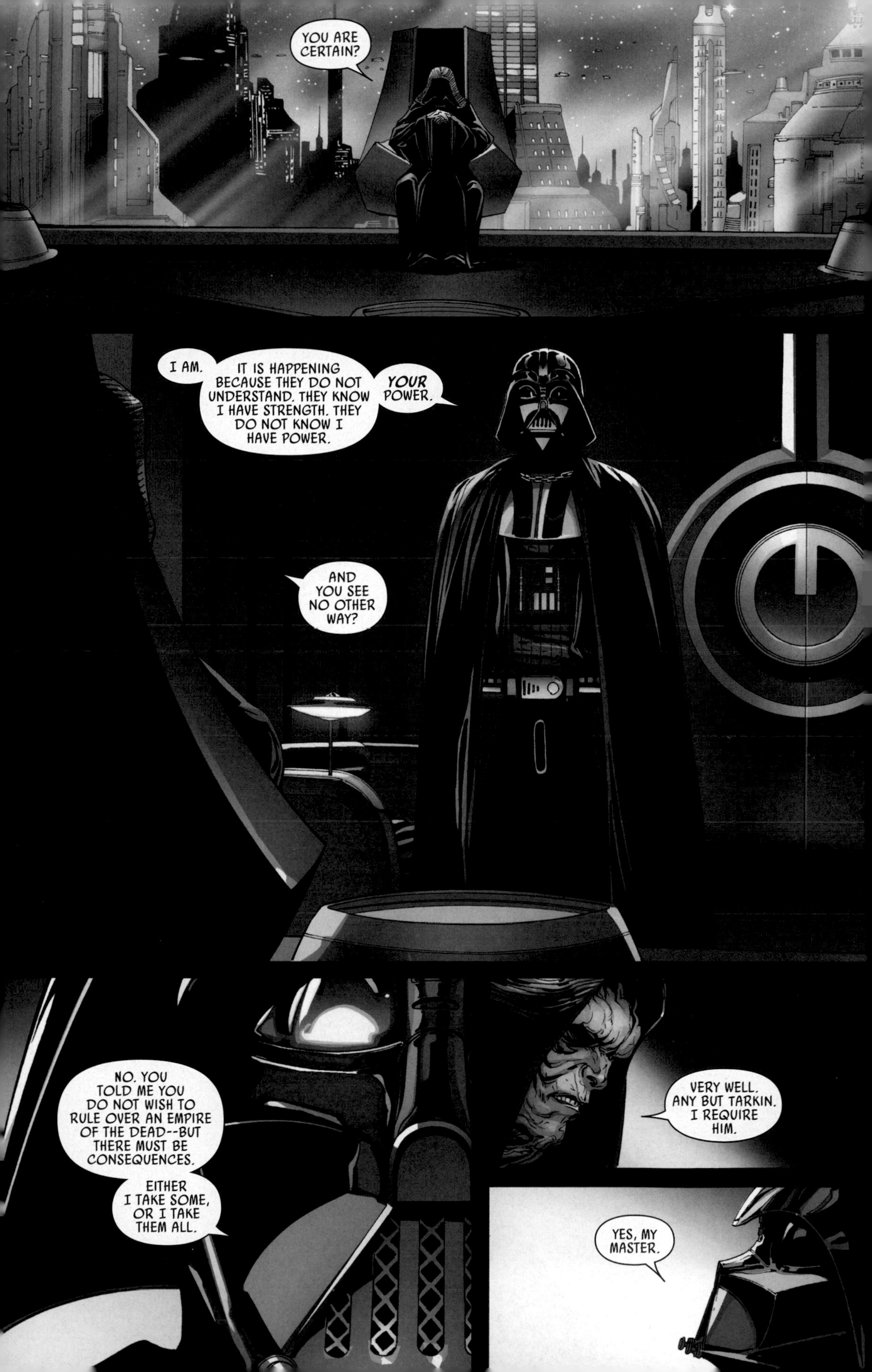

YOU ARE CERTAIN?
I AM.
IT IS HAPPENING BECAUSE THEY DO NOT UNDERSTAND. THEY KNOW I HAVE STRENGTH. THEY DO NOT KNOW I HAVE POWER.
YOUR POWER.
AND YOU SEE NO OTHER WAY?
NO. YOU TOLD ME YOU DO NOT WISH TO RULE OVER AN EMPIRE OF THE DEAD--BUT THERE MUST BE CONSEQUENCES.
EITHER I TAKE SOME, OR I TAKE THEM ALL.
VERY WELL. ANY BUT TARKIN. I REQUIRE HIM.
YES, MY MASTER.

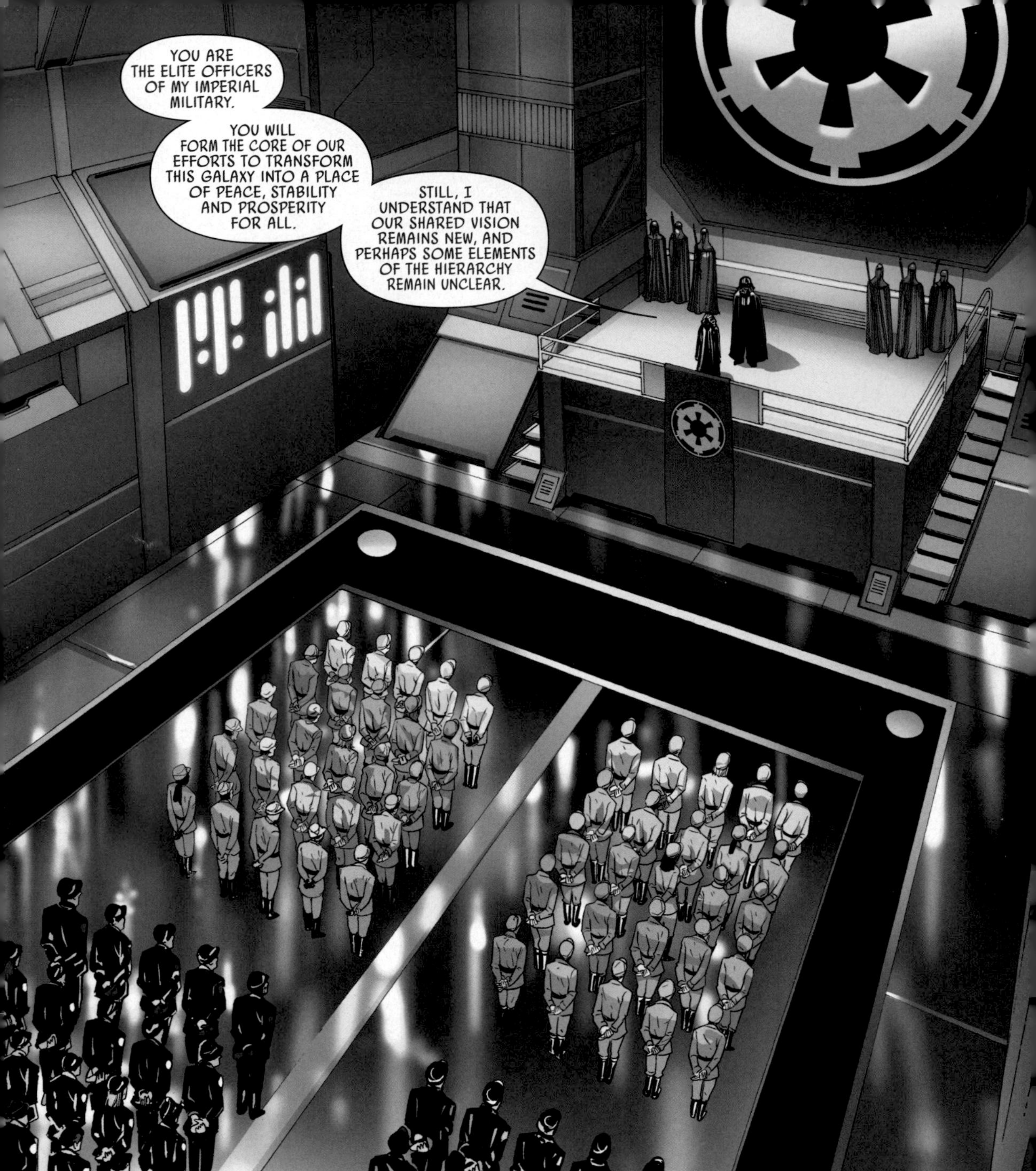
YOU ARE THE ELITE OFFICERS OF MY IMPERIAL MILITARY.
YOU WILL FORM THE CORE OF OUR EFFORTS TO TRANSFORM THIS GALAXY INTO A PLACE OF PEACE, STABILITY AND PROSPERITY FOR ALL.
STILL, I UNDERSTAND THAT OUR SHARED VISION REMAINS NEW, AND PERHAPS SOME ELEMENTS OF THE HIERARCHY REMAIN UNCLEAR.

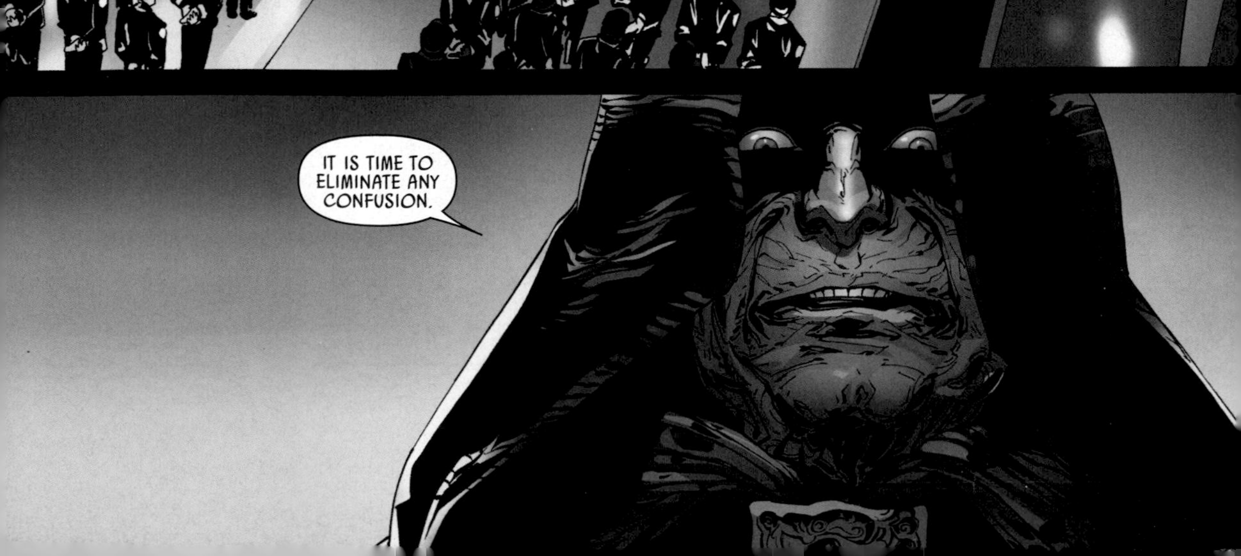
IT IS TIME TO ELIMINATE ANY CONFUSION.

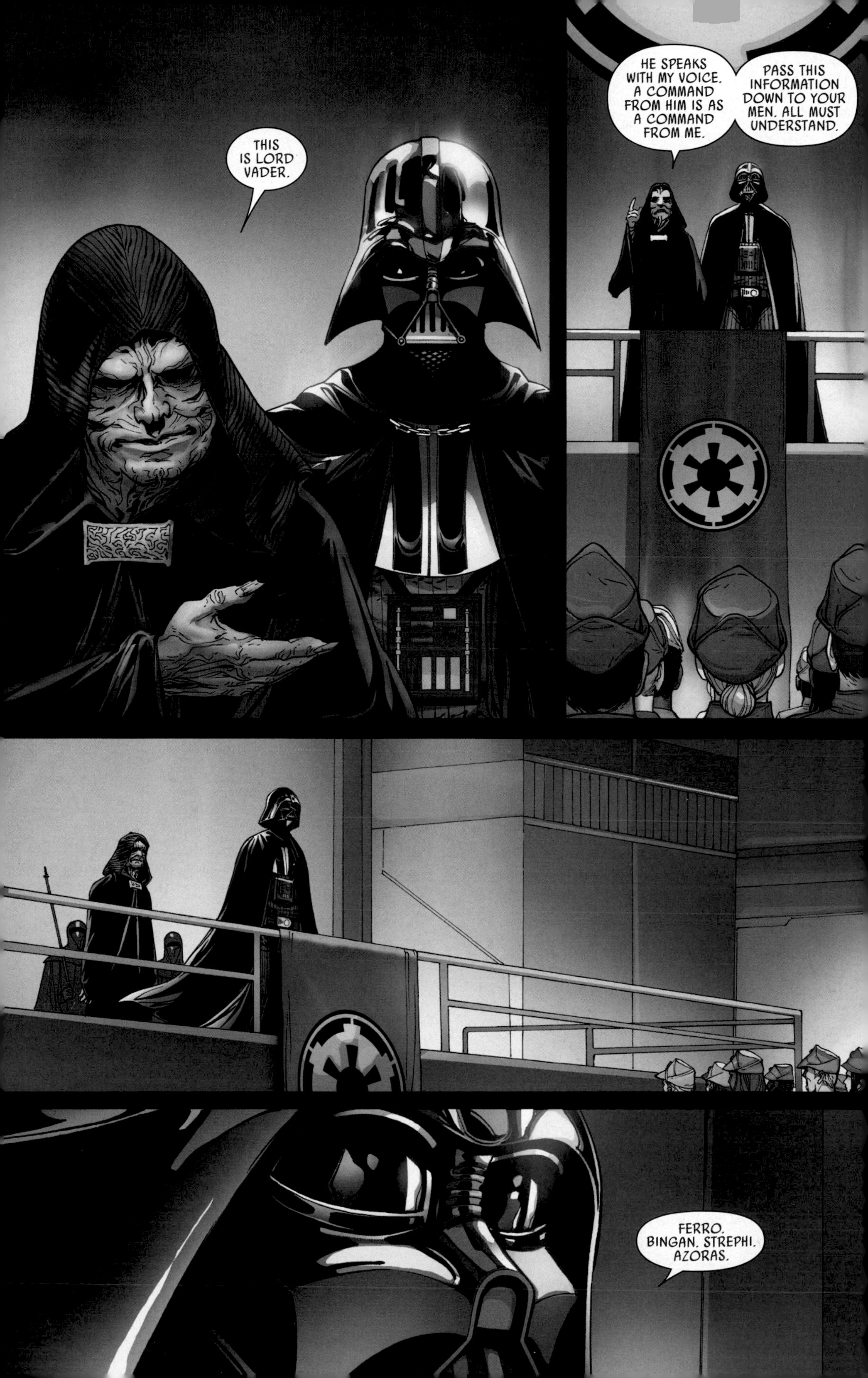
THIS IS LORD VADER.
HE SPEAKS WITH MY VOICE. A COMMAND FROM HIM IS AS A COMMAND FROM ME.
PASS THIS INFORMATION DOWN TO YOUR MEN. ALL MUST UNDERSTAND.
FERRO. BINGAN. STREPHI. AZORAS.

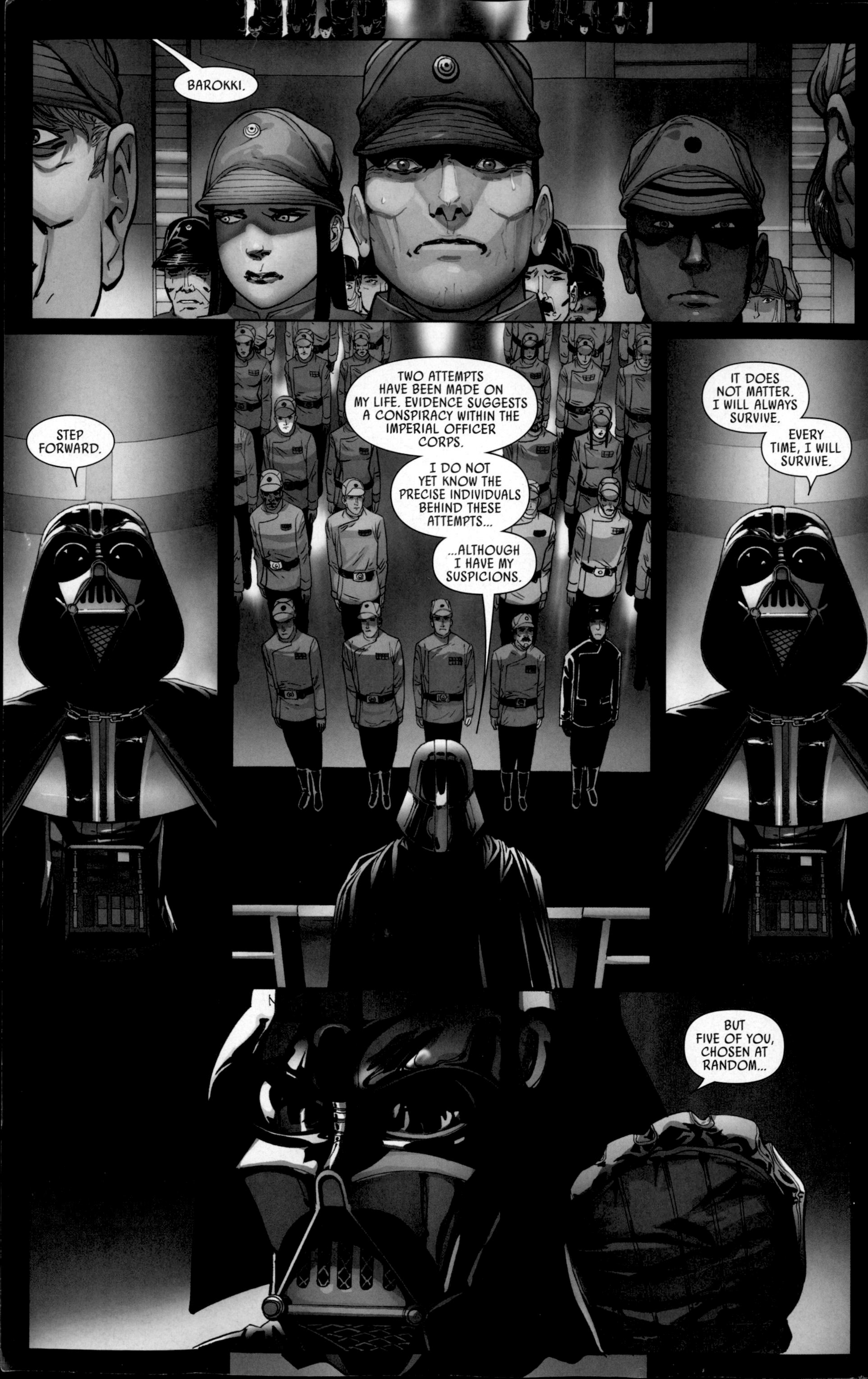
BAROKKI.
STEP FORWARD.
TWO ATTEMPTS HAVE BEEN MADE ON MY LIFE. EVIDENCE SUGGESTS A CONSPIRACY WITHIN THE IMPERIAL OFFICER CORPS.
I DO NOT YET KNOW THE PRECISE INDIVIDUALS BEHIND THESE ATTEMPTS...
...ALTHOUGH I HAVE MY SUSPICIONS.
IT DOES NOT MATTER. I WILL ALWAYS SURVIVE.
EVERY TIME, I WILL SURVIVE.
BUT FIVE OF YOU, CHOSEN AT RANDOM...

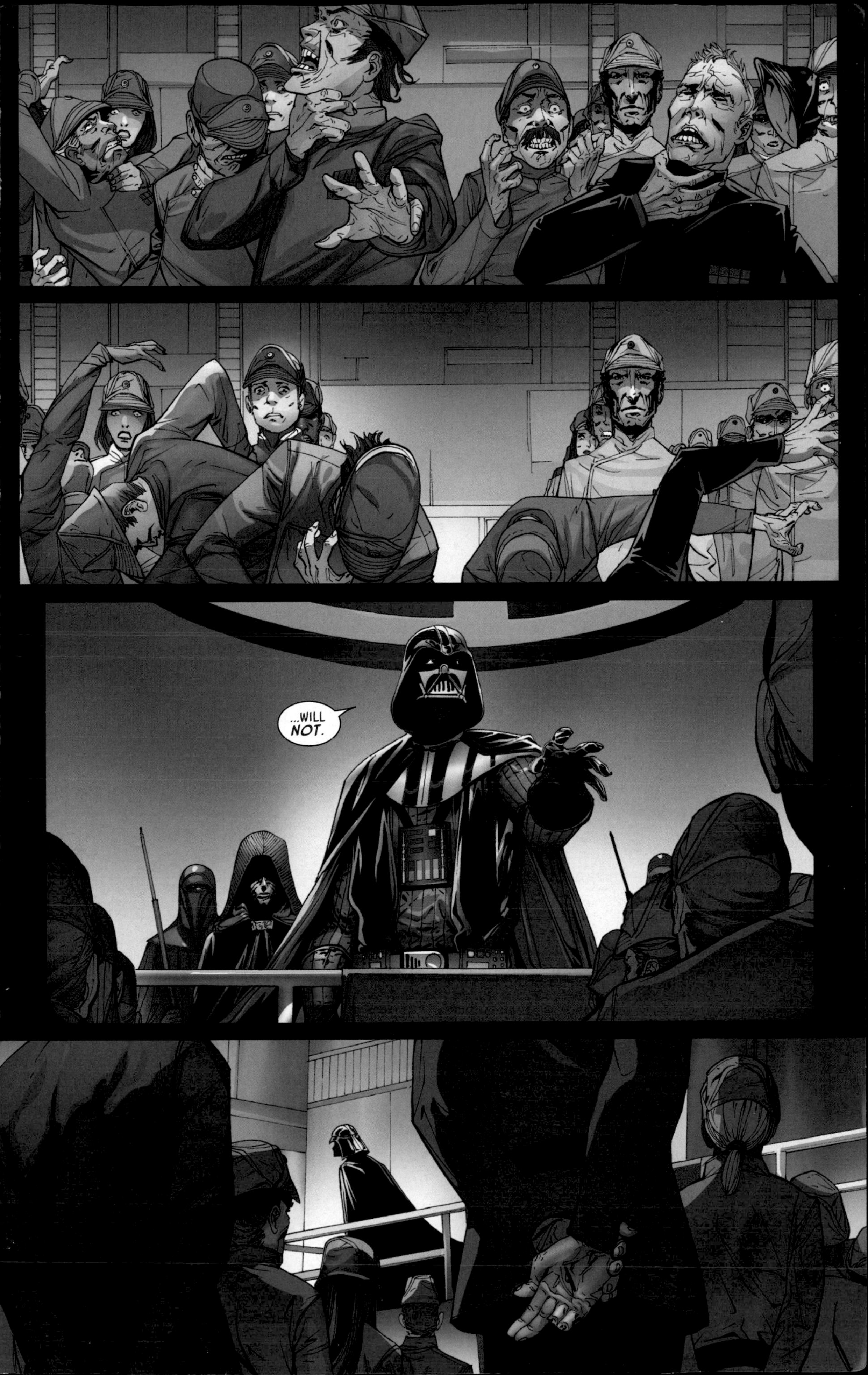
...WILL NOT.

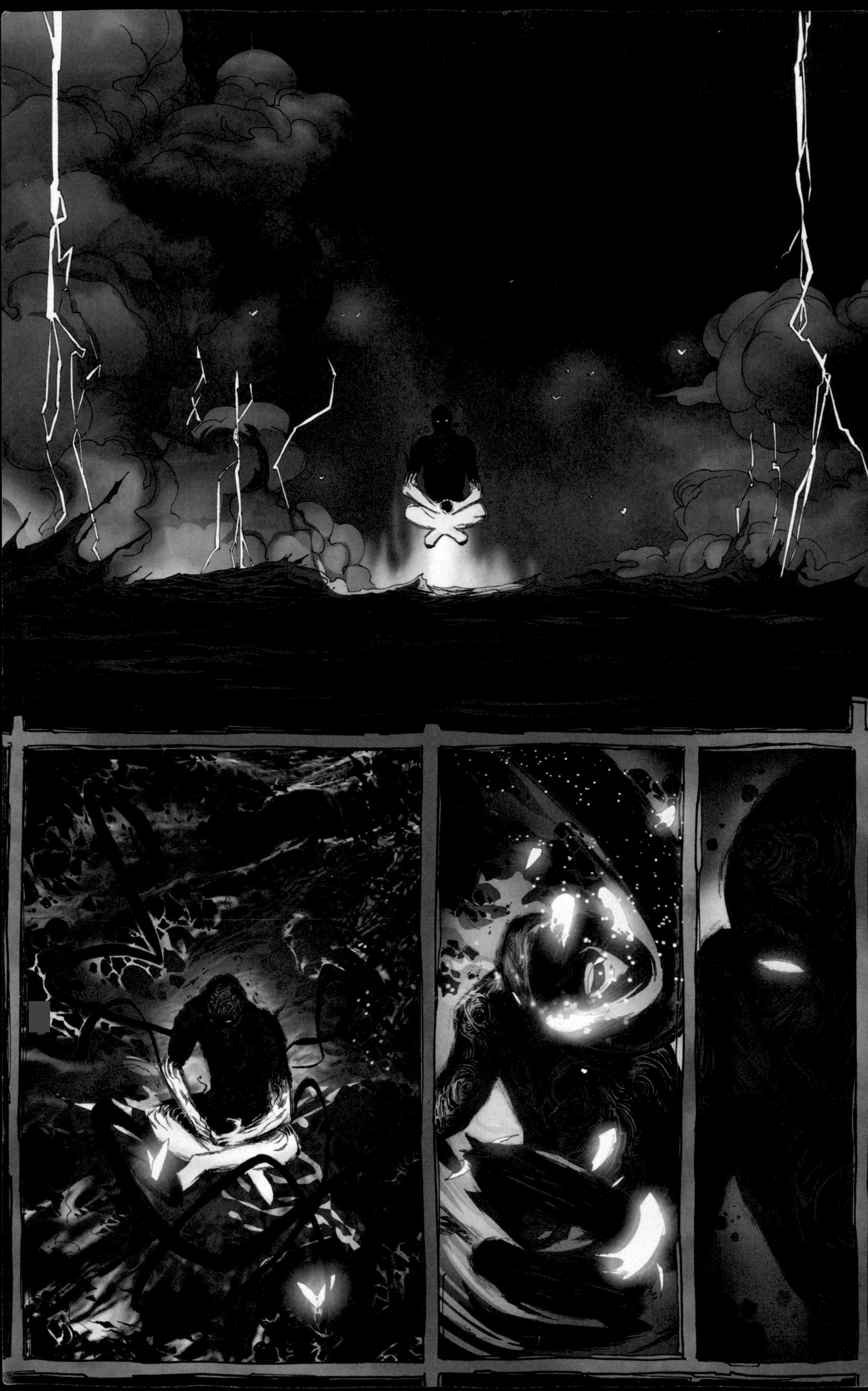

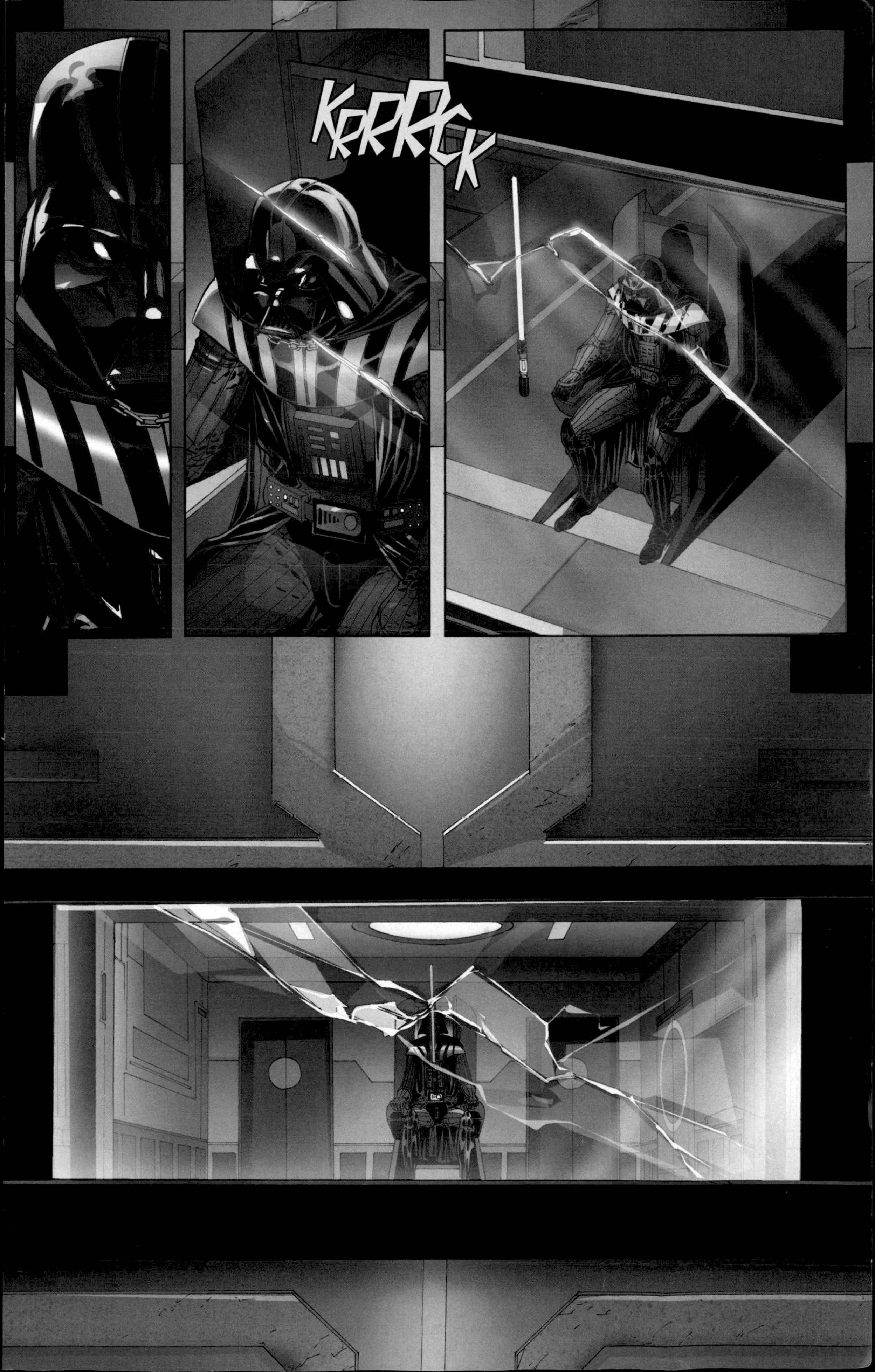
KRRRCK

RETURN TO A GALAXY FAR, FAR AWAY!

STAR WARS: THE FORCE AWAKENS ADAPTATION HC
978-1302901783

ON SALE NOW

AVAILABLE IN PRINT AND DIGITAL WHEREVER BOOKS ARE SOLD

WHAT IS A PRINCESS WITHOUT A WORLD?

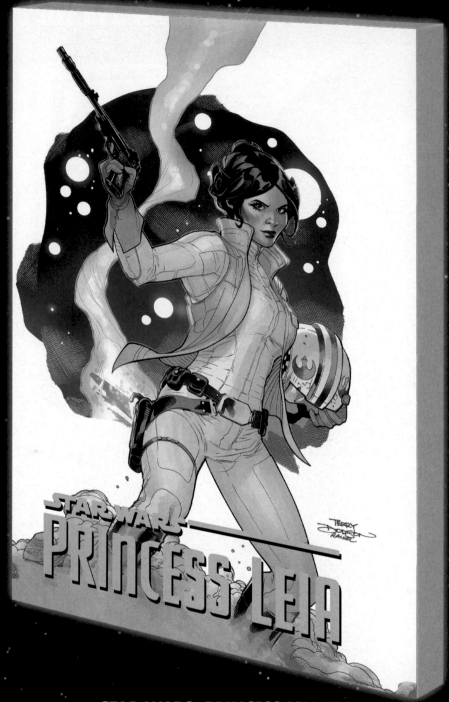

STAR WARS: PRINCESS LEIA TPB

978-0-7851-9317-3

ON SALE NOW!

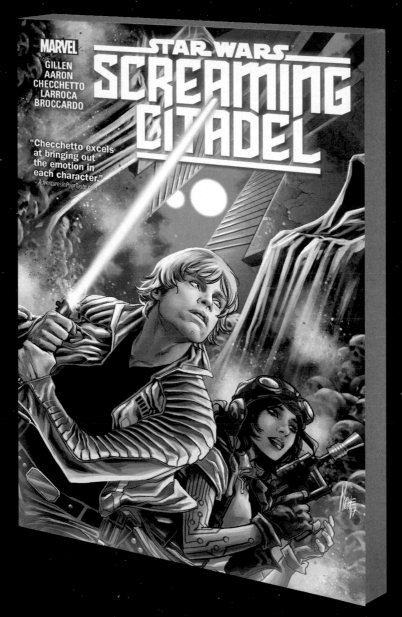

OR THE FULL STORY, READ

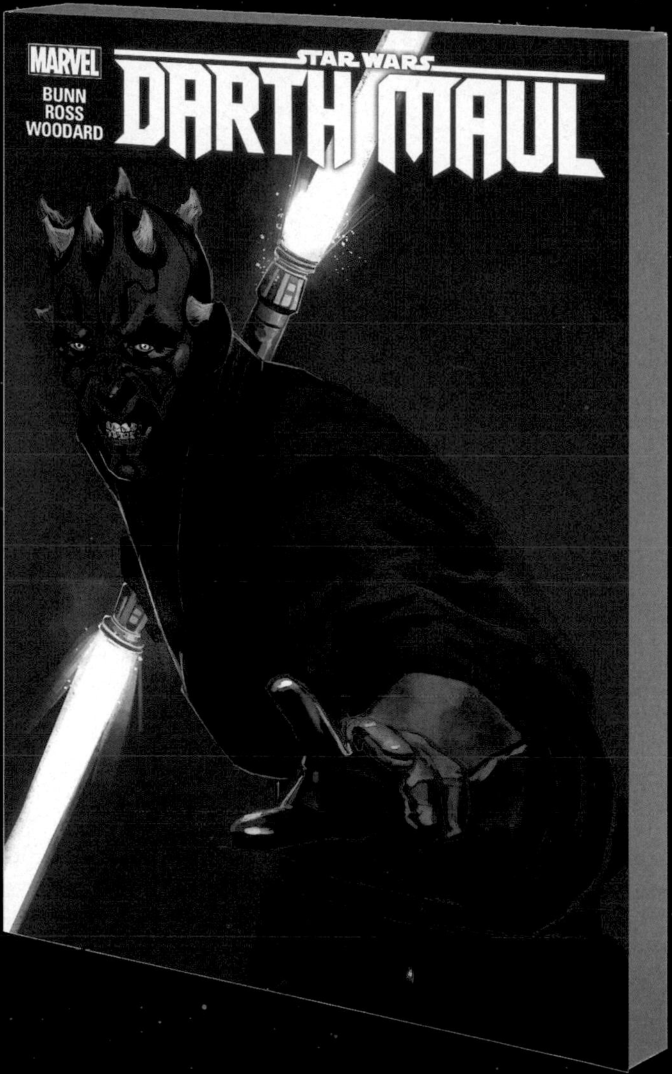
MARVEL
BUNN
ROSS
WOODARD
STAR WARS
DARTH MAUL

STAR WARS: DARTH MAUL
978-0785195894

ON SALE NOW

WHEREVER BOOKS ARE SOLD

TO FIND A COMIC SHOP NEAR YOU, VISIT COMICSHOPLOCATOR.COM

MARVEL Disney LUCASFILM

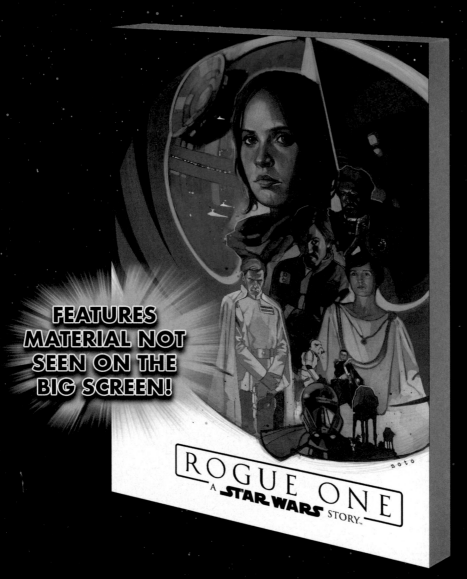

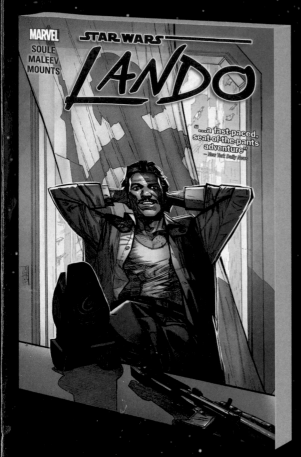